The Frontier Within

WEATHERHEAD BOOKS ON ASIA
WEATHERHEAD EAST ASIAN INSTITUTE, COLUMBIA UNIVERSITY

WEATHERHEAD BOOKS ON ASIA
Weatherhead East Asian Institute,
Columbia University

LITERATURE
David Der-wei Wang, Editor

(Continued following the index)

The Frontier Within
Essays by Abe Kōbō

Abe Kōbō

EDITED, TRANSLATED, AND WITH AN INTRODUCTION
BY RICHARD F. CALICHMAN

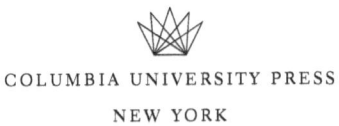

COLUMBIA UNIVERSITY PRESS
NEW YORK

Columbia University Press
Publishers Since 1893
New York   Chichester, West Sussex
cup.columbia.edu

Copyright © 2013 Kobo Abe
Paperback edition, 2016

Library of Congress Cataloging-in-Publication Data
Abe, Kobo, 1924–1993.
[Works.   English.   Selection.]
The Frontier within : Essays by Abe Kobo. / by Abe Kobo; edited,
translated, and with an introduction by Richard F. Calichman.
pages cm — (Weatherhead books on Asia)
Includes bibliographical references (pages) and index.
ISBN 978-0-231-16386-6 (cloth)—ISBN 978-0-231-16387-3 (pbk.)—
ISBN 978-0-231-53509-0 (e-book)
I.   Calichman, Richard.   II.   Abe, Kobo, 1924–1993. Shi to Shijin.
English.   III.   Title.
PL845. B4A2   2013
895.6'45—dc23

2012039752

Cover design: Noah Arlow

CONTENTS

ACKNOWLEDGMENTS

I am grateful to a number of individuals for helping me secure the copyright to Abe's essays: to Carol Gluck, first of all, whose enthusiastic support and timely interventions made this project possible; to Donald Keene, who kindly contacted Abe Neri about the copyright; and finally to Abe Neri herself, who generously granted the copyright. Particular thanks go to Toba Kōji of Waseda University, whose warm collegiality and thorough knowledge of Abe made him both a friend and an invaluable resource. I am indebted to the two reviewers of the book, who offered incisive comments, and to Jennifer Crewe of Columbia University Press for her ongoing editorial assistance. Finally, let me express my deepest gratitude to Hirayama Keiko and Hirayama Yōko, whose patience, support, and hospitality sustained the project throughout, from Paris to Tokyo.

The book is dedicated, with affection, to K.

INTRODUCTION

In the English-speaking world, the name Abe Kōbō typically evokes images of an existentialist author, one similar to such European writers as Franz Kafka, Jean-Paul Sartre, and Alberto Moravia in his depiction of the themes of alienation and the absurd. Abe appears, as several have remarked, as the most un-Japanese of writers, at least in comparison with such other writers of his stature as not only Mishima Yukio, his near exact contemporary, but also Kawabata Yasunari and Tanizaki Jun'ichirō. Clearly this reputation can be attributed in large part to a certain politics of translation, in which "western" readers and translators both actively—if unconsciously—sought out those texts of Japanese literature that appeared most exotic and different from themselves. With his strange landscapes, abstract allusions, and theoretical meditations, Abe's fictional texts struck readers (beginning in the mid-1960s, with the appearance of his work in English) as utterly unlike the traditional scenes of cherry blossoms and geisha that they had come to expect from the various translated novels then in circulation. These works provided the background against which Abe's writings were read and interpreted, with not a little sense of puzzlement. If these novels helped satisfy a certain craving for the exotic and culturally heterogeneous, thereby confirming, in ricochet fashion, the sense of western culture as essentially uniform and homogeneous, then Abe's texts provoked a momentary unsettling in appearing insufficiently different and rather too close for comfort. This incongruity was soon enough resolved, however, through a notion of influence in which Abe was seen as artistically and intellectually indebted to those western ideas that were then widely visible in avant-garde literature and cinema. Although dissimilar in themes and treatment to much Japanese fiction then being read, Abe nevertheless joined his contemporaries in confirming a western sense of dominance implicit in the consumption and evaluation of Asian art. That is to say, whereas the focus on tradition and Orientalist aesthetics in certain novels allowed for an exoticization that effectively reinforced a framework in which western modernity saw itself inversely reflected in the premodern East, the understanding of Abe's texts as a product of western artistic and philosophical influence underscored Abe's credentials as an avant-garde writer strictly at the cost of relegating his work along these geopolitical coordinates of East and West as necessarily secondary and derivative.

In order to more effectively problematize the various assumptions regarding culture and geopolitical and literary modernity implicit in the translation and reception of Japanese fiction, and that of Abe's works in particular, it seems important to examine the ways in which these texts themselves often draw attention to such assumptions and call them into question. A study of Abe's novels, plays, and short stories consistently reveals a heightened sensitivity to various hierarchies and power relations that serve to legitimate social formations. One thinks, for example, of the insight found in *Suna no onna* (*The Woman in the Dunes*, 1962) that various parts of the countryside, unlike the city, regard themselves as outside of and hence potentially resistant to the overarching framework of the nation-state; or of the understanding in *Tanin no kao* (*The Face of Another*, 1964) that the foregrounding of subjective identity in society is indissociable from the problem of the minority. However, it is far less widely known that many of Abe's ideas concerning social relations are set forth quite explicitly in his essays, which often lay out in detail certain notions, strategies, and logics that are merely alluded to in his fiction. The reason for this disparity of knowledge in the "West" between Abe's fictional texts, which have been studied and discussed for nearly fifty years now, and his critical essays refers, I believe, to another aspect of this politics of translation in which literary discourse has long been privileged over, and seen as inherently distinct from, theoretical-critical discourse. Doubtless there are various reasons behind this imbalance (broader commercial factors must be taken into account in addition to those involving, more narrowly, academia and the institution of Asian studies), but it must be said that such division makes little sense when examining Abe's oeuvre: at its worst this split can lead to a form of aestheticism divorced from historical concerns, but even when literary analysis is guided by attention to history, the risk is that it remains theoretically naïve and insufficiently aware of its own institutional biases. Abe himself warned of this risk and sought to elaborate a form of writing that was at once literary, historical, and theoretically informed.

Abe's main concern lay in articulating a notion of the social in which individuals are not co-opted or appropriated strictly as parts within a unified and comprehensive whole but are rather granted a measure of freedom through which to explore the world and others (including, significantly, the self as other) in all their alterity. This concern appears in various guises throughout his fictional works, but the following essays, each responding at different historical junctures to a range of distinct problematics and injustices as perceived by Abe, offer an opportunity to examine how this and related themes are reworked and consolidated over the span of a quarter century, from his 1944 "Shi to shijin (ishiki to muishiki)" (Poetry and Poets [Consciousness and the Unconscious]) to his 1969 "Zoku: uchi naru henkyō" (The Frontier Within, Part II).

The realm of the social, Abe argues, must not be conflated with or reduced to the state and its various institutions. The state attempts to suture this gap through an array of ideological mechanisms all oriented toward establishing a smooth and ordered passageway between the mediating bodies that connect the individual to the totality. It is these mediated institutions that serve the state in marking, or in some sense imprinting, the individual as belonging to it. Abe cites several examples of such institutions, broadly defined: that of the school system (in the 1965 "Gendai ni okeru kyōiku no kanōsei: Ningen sonzai no honshitsu ni furete" [Possibilities for Education Today: On the Essence of Human Existence]), popular culture (in the 1957 "Amerika no hakken" [Discovering America]), and establishment literary criticism (in the 1954 "Bungaku ni okeru riron to jissen" [Theory and Practice in Literature]). Yet it is the institution of the military that seems to draw Abe's strongest fire, as can be seen in such essays as "Miritarī rukku" (The Military Look, 1968) and elsewhere. Without question, Abe's sharply critical views of the military were fostered during the end of the Fifteen Year War (1931–1945) and its immediate aftermath, which he spent in Manchuria and where he witnessed various atrocities committed by Japanese soldiers.

More generally, however, the institution of the military appears from Abe's perspective to represent in especially clear form the dynamics of all social institutions in their role as mediating organs of the state. This explains why Abe chooses to focus on the military from the particular vantage point of its uniforms, for these function to transform the individual who wears them into an agent or instrument of the national polity, one charged with the specific task of protecting and perpetuating state rule through the exercise of violence. Abe surveys the gradual evolution of the state through the changing style of military uniforms from the more traditional warning coloration to protective coloration, seeing in this development evidence of the state's modern hypocrisy and chameleon-like ability to blend in with its surroundings. These uniforms operate in the manner of a lure, enticing those who wear them to internalize those particular attributes that the uniforms represent, as for example loyalty and patriotism. The military uniform seems to contain certain expectations that the soldier, upon wearing it, comes to claim as his own. In focusing on the importance of this costume, Abe discovers an often overlooked commonality between the soldier and the actor. As he writes in the context of German soldiers during World War II, "I am now holding two photographs in my hand. One is of several Nazi soldiers immediately before they storm into Stalingrad. . . . Like seasoned actors, they appear in the photograph to be intently performing the role suited to their Nazi uniforms. . . . The other photograph [is of] surrendering Nazi soldiers. Or more accurately, they are two Germans who have just ceased being Nazi soldiers. . . . The change these soldiers underwent is quite striking. It is like an actor's face, vivid and real, after he has returned to his dressing room and washed off his role together with his makeup . . . making his Hamlet costume now appear false. . . . Defeat robbed these soldiers of more than the will to fight. It also stripped them of the meaning and idea behind their uniforms as well as deprived them of the state itself, which gave these uniforms their own identity as uniforms."[1]

The uniform makes the man, as the saying goes, and Abe interprets this expression quite radically to suggest a form of subjectivity in which man exists largely devoid of any inherent content, that he is on the contrary akin to an empty shell or vessel in which the potential for becoming and self-transformation exists inseparably from the state's capacity to fill this space with its own ideological elements. Abe rejects any essentialist conception of man that would locate an ultimate ground or substratum that anchors the various qualities, roles, and identities that man comes over time to internalize and adopt as his own. In such an understanding, the transforma-

tive nature of identity is restrained by the distinction between man's qualities, which are multiple and constantly changing, and that more powerful
internal essence that remains itself unchanged. Exposure to the world and
its alterity demands a shift of focus from the internal to the external, Abe
argues, and the fragility of the former can be seen in the dominance wield-
ed over it by the superficial garb that is the military uniform. Any subjective
identity assumed by man must thus be regarded as nothing more substantial
than a role performed by an actor at a certain time and place; this identity
lacks the permanence to ever transcend these spatiotemporal limitations
and become one with the actor himself. The role and costume can always
be replaced by others, which suggests that they are in fact historically contingent. For Abe, recognition of such contingency marks the beginning of a
critical consciousness vis-à-vis the lure of subjective identity. In the example
he provides, the German soldiers appear to belatedly realize through defeat
that they have fallen prey to the manipulations of state ideology by regarding their identity strictly in terms of the uniforms they were required to
wear. These uniforms hold out the promise of identity to the wearer, offer-
ing the security of profession (soldier), nationality (German), and political
ideology (Nazism). Through this promise, Abe suggests, individuals are led
to see such objects and the institutions they represent as a means through
which to actualize their own inner potential. Ironically, it is by fulfilling
their potential as individual subjects that they come to be most beholden
to—that is to say, subjugated by—the state.

Abe refers here to the problematic of fascism, but it is crucial to realize
that this term "fascism" for Abe is not limited to the particular case of Nazi
Germany. Deeply suspicious of all national-cultural particularisms, Abe
instead seeks to explore a more general form of fascism, one that, as Michel
Foucault writes in his preface to *Anti-Oedipus*, exists "in us all, in our heads
and in our everyday behavior, the fascism that causes us to love power, to
desire the very thing that dominates and exploits us."[2] One must of course
pay rigorous attention to the specific historical manifestations of fascism, but
the danger here is that such focus blinds one to other, at times equally virulent, forms of fascism. Indeed, Abe depicts the contestation and hypocrisy
often surrounding this term or notion in his 1951 short story "Chinnyūsha"
(The Intruders), where figures clearly suggestive of the U.S. Occupation
authorities attempt to dissimulate their own quasi-fascist tendencies in their
repeated condemnation of the central Japanese protagonist as fascist.[3] In
this sense, it is no accident that Abe's point of comparison of Nazi uniforms
in "The Military Look" is the fatigues-style uniform worn by the U.S. mili-

tary, just as it is significant that Abe makes frequent reference to neofascist movements in the United States in his 1968 "Uchi naru henkyō" (The Frontier Within). Such comparison between Nazi Germany and the postwar United States, however, in no way implies any facile equivalence between these two political entities. Rather, Abe's point is that fascist elements are intrinsic to all modern forms of power, that they can potentially be found in democratic and totalitarian societies alike, and that any attempt to delimit their appearance to certain national contexts as opposed to others reveals, if not a willed ignorance or denial, then certainly an underlying attitude of cultural particularism.[4]

Yet Abe's critique of the United States is worth dwelling on, partly because such criticisms on the part of Japanese writers have often been dismissed or overlooked by American scholars of Japan studies, but also because, more specifically, Abe believed that the widespread notion of "American democracy" contains certain mythic or propagandistic elements that serve to conceal more than they reveal about the workings of state power. It must be remembered that Abe was writing during the period of the Cold War, and that as a former member of the Japan Communist Party (before being expelled in 1962) whose political allegiances remained firmly leftist throughout his life, he was sensitive to the various injustices of American imperialism and viewed U.S. global ascendancy in the postwar years with profound distrust. Along with many other Japanese critics of U.S. foreign policy, Abe strongly denounced the United States for its postwar occupation of Japan as well as for its continued military aggression in Asia, both in the Korean War and Vietnam War. Yet Abe was similarly critical of events taking place within the United States as well. He specifically draws attention to the discrimination against minorities, emphasizing the persistent force of anti-Semitism and racism against blacks. While it is important to recognize that anti-Semitism in the United States never came close to reaching the depths of violence and atrocity as it did in Nazi Germany, the fact is that Jews were actively excluded from broad swaths of American life. The treatment of blacks was even worse, as Abe realized, and here again, interestingly, he turns to the example of Nazism to illustrate their plight: "Prejudice against blacks is far more virulent and nihilistic than anti-Semitism. The Nazis believed that Jews had to be killed, whereas American farmers never even saw the need to kill blacks."[5]

The question thus arises as to why Abe repeatedly points to the presence of certain commonalities between fascist Germany and American society. Beyond the specific historical circumstances behind several of Abe's more pointed critiques of the United States (both "The Military Look" and "The Frontier Within" were written in 1968, when U.S. involvement in the war in Vietnam was at its height), he seems to impugn both entities as exemplars of state violence. Abe fully understood that the horrors of the Holocaust extended beyond measure, but he reserves particular contempt for the United States for its sophistication and cunning in disguising the various ideological mechanisms at its disposal. Whereas violence in the case of Nazi Germany was undoubtedly greater in scale—if it is indeed even possible to quantify such things—American state violence was in certain respects the more insidious in its capacity to conceal itself often even from itself, and this effacement or denial of violence amounted to a doubling of violence that Abe regarded as a new development in modern power. Such self-concealment (in the double sense: both as concealment *of* itself and concealment *from* itself) was, at bottom, made possible by the widespread sense of fear or anxiety in society on the part of the individual vis-à-vis the totality that he believes is judging him negatively, finding him to be, in one manner or another, insufficient. Clearly this anxiety is not something that can be understood as a mere flaw or shortcoming at the level of individual psychology. To be sure, such conceptualization itself stands as evidence of the capacity of the state to efface its presence. Rather, individuals come gradually over time to be inculcated with a sense of anxiety through a range of ideologies as transmitted by those institutions representative of the totality that is the state. It is through these ideologies that they are forced to confront their own putative insufficiency or inadequacy according to the standards set forth by the whole, of which they are but a part. In this respect, Abe would have agreed completely with Jean-Paul Sartre's articulation of the relation between individual American citizens and what he calls Americanism: "An American told me in Berne, 'The problem is that each of us is eaten away by the fear of being less American than our neighbor.' . . . There is an anxiety on the part of the American when faced with Americanism."[6]

The individual, in this case, finds himself confronted with an idea or ideal of what it means to be an authentic national citizen. Such ideal, which is the generating force behind all ideology, has by definition no actual or concrete existence. It is in principle impossible for any living individual to ever fully attain this ideal, and therein, ironically, lies its power. Once this ideal is internalized and accepted as the implicit standard by which all authentic citizenry is judged, one can only be found deficient. In this way, as Abe reveals time and again in both his fiction and essays, social existence comes to be ideologically determined by the notion of lack. Just as actual existence can never entirely overcome its vestiges of materiality, thereby revealing its flawed status vis-à-vis ideality, so too is the individual helpless to erase what might be understood as the surplus of his singularity in his desire for the totality. This desire is effected and mediated by an ideal of authenticity in relation to which individuals cannot but feel themselves lacking. This lack, as I have stated, comes to be erroneously attributed to individual failings rather than properly seen in structural or formal terms as instrumental to the formation of social order. Here we can better understand why Abe places so much theoretical weight on the distinction between the authentic (*honmono*) and inauthentic (*nisemono*) in social relations. In the case of the United States, for example, those who are represented as ideal citizens are regarded in their authenticity as necessarily part of the majority, regardless of whether or not this is factually accurate. Those who are seen for whatever reason as lacking the requisite traits to be determined in this manner fall into the class of minority, as Abe demonstrates through the example of Jews and blacks. In their inauthenticity, Jews and blacks can never truly be understood as Americans. (The same holds true for Korean residents in Japan, as Abe quite brilliantly illustrates in *Tanin no kao*.)[7] Their perceived deficiency and falseness comes easily to be internalized and manifested as anxiety in regard to their rightful place in society: how can they acquire a sense of security, in other words, when the fact of their physical residence in the United States is belied by their knowledge that they are somehow other to or less than American? What is crucial to understand in this context is that the situation of the minority ultimately depends far less on content than it does on form. The definition of Jew or black (or Korean resident in Japan) is historically variable, and these determinations have far less to do with such "biological" factors as ethnicity or race than they do with perception, and hence representation at a social and ideological level. Yet the fact is that the notion of the minority must remain empty and free of all content in order for the state and its institutions to exercise the greatest degree of power. In principle, anyone in society can potentially be regarded as a minority, someone whose national or cultural authenticity comes to be threatened and placed in doubt, and the anxiety or fear this generates is effectively mobilized by the state in reinforcing the hold its institutions maintain over the individual. As Abe shows, the state cannot enforce loyalty to itself as totality without recourse to the mechanism of the minority, who, regardless of content or specific determination (as Jew, black, resident Korean, etc.), represents the threat of punishment and exclusion potentially reserved for every individual.

How then can individuals articulate a form of existence that recognizes the domain of the social as primarily a site of alterity, one that resists absorption within the logic of the whole-part relation that undergirds the entire edifice of the state and its institutions? Abe appears to offer a tentative answer to this question in his thinking of the notion of sustained flight (*nige-dashippanashi*): "The notion that we need to cultivate concerns the state of sustained flight. What does this mean? Whereas settling down somewhere is a basic condition, remaining in a state of sustained flight is a process. We carry within ourselves a prejudice that this process invariably involves settling down somewhere. My point here consists in shedding doubt on this prejudice."[8] Throughout his essays, Abe focuses on various figures who are in some sense marked by this notion of sustained flight, as for example the Jew, the Gypsy, the war deserter, and the nomad. These figures are linked together by their shared refusal to submit to the various mechanisms of state power. These mechanisms or structures, Abe emphasizes, no longer simply exist outside the individual in the bare form of coercion. Rather, state power in the modern era has developed in such a way as to achieve through internalization—that is to say, subjectivization, what the postwar critic and China scholar Takeuchi Yoshimi has referred to as the "process of subject formation" (*shutai keisei no katei*)[9]—what had hitherto been possible only externally through brute force. Abe's concept of sustained flight must be understood in its most general aspect, beyond the limited sense of mere physical escape (as, for example, the crossing of national borders), to signify a resistance to the lure of subjective identity as centered on ideals propagated by the state and reinforced by the correlative notions of authenticity and inauthenticity. Abe's privileging of such expressions as "flight" and "process" as elements of resistance in no way implies a naïve conception of the state in terms of stasis; on the contrary, the state's active dissemination of fear or anxiety throughout society creates an apparatus that is in constant motion. Yet this work of the negative comes ultimately to be itself negated by the synthesis that is the state's own existence. What Abe terms here "settling down" refers to nothing other than the subject finding his proper place within the state's comprehensive framework. Here the subject obediently accepts his status as functioning part within the state's totality. The state's goals become his own individual goals in, for example, its global competition with other states. It is precisely this permeation of the whole within the part from which Abe seeks to flee, and this is achieved by first of all refusing the state's lure of becoming one of its own by means of actualizing one's own subjective potential and becoming oneself.

In conclusion, the essays collected in this volume reveal Abe's importance as a thinker of the social. To read Abe as a *Japanese* thinker of the social, or as one whose writings can better teach one about various matters particular to the geopolitical entity of Japan, is to in effect not read Abe. However, this is not to suggest that the trap of particularism can be simply overcome by appealing to a vaguely universal notion of humanity or mankind. Rather, the point, as Abe insists at the most urgent moments of his text, is to gain a greater awareness of those institutions that bind us to this limited—and, to be sure, self-interested—way of thinking. The critique of the nation-state that Abe elaborates throughout his writing is in fact contradicted by a particularist conception of Abe as belonging to the corpus of Japanese literature and thought. The "flight" from such conception is effected by an understanding that it is the perceived unity of the nation-state that grounds and legitimates the very category of national literature. To read Abe, then, is to acquire a sense of the complicity that links these two entities together.

The Frontier Within

POETRY AND POETS (CONSCIOUSNESS AND THE UNCONSCIOUS)*

My beloved friend,
In this text is told
Of the night that brings all things into existence
And of man's being,
And through these things,
Of every manner of affirmation and loud laughter
And songs of heroes.
All fog and dusk open up
And a celestial body, glowing and eternal,
Enveloping all noble souls,
Will finally emerge.
At that time
This text will burn away
Through its own heat.

*Written on June 8, 1944.

SECTION I

1. WHAT IS TRUTH?

Consciousness of existence is always in one form or another accompanied by the desire to question. Consciousness attempts to confirm that its own concerns (in the simple sense of this term) are highest. It is inclined to disregard the matter of "for what purpose" and take up the question of "what is first of all necessary."

Yet we are not utterly blind or indifferent to what lies behind the issue of "for what purpose." The common and self-evident orientation of this metaphysical questioning can always be summed up in the words "for truth" or "for life."

Although truth itself is not necessarily questioned, it always remains the driving force behind man's spiritual and cultural life. No matter what the question is, it can never be entirely indifferent to truth. Truth is always one element in the drama of life, whether as theater, stage, script, writer, critic, or actor.

As every serious thinker today knows, however, the idea or ideal state that is truth does not exist objectively outside us in the form of something fixed or stable. Yet when one asks whether what has been categorically termed as truth is either analogous or homologous (to borrow terms from biology), then truth inevitably disappears in the vague fog as a symbol of fanciful myths.

But this disappearance is a result of neither man's imperfection nor insufficient analysis; rather, it is the necessary fate of truth. Why is this? Such anxiety appears on the basis of various actions as a premonition. A kind of "rational" judgment attempts to bring about the fall of all things into a single point floating in infinity. Immersed in the grief of its own self-doubt, consciousness tries to find something that precedes it. Reason falls while unreason dissolves. Everything then melts into the chaos of creation. Light seems to shine forth when all things become entangled and align with the depths of a single night. Like the coming of spring, a kind of hope and joy flits by within the symbol of the night.

But it then strikes one that truth is yet once again left behind in winter, teased by the freezing wind. Why is this?

In order to answer this question, I will first level a charge against the traditional errors and unclear definitions concerning the notions of subject and object. I will then conclude that truth can never be questioned in this manner. Yes, the question of truth must be posed once again in the faraway skies.

2. SUBJECT AND OBJECT

Subject and object have been the target of mankind's most brilliant battles over knowledge since ancient times. Each has tried to usurp the absolute throne and negate the other, but with few exceptions the battle finally appeared to end with the pure object falling to its knees before the pure subject. However, ontological *existence*, which precedes this division between subject and object, has been allowed to reign over both of these by virtue of the fact that man's suffering has sunk more and more deeply within the infinite realm of intuition. Unknown, anxious expectations have been presaged in several souls as the comprehensive source of life. Within the night of deep souls, in which there is nothing to question or criticize, higher souls have identified the voice of production.

Nevertheless, subject and object have not disappeared from our view. When the night of deep souls rose to a testimonial of life via the form of consciousness, subject and object remained unresolved in the hollows of both outstretched hands. As always, these two were conflated in various ways.

As champions of life or higher knowledge, we must of course break with the global dimension of subject and object so as to live within the deep night—that is, the existential nothingness where reason and unreason coincide. All affirmations must then reemerge in the instantaneously heroic or tragic transformation, and we must find our own correct path within our incessant falling.

Yet when experience-based philosophers and poets of the cosmos (Dionysus) encounter language in the form of consciousness, which is the necessary restraint on human relations, is it possible to completely abandon the dimension of subject and object? For the highest souls that fall into the everydayness of existence, is that dimension merely a meaningless specter?

Yes and no, as is most certainly the case. We encounter here a double response that involves both negation and affirmation. Yet there is no contradiction here.

First, let us consider the case of negation. The fixed pressures and faith with which we are burdened certainly disappear without a trace before our premonition of the deep night, and only poetic ecstasy overcomes suffering to instantly plunge us forward into the dawn of affirmation. Yet what should we do with the daily reflection of our humanity, a humanity that cannot be God precisely because it desires to be God? Worldly existence cannot be forever condensed into one high dimension. Lower dimensions are invariably rooted to the increasing depths of the world as the essence of the night, and constantly sustain themselves via the ever higher unfolding. Is it not then natural for the dimension of subject and object to remain as one element of life?

Second, a brief matter can be considered in the case of affirmation. A transformation is demanded—that is, an incessant separation and departure—through which we can seek the life of the self that flows among all everyday things as something unfolding within a cosmos that transcends subject and object.

Considered from two distinct standpoints, the subject and object that had once rippled identically upon the same dimension now appear clearly as utterly different and irreconcilable dimensions. The language might be the same in these two cases, but their form and character are revealed to be completely different.

Yet I shall introduce a third subject and object that comes about at an even higher level of unfolding. It is this that must truly be questioned, for it requires a great leap in our attitude regarding such things as truth and life.

Think about it: what has traditionally been handed down to us through these words "subject" and "object"? "Object" refers to a notion that is shared by all, that is, possesses universal validity, whereas "subject" indicates a particular notion that is unique to each individual. From our standpoint, however, the notion of universal validity itself already involves the loss of objectivity. If the object is to reacquire a forceful standpoint before thought, then it must be reconsidered on the basis of a definition other than that of universal validity. The object must now be critically reappraised from an existential perspective.

All kinds of voices begin from the point where our souls come in contact with the essence of the night. These voices unfold in various dimensions and become words. They can be grasped within consciousness in the form of self-negation or self-transcendence. The thing in itself—that is, intuition of the night—spawns a kind of symbolic premonition in the very form of unfolding itself. It is here where one glimpses the third object, which neither loses its existential significance nor violates the original inner unity that produces objective language.

It is clear that all expression necessarily takes place through the subject. Only subjective experience can transform all consciousness into language.

Of course the differential weight of words (i.e., the dimensionality contained within them) can be understood in accordance with the different dimensions of the internal unfolding of each person as existent. The weight of words varies among subjects depending on the degree to which their souls come in contact with the essence of the night.

Now what is the significance of the ultimate point in the subject's ever increasing dimensional unfolding? Man's soul then experiences the approach of the infinite night. Intuition of the night is not merely conceptual; it appears in practical form within actions, experience, and methods. Can we not define this ultimate point, which is eternally distant and far away, as the third object?

The traditional notion of the object held that it exists outside us as a hypothetically independent entity, one whose form is eternally maintained. According to our definition, however, the object is internal but also forms part of the eternal form of the deep night that is both grasped as a symbolic mark and stands within our longing for life, which extends throughout the cosmos as a whole. *Our original voice* can be found therein. Despite the fact that this voice is the most subjective, it nevertheless goes far beyond the subjective and shudders within its premonition of the eternal. Here one finds existential eternity as condensed in the instant. Is this not the correct ontological interpretation of the object?

Only the perfected poet of the cosmos can clearly grasp this kind of object as his own. In other words, only the highest subject can approach it. Setting aside the question of the madman, souls, no matter how healthy (?) they are, perceive the object merely as an eternally unknown and illusory concept when their own subjective unfolding remains yet undeveloped. Eternity is possible only for those who know the night. As ever, the ancient dream of the object preserves its iconic status as something that makes ordinary people smile and cry.

3. WHAT IS TRUTH? PART TWO

Truth is the sound of a reed flute playing in the wilderness.
Truth is a disguise of the mind.

If we, while passing through various dimensions in our role of adjudicator, look closely at truth, which lingers coldly at times outside and within us, we immediately realize that it manifests our desire for self-sustenance. As

Nietzsche said, we often mistake cause and effect. In such cases, the cause comes to be created in the service of the effect through a desire for explanation or solace. I have just made an assertion. Yet is not the assertion that "the cause comes to be created in the service of the effect" not an utter self-contradiction? Here the assertion already demands truth. To state that something is true is a kind of affirmation, an original cause. But isn't this cause already nothing more than an explanation for the effect? Such suspicion renders the following observations completely meaningless, bringing them to a standstill by reducing all language to a mere excuse. Is truth then only an excuse for life?

Yet even this ambitious rhetorical question no longer waits for a response; instead it disappears in vain, unable to sustain its own excess weight. This question already conceals the desire and hope for a newer truth even if that means abandoning the truth one has hitherto maintained, which relates to the nature of truth as lacking any basic differences in dimension. The contradictions and deceptions contained in this question are the very elements of the guilty, mistaken notion of truth (?) that previously lured truth into a vast maze.

Truth thus floats up and sinks down, approaches while remaining inaccessible, already spectacularly fleeing beyond the range of negation and affirmation, but I wonder if we can't recover it ourselves with the aid and method of the third object, as defined in the previous section.

Yet it would be both impossible and unjust to complete this task without critically appraising its own character. All questioning has its sources and goals. For all true thinkers, this point can never be overlooked. Now what is the ground from which our own questioning emerges? Are there any reasons why we find in this third object a premonition or expectation that truth can be recovered? Without first resolving these issues, our questioning can never rise beyond empty, diversionary logic.

Truth appears within all dimensions in many diverse forms. Truth first began in the affirmative form of judgment. The expressions "a . . . b . . . c is true" and "it is true that α . . . β . . . γ is true" potentially correspond to each other as based on the method of undetermined coefficients. That is, "a . . . b . . . c" can be replaced and fulfilled only according to the form "α . . . β . . . γ is true." In other words, truth is the criterion of truthfulness. In this case, it is nothing other than objectivity that functions as the scale. This represents the first relation between truth and object.

Next let's focus not on truth but on the disclosure of truth itself. (This also signifies the presence of dimensional stages of unfolding.) Truth itself is always disclosed as that which unfolds. This is precisely the reason why truth previously fell into a maze. Insofar as we recognize the necessity of the hermeneutical standpoint, we must acknowledge that truth goes beyond the constraint that something be true and requires meaning and value as well. In other words, truth is the self-perfecting unfolding of the principle of life (in the broad sense), which contains the highest meaning and value. In this sense, we can methodologically introduce the (second) relationship between truth and object.

In any case, truth exists outside the range of negation or affirmation. Truth itself is neither existence nor nonexistence. It preserves its character of relating to man, regardless of its importance or unimportance, or whether it relates to friend or enemy. Truth does not relate individually to individual instances but rather strictly on the basis of its own principled validity. It attempts to essentially govern all phenomena, regardless of dimension. As generally conceived, truth takes the form of philosophical principles.

In fact, however, truth is absolutely not a philosophical principle. Philosophical principles consist simply of laws that govern, but truth can never be limited to the form of a law. Like truth, philosophical principles might also represent an incessant advance toward a certain goal or direction. Although they follow the same movement, philosophical principles are an advance forward. In this sense, however, truth clings to one point. The movement of truth is discontinuous, to be found in leaps. Truth always changes dimensions through self-negation.

In other words, truth is a character of man's being. Everything that I have stated above regarding the various tendencies of truth can be summarized in this one phrase. But this phrase is in no way self-contradictory (in relation to truth).

Let me provide an example in which everything that I have stated above can be brought together: "Truth is contained in the phrase 'Truth is man's aspiration.'" What is the relation here between the first truth and the second? Two cases can be discerned: one cyclical, the other dimensional unfolding. If the fact that truth is man's aspiration signifies man's aspiration, then this involves a cycle; otherwise it involves dimensional unfolding. One would be committing a serious error by considering this phrase to be merely cyclical. That is, truth understood as man's aspiration invariably conceals within it will or intentionality. Truth can never be under man's control. In the case of "A is truth," however, truth is subjugated to reason in the form of a law. These two truths clearly possess different dimensions. Formally they represent an ascending unfolding, but in content they reveal a descending unfolding or closure. In its essence, however, the self-perfecting leap of truth does not restrict itself to either of these two truths. Rather it seeks itself in the small space between these two phrases. This gives rise to various possibilities, as follows:

"The claim that 'truth is man's aspiration' itself may not be true. But might there not be some trace of truth concealed in the *thought* that truth is man's aspiration?"

"Rather than claiming that truth is man's aspiration, shouldn't one conceive of truth as that which discloses itself as what must receive man's aspiration?"

"There is already concealed in these phrases a longing for truth. The departure point of these phrases is nothing other than man's being."

"That is to say, truth is man's being. This understanding of truth circulates infinitely, without any contradiction."

"All (individual or dimensionally different) truth corresponds to its cyclical stage, as mentioned above. To claim that truth is one character of man's being is to say that it can be obtained through the first cycle on the basis of a certain method. The two phrases presented at the beginning of this section correspond to a certain cyclical stage. At the same time, they also refer back to the one phrase above. All truths begin from 'truth is man's being' and revert back to 'truth is man's being.' This fact must be described as truth in the form of man's being."

"The claim that truth is man's being itself undergoes infinite dimensional turns. This incessant turning takes place at infinite speed as compared to the path of negation and affirmation."

(The phrase "man's being" must be rigorously distinguished from that of "existing a priori within man.")

Albeit in a very different form, we have finally reached this conclusion by following the method that departs from the subject to arrive at the third object. By focusing more closely on this conclusion, however, we realize that it has brought about a loss of value in truth. Truth that contains value is no longer the bare form of truth itself. Value itself is, like truth, man's being, but it is completely independent of truth. When these two coincide, what is called truth is really an error caused by conflating these two through imperfect understanding, and this should be referred to rather as a *desired* object. From our standpoint, however, the classical notion of the object has already perished and been replaced by a new understanding of the third object, which must be described as an emissary of the night. Would this be applicable to the third object here? Such object represents the very limit of the ascending dimensional unfolding of the subject. Here a kind of poetic experience becomes necessary. The third object chooses its recipient. Just as a child selectively belongs to its mother before separating from her and becoming independent in a new generation, so too does this object separate from the individual character of the subject so as to be eventually raised to the level of pure human being in the form of cosmic poetic experience.

At the limit of various dimensional unfolding where "being-in the world" and "being in-the world" coincide, object and truth are recognized simply as different expressions of man's being.

Thus all representations of phenomena refer back to the dimensional cycle of this one instance that is man's being. In order to further clarify this matter, we must now more critically develop the representation and substance of this notion of "man's being."

4. MAN'S BEING

Man's being: in the previous section we discussed the *inner* self-circulation of the representation and substance of man's being. In this way, however, such an imperfect symbol inevitably perishes in nihilistic skepticism as a mere subjective idea. We now confront that danger. We must advance critical logic in order to avoid falling into the trap of reversing cause and effect.

The question of attitude must first be considered. As should be clear from the foregoing, those who critically approach this problematic must always put themselves in the movement and leap of incessant unfolding while keeping in mind the ultimate reflection of the dimensional stages, which is so easily lost sight of. Any hypotheses of one fundamental idea must here be absolutely avoided. Watching, learning, and critically appraising are far more important than thinking. What is required, in other words, is an attitude based on experience. Lacking any specific departure point at present, all deductive reasoning can rely only on the self-unfolding of our own attitude. That is to say, the notion of attitude does not refer simply to the attitude of the questioner, for this notion itself must be questioned in its essence. The being of the question—that is, its rise to the level of attitude— is what determines man's being.

Nihilistic skepticism (the skeptical negation of all assertions) grounds itself on its own imperfect methodology, since it cannot maintain any of its own assertions or conclusions. Even if it transcends that character, however, it cannot negate it. Furthermore, even if nihilistic skepticism negates its own nihilism through self-skepticism, it cannot negate skepticism itself so as to affirm something new. Yet the incessant pursuit of this method eventually leads it to sublate its own status as skepticism and approach a state of Buddhist emptiness or a chaos that transcends both negation and affirmation. This method in fact coincides with the method of infinite dimensional unfolding that we have been following.

What we find here is chaos, a vast night: a night that conceals within itself numerous lives and sinks within its own horrible silence, an intense thermal mass that melts all. Here there is neither past nor future nor dream, for chaos is present and real. This chaos remains indifferent to individuality. A stifling indifference surrounds us. All words are commanded to be silent. Can anything possibly emerge from this chaos? What can we expect by standing here? What kind of premonition awaits order? Might there not be a secret concealed here somewhere? Or is that merely a specter of death and anarchy? Doesn't everything slip away from my own two hands until finally I myself fall into falsehood?

These are criticisms, for here we must attempt the final unfolding. Such criticisms are not logical but rather experiential, as based on attitude. Our concern must be questioned and nihilism and the fall endured. We must experience the night ourselves, and even within our everyday lives breathe in the night and listen to its self-unfolding.

The night in no way signifies a conceptual state. Nor is it the target arrived at by criticism, negation, and affirmation. Such arrows lose their way in the night and drift off. The night cannot be defined. Rather it must be presaged and perceived firsthand as an urgent experience in an infinite dimensional unfolding. It can be grasped only instantaneously. Within this grasping, in fact, there exists a light that must be considered. What is to be critically approached, in other words, is the night in terms of its self-disclosure, imminence, and inner character.

To symbolize the night by that name is merely our interpretation. The desire to fall into truth, which might also be called self-recognition, is nothing other than an expression enabled by reason, which is the surface of the night. Such self-recognition is the ethical expression of man's being, but it can never be governed by value. Rather, it precedes value as that which produces value, and must of course be rigorously distinguished from such things as self-complacency, self-sufficiency, and happiness. Self-recognition is not an action but rather the principle of action. Heidegger speaks of the everydayness of existence, that is, the primacy of *Dasein*. Self-recognition can be seen when this everydayness is purely taken up and the choices of the existent are unfolded and grasped in their essence. This is what I am referring to when I speak of "self-recognition." It must always be grasped within the unconscious and irrational by tracing actions dimensionally back to their origin. As goes without saying, psychological interpretations are here completely invalid.

Seen in this way, self-recognition is precisely the night's self-disclosure, immanence, and inner character. Because there is here true apprehension as based on experience, any negation through cyclical interaction is inapplicable. Thus it becomes clear that the self that experiences the night is ontologically privileged. The concrete experience of the night raises the questioner to the highest level. Nevertheless, we have not yet arrived at any conclusion but merely explained the notion of attitude. Keeping this notion in mind, let us now turn to the question of the night and man's being.

The night is in no way the work of reason, nor is it deduced from experience. It is experience itself. The night is not an invited guest but rather the air that fills this room. It is *that which thus brings all things into existence*. Our judgments, expressions, lives, actions, fantasies: everything is brought into existence by the night. Hermeneutical experience: the blank space in the following lines is filled by these silent words. (I have prepared this blank space for the purpose of your own self-experience.)

....

....

....

Man's being is clearly revealed by these several lines of blank space. The night is *that which thus brings things into existence*.

(Let me provide a bit more explanation of this point in anticipation of the many criticisms that are likely to be directed at these words. Such criticisms will no doubt claim that the notion of "that which thus brings things into existence" represents a subjective, arbitrary judgment. What is "thus"? What is "brings things into existence"? What is "that which"? But these criticisms easily fall to the ground due to the self-experience of those who launch them. All we have to say here is that such experience is not merely our experience of the night but rather the experience of the night's self-experience. The many conflicts unfolding here in this text; my silent dialogue with the imaginary reader who exists in my mind; your debate as reader with the imaginary me; the skeptical critic; the criticisms he launches; what I will write now; what I have written; the expression "thus brings things into existence": all of these infiltrate the word "thus." The phrase "brings things into existence" is enveloped within the judgment "thus," but when it is experienced as the self-experience of the "thus," it goes beyond the range of such criticisms as a new self-experience, that is, the productive principle of the experiential "thus." Clearly this notion of "thus brings things into existence" eludes consciousness. Given that consciousness represents the law of restrictive interaction between one person and another, this notion can also be described as inexpressible. In other words, the night cannot be objectified by this expression, only symbolized. Precisely for this reason, any criticism of the phrase "that which" necessarily loses its effectiveness. "That which" does not indicate the night itself; rather, it merely signifies a symbolic expression. Thus what appears to the critic as a target reveals itself to be simply a mirage.)

How must we interpret man's being in relation to the night as "that which thus brings things into existence"? It is clear both from the nature of the night and the ontological status required by man's being that these two things are identical in essence. Yet where does their symbolic difference originate? This difference can be found in the fact that man's being is the active expression itself of "thus brings things into existence," whereas the night is enabled by the objectified method of the "that which." The departure point and passage may have been different, but it is clear that ultimately these two things and the unfolding development of their passage perfectly correspond to each other. In other words, man's being is the night and the night is man's being.

However, we must not forget that the expression "man's being" is an utter symbol. The people who stand before us as existents have not yet made their appearance. These people are enveloped in a fog of the unknown, they are a premonition of the ego. They experience things, they are the experienced cosmos; they are part of being-in-the-world, which exists prior to subject and object; they are action. They can be grasped only within their fall into this *unfolding everydayness*. When people are connected to the word "being," even the foregoing meaning virtually disappears and the single phrase "man's being" becomes an experiential symbol that cannot be broken down and discussed, like a chemical bond that cannot be reduced to its constitutive elements through any simple method since those elements have now bonded to become different from what they were originally.

Our point here is that reason, interpretation, and language are all meaningless. Man's being is also a mere symbol, like the night. The interpretative attitude regarding language is necessary. Yet interpretation must not become analytic. What is needed is experiential interpretation, especially with regard to symbols.

We have thus discussed man's being and the chaotic origin that brings into existence all manner of concepts and actions. In the foregoing four sections, I have explained my nature and attitude in this text.

SECTION II

1. BEING-IN-THE-WORLD

Longing for interiority, one becomes aware of the division between the chamber of the mind and the utterly indifferent external world. One then repeatedly tries to force open the eternal window separating these two. But the hand reaching out to open that window is always powerless, and like an incorporeal specter one must give up in dejection. This window is forever closed.

We are troubled by this division, but does the desired outside of the window really exist in the form in which we now see it? Does this window glass ever transparently allow for the figure of the external world as such to be sent into our solitary chamber? Is that variegated external world not merely an apparition that is skillfully depicted or traced out by this window glass? Is this window not a mirror that reflects our mind?

Is it not reasonable that we think this way? All rulers have now vanished, and even the self has lost its meaning as ruler. Like the "locus" defined by Aristotle as the internal surface that envelops things, only a cold, indifferent diamond remains in our hands: this diamond may be the primary intuition of experience and possibility, but it cannot be the cause of anything. In the realm of existence, we can harbor no hopes or expectations, like an exile on a deserted island. A diamond only pierces our mind with its hard, sharp edges. Come now, quietly return to your assigned chamber and look around. Is this window not the mirror that reflects our mind?

Surely anyone can see that this window is *man's being*. As such, must we not also conceive the figure of the external world as seen (putatively) through that window as belonging to it? Regardless of whether or not that world exists, the particular restriction that it be seen through the window has already been added, and that window represents the experiential interpretation of man's being. Because of this, the external world reveals itself to be nothing other than that which is glimpsed through our experiential inter-pretation. Precisely for this reason, the external world is "thus seen." What is this "thus seen" if not the nature of the window? As that which is "thus seen," the external world belongs to the window. An external world that did not belong to the window might of course also be possible. However, such world would never be "thus seen"; it would be forever unknown, noth-ing more than an irrelevant fantasy. For an immature soul, thinking about such a world would be complete reverie, a fleeting, naïve, and anguished longing, but this would be a clumsy or even harmful misapprehension. What could this external world as "thus seen" be if not the reflection of our minds? What could that window be if not the mirror that reflects this world?

Until now, however, the object of our thinking has been the figure of the external world. Yet this world does not only appear as a figure. The fig-ure that exists outside, separated from the chamber of our mind, has now disappeared, but what of the meaning of the external world that is revealed together with the figure?

Of course the figure itself is a kind of meaning. Yet this meaning repre-sents the meaning of the night as that in which the figure appears, which is completely different from the meaning of value that we are here problema-tizing. I am trying to explain the meaning of a kind of judgment, the con-tent as opposed to the figure. This can also be described, in certain cases, as active.

Examining this closely, we find an unspeakably drastic transformation that begins suddenly in our soul or chamber of the mind. We suddenly real-ize that the meaning or content that is believed to appear strictly along-side the figure has at some point separated from it and is drifting in infinite space. It has sunk into an inaccessibly distant sky, a chaos where it mixes together with stars. Realizing this, we look around at the dark expanse, our skin crawling, as if awakening from a nightmare. The darkness sud-denly appears horrible. The dark expanse constantly increases in depth and becomes heavier at every moment, appearing about to crush us. Thinking that it would certainly be possible to relax if a light were turned on, we rise to switch on the light.

Yet no relief comes to mind. Rather, we are beset by a terrible fear as we bitterly regret the fact that we didn't endure the oppression in the dark-ness. What has happened? One imagined oneself sleeping quietly and safely ensconced behind solid wall when suddenly all walls vanish and one is alone floating adrift in the darkness. What fear can be greater than this?

But take courage! This courage will surely help you adjust to the dark. And you must question! Gaze into the darkness and ask what has happened!

When one thinks about it, meaning is always solitary. When it appears alongside a figure, that is less the nature of meaning than it is of man's being. Meaning appears as man's being and the night's self-disclosure: it wanders among the solitary night together with value, it is a cluster of stars. Meaning is a constellation that takes the form of a spear. And the sharp tip of this spear pierces the various figures, finally cutting away the hostility of the external world, which had so heavily pressed in upon the surrounding chamber of our mind. The walls that we sadly accepted lost the external pressure that had hitherto maintained equilibrium, and with frightening speed expanded outward. They simultaneously lost all materiality, becoming part of the night. Although the cosmos floats in darkness, it confronted us without being in any way distant from us. The various figures were the media that filled the stars.

One after another, all figures are brought within the self when they come in contact with the solitary spear constellation. In order to see this, of course, one needs the light of unfolding. The chamber of the mind then expands increasingly outward. Before this unfolding deepens, the chamber of the mind functions as an intuition of an eternally fixed immobility: the external world as reflected in the window is enveloped in the sad light of dusk as the self's own reflection as this self continues to reject all meaning and expectation. As the storm of unfolding gradually moves in the direction of purity, however, it finally destroys the walls that define the self as finite and the border between inside and outside that brings us into existence as "being-in the world." The chamber of the mind thus comes to be dispersed in the infinite night of man's being. As eternally unknown, the external world acutely provokes our longing. When we realize that the world's brilliant coloration is nothing other than the radiant spear constellation that exists within it, the unknown external world loses its quality as mere figure and is reborn as a new element that is completely inseparable from its meaning within the infinitely expanded chamber of the mind. After so long, the stars then shine. And it is the darkness surrounding these stars that allows them to shine so brightly. We do not see stars; we see stars shining in the dark night.

Thus the self understood as a "being-in the world" expands to the level of "being in-the world." Rilke conceived of *Dinge*, or things, as flowing with life and celebrated them in verse so grandly and beautifully because he accepted them with a love that inflamed the spear constellation shining in the dark night. Yes, heavy stars fall, as does the heavy, dark night. These are not something that can be seen; rather, they must be accepted.

Yet is the self as a "being in-the world" really the collection of various unfolding dimensions? What exactly is "being in-the world?" Is it truth? Or would that also be an illusory misplacement of cause and effect? Would it not be strange if our unfolding were to stop here? The night would vanish if our unfolding were to end. If we are to maintain the same standpoint as defined in section 1 above, then it would be absolutely impossible for us not to doubt this strange ending or midway point. Where is the mistake? Where is the end or inadequacy of this unfolding?

What could these questions be if not the tragedy of life? We are engulfed by a horrible premonition that the false mark of subject and object that erases all things in the darkness is burned into our forehead.

In fact, this begins in the following way: meaning was at a standstill. Like a thermal mass on thin ice, however, it quickly sank and disappeared. For there was clearly a mistake here. Had we not already enclosed some kind of affirmation *within* meaning? Weren't we unable to distinguish meaning and value in the faint light, despite the fact that they belong to completely different constellations, which unfolded to this point and yet remained at a lower, impure dimension? Meaning and value, which are independent of each other, are elements of a cosmic structure; they do not emit the eternal light of truth. They represent (different) ways for chaos to disclose itself, as apprehended strictly by the experiential and symbolic intuition that is man's being. Meaning must once again become the jewel of an uninhabited land that is completely indifferent to us. It must be raised to the level of man's being in its endless unfolding.

But look! These stars separated from the figure more than they have ever done before. Meaning and figuration are of completely different dimensions: one vanishes on the basis of the other, while this other disappears from view if one fixes one's gaze on the first. These two appear to coexist, but is it the case that Rilke's *Dinge*, which are rendered possible strictly by this coexistence, are a dreamlike rapture that transcends all judgment?

However, this question discloses the following formula and is itself clarified by it: namely, *Dasein* represents a gap of countless different dimensions. And intuition consists of an elevated viewing of this multilayered, transparent plate glass. The night is precisely this lightless totality.

Seen in this way, the world increasingly reinforces its infinity together with man's finitude. Although the world is man's being, it is not *man's* being. It never stops at the level of "being in-the world." Man can never restrict or govern his being. Rather, it is this being that first assigns man the status of a being-in-the-world. The world is the totality, an infinity bound up with the night. In which case, wouldn't it be "being-in the world" that actually comes to the fore? Yet the unfolding of a higher level of man's being advances in and of itself ever higher, revolving endlessly around a circle. Man's being remains neither at "being-in the world" nor "being in-the world," but rather passes silently through a light that flickers rapidly from one to the other.

The night and world can be perceived only by the actant in his transformative actions, passing from one dimension to the next in the course of his unfolding. There is nothing that is at a standstill, for everything goes around. This rotation itself then vanishes as a fixed idea. All flows are a line of discontinuous points.

When the night is instantly captured as the intuition of experiential *Dasein*, both "being-in the world" and "being in-the world," with their endlessly repeating movements, are sublated in that instant and become pure being-in-the-world as man's being. Here being-in-the-world is no longer a combination of individual words. It is precisely in this sense that Rilke's *Dinge* possess eternal objectivity. Being-in-the-world is the instantaneously concrete intuition of the night. The grievous reflective oppositions vanish, the wordless night closes in, and the eternal instant envelops the flesh.

THEORY AND PRACTICE IN LITERATURE

I

Do such questions as "What is literature?" and "What should literature be?" really have any meaning? There are those who claim that literature is something to be felt rather than discussed. Certainly any literature that can be replaced by several lines of plot cannot be described as literature. Indeed, no matter how detailed or accurate the commentary on the work, literature is that in which such replacement is impossible. This is its essential point of difference with other forms of written expression.

In the case of geometry, for example, one finds the following proposition: "Draw any circle around point A." Regardless of whether this circle is drawn with a compass on a notebook, by a teacher in freehand on a blackboard, or is simply imagined by a lazy student in his head, they all carry the same meaning. Also, regardless of whether one speaks of "the line segment contained within a circle's circumference that passes through the center"

First published June 30, 1954, in *Iwanami kōza: Bungaku*, vol. 8.

or "the circle's largest chord," the reference to the diameter is the same. This point likely applies to all scientific description. Such expressions are a pure means in relation to content, they are transparent as a vacuum, and necessarily must be so. If it is possible to speak here of skill or clumsiness of expression, this would refer strictly to the degree of transparency.

Yet this is not the case with literature. Even if the expressions "that long-faced woman" and "that horse-faced woman" referred to the same woman, they carry a completely different meaning. But perhaps this is not a very suitable example. The modern novel has advanced in such a way as to minimize such differences in meaning as much as possible. As Sartre points out, the language for prose should ideally be as transparent as possible (Sartre, "What Is Literature?"). In the world of prose today, it has become commonsense to scorn an ornate style and favor simple, dry expressions. One persuades not by expression but by the expressed content. Yet isn't there an essential difference between scientific expression and literary expression? Some people distinguish between these two by claiming that the former involves general knowledge whereas the latter involves the writer's own individuality, but this distinction appears inadequate to me. The notion of individuality is still too vague here. It probably refers to something like a creative subject, but if that is the case, wouldn't this also apply to, say, brilliant philosophical essays?

Actually, the notion that it is the prerogative of literature to emphasize a writer's individuality is to a certain extent bound up with a conservative way of thinking. Of course this is not to say that this notion is conservative in full. Claims in favor of the writer's individuality do carry a certain meaning in response to criticisms that take the form of official "discussions," in which literary works are judged peremptorily through ideologically driven assessments, as for example, "This work contains no revolutionary vision" or "No mention is made of workers." And yet the significance of such claims lies strictly within these limits. A method that classifies works on the basis of whether or not they involve the writer's individuality ultimately represents nothing more than a subjective organization of phenomena. If that is the case, wouldn't it be better to classify things based on something like the statistics derived from the comparative grammar of literary works and scientific essays? Discovering the percentage of parts of speech, for example, would surely reveal the difference between these two.

If what is called literary theory were actually at this level, then it might well be that literature has no need of theory. Even without going that far, literary theory might simply operate on the basis of its own intellectual curiosity, unrelated to literature itself. Since literature, as with certain kinds of social phenomena (e.g., a university professor's academic ability vis-à-vis his salary), can be said to possess relative autonomy vis-à-vis other social phenomena, such a claim is not so far-fetched. In Japan, actually, true literary theory continues to be ignored and pushed sadly aside in that world of writing that, while dealing with literature, remains yet outside it (generally referred to as literary criticism). A writer's activities were generally seen as a kind of moral practice, a personal protest against the everyday world, a highly individuated expression of the world of "art" that could be attained only by intense individual training, and thus something in which no theoretical intervention was ever possible. ("*Were* generally seen": I use the past tense here since this tendency has changed quite a bit in the postwar.) For example, the expression "Literature cannot emerge where there is no pain" is very easily accepted. If a writer were to speak of his writing like office work, for example, he would no doubt cause great disappointment among his listeners. What appears writerlike consists simply in the writer reducing as much as possible the distance between his work and personal life, and also in his taking whatever drastic steps possible to ensure that the substance of his personal life functions as a proxy in resolving the troubles in the lives of his readers. (Itō Sei regards such a writer as an escaped slave, but this escape itself would be a drastic act for most people.) Virtually no distinction is made between the *putatively writerlike* and the value of the work. In fact, I suspect that most so-called literary youths feel less passion for creating works than they do for those efforts required to become *putatively writerlike*. As goes without saying, this is the very foundation of I-novel culture.

Rather than devoting itself to creating theories, therefore, most literary criticism takes the form of simply commenting on current topics or discussing life from a literary perspective for the purpose of creating a commodity value for literature. Indeed, it might be too much to describe commentaries on current topics in this manner. Even such commentaries should have educational meaning apart from the market. No matter how we might consider them subjectively, however, the role objectively played by most commentaries consists simply in the free competition of bourgeois trade. Insofar as literary criticism takes part in this, writers (if simply in appearance) could pretend to ignore this genre. For example, the following unpleasantly bizarre commentary is openly published in first-rate newspapers: "This month Mr. So-and-so's work is the most worth reading. It is an *extraordinary example of middlebrow fiction*." No real effort is required to pretend to ignore this. If the organic association that is the literary establishment comes to be formed by the joining of this totality with the (capitalist) and relatively autonomous movement of commercial journalism, then it would hardly be surprising for there to be absolutely no space for theoretical reflection.

But perhaps it would be slightly premature to describe the contempt for theory only in these terms. This same tendency can be found in no small degree among the writers of so-called democratic literature, who flatter themselves into believing that they exist outside the literary establishment. As goes without saying, I am not trying to prove here that theory is unnecessary. My aim rather is to emphasize its necessity. If, according to Marx, "Mankind always takes up only such problems as it can solve,"[1] then my conclusion regarding these writers of democratic literature—namely, that if literary establishment writers who reject the necessity of theory are ruled by literature's commodity value, then what value rules over the writers of democratic literature who reject the necessity of theory?—has already been prepared. However, I needn't touch upon it now. Let me simply repeat the excuse these writers have for holding theory in such contempt. These intellectually progressive but literarily conservative (there is no need to explain here that the rejection of theory is conservative) writers are fixed on the idea that the relation between theory and practice is one of antagonism. They claim that theory is conceptual, intellectual, petty bourgeois, and western, whereas practice is realistic, popular, and revolutionary. Of course it is correct to privilege practice over theory. In his *Materialism and Empirio-Criticism*, Lenin himself writes that, "If we include the criterion of practice in the foundation of the theory of knowledge we inevitably arrive at materialism."[2] Practice is clearly the foundation of man's cognitive activities and the driving force behind the development of knowledge.

Yet isn't it strange that such unilateral emphasis on practice on the part of these writers of democratic literature renders them no different from the I-novel writers, as we saw earlier? If that is the case, can we then say that it is not necessarily wrong to see the I-novel in terms of Japanese national particularity?

When one thinks about it, there are various nuances as to why the I-novel gained acceptance in Japan and was recognized as progressive. Was there not a kind of moral deification of practice at stake here? Even if these writers acquired a certain knowledge and critical ability, were there not also some deeply rooted feudal feelings that remained? In addition to these more passive reasons, however, one must also take into account the following active ones.

Unable to fully resist the policies of class division as established by those in power, European rationalism could not be assimilated as national property and remained, like a *lump*, in the form of intellectual satisfaction among the petty bourgeois intelligentsia. This brought about a sense of rupture with the masses, and from this a feeling of emptiness. Two different tendencies thus came to emerge from within the intelligentsia.

The first is that of practice as panacea, which we have been discussing, and the other something that might be called introverted naturalism. Even though the aims of naturalism are indeed quite assertive, this was originally a method that established as its axis the standpoint of the observer. Once its search turned inward, naturalism immediately became a bystander of reality. The evaluative criteria of literature came to be determined by this method, or perhaps this method's self-awareness. The ideas of Flaubert would be the exemplary type here. In its privileging of methodology, one of the characteristics of naturalism was its distinction between expression and knowledge. Perhaps it is not quite apt to speak here of distinction, but naturalism essentially sought to detach expression from knowledge.

This notion is quite deeply rooted among literary theoreticians, and even Sasaki Kiichi, for example, seems to make the same mistake. In Sasaki's case, however, a critique is made against idealism in its neglect of the particularity of literary knowledge, but I wonder if he doesn't fall into idealism of another sort. Expression inheres within knowledge, and knowledge cannot be formed without recourse to expression. Knowledge and expression are simply two names for the same function as brought about by the abstractions of the brain.

The notion that expression can be detached from knowledge is idealist, as has already been illustrated by the dual-system theory of Pavlov's conditioned response.

This dual-system theory refers to something like a physiological superstructure, as it posited a second conditioned response formed on the basis of the (first) conditioned response, in which the innately unconditioned response seen in all dogs that begin salivating anytime and anywhere when fed comes to be associated with the sound of an electric bell (conditioned stimulus). As the physiological basis for consciousness, this is comparable to Darwin's theory of evolution in its revolutionary impact.

The second conditioned response can be found only in humans. This response is generally highly unstable and becomes stable only through the formation of language. Language is the sign of a sign. Through this sign of a sign, man acquired the ability to generalize—that is, to render abstract— the reflex activity of the cerebral cortex. It is already clear that abstraction or knowledge depends upon language and thus expression, and also that expression is a form of knowledge.

As Marx also points out, "Ideas do not exist separately from language."[3] In Stalin's recent treatise on linguistics, he emphasizes the corporeality and materiality of knowledge as follows: "It is said that thoughts arise in the mind of man prior to their being expressed in speech, that they arise without linguistic material, without linguistic integument, in, so to say, a naked form. But that is absolutely wrong. Whatever thoughts arise in the human mind and at whatever moment, they can arise and exist only on the basis of the linguistic material, on the basis of language terms and phrases. Bare thoughts, free of the linguistic material, free of the 'natural matter' of language, do not exist."[4]

The most important issue here concerns the reason why, in viewpoints that privilege methodology, a need has been created to distinguish expression and knowledge. This question would not arise in the case of idealist aesthetics, which mystifies and absolutizes knowledge, but that is not necessarily the case here. From the standpoint of materialism, what is the reason behind the emergence of this need? The answer is simple. Intellect that is severed from the masses, and that can no longer identify history within their real movement, necessarily forfeits real practice, with the result that practice comes to be confined to the center of one's personal life. In the case of writers, then, practice comes necessarily to be placed within their work of expression. A writer's practice becomes reduced to his expressive activities.

The writer thus replaces the indispensable circulation between practice and knowledge, which is necessary for man to increase and deepen knowledge, with a self-increasing circulation between expression and knowledge. This would be the equivalent of Mao Zedong's notion of the prodigy's self-circulation of indirect knowledge.

Of course knowledge is different from the static images of film. It possesses its own law of movement that allows it to deepen and increase. Mao Zedong concisely expresses this law of the deepening of knowledge: "Man's knowledge depends mainly on his activity in material production, through which he comes gradually to understand the phenomena, the properties and the laws of nature, and the relations between himself and nature; and through his activity in production he also comes gradually to understand, in varying degrees, certain relations that exist between man and man."[5] Of course the practice of production is not the only form of practice, which "takes many other forms—class struggle, political life, scientific and artistic pursuits." Through these, man, "in varying degrees, comes to know the different relations between man and man."[6]

Knowledge thus *accompanies the development of production*: it "develops step by step from a lower to a higher level, that is, from the shallower to the deeper, from the one-sided to the many-sided," until finally "the modern proletariat emerged along with immense forces of production (large-scale industry)."[7] Knowledge of society thus becomes a science.

Yet what is the law of the deepening of knowledge and the relation between theory and practice? Knowledge first begins in experience (perceptual knowledge): "this is the materialism of the theory of knowledge." It then needs to be deepened: "the perceptual stage of knowledge needs to be developed to the rational stage." And "this is the dialectics of the theory of knowledge."[8]

These statements might not appear especially new. The critique of dogmatism and empiricism as well as the lesson that knowledge is not used simply to understand and explain reality but also to functionally re-create and transform it: these lack novelty, however, precisely because they are already established truths. The deepening of knowledge is completely different from the prodigy's self-circulation of indirect knowledge. Of course Mao Zedong's "On Practice" represents a general definition of knowledge, whereas a particular law of movement regarding literary knowledge must establish a particular definition through particular research. Although Mao's theory is incomplete in this sense, the particular is always contained within the general, such that general laws should inform particular laws. Of course research into what exceeds such general laws is necessary, but let us here simply be clear that the prodigy's self-circulation of indirect knowledge is qualitatively different from a deepening of knowledge for the purpose of actively re-creating and transforming reality. Dialectical leaps in development are always taken from the viewpoint of concrete practice. Even if in collective practice these dialectical leaps do not necessarily take the form of direct, concrete action, they always contain the viewpoint of practice. Is it not obvious that any movement of knowledge that has lost this viewpoint is nondialectical?

An increase in nondialectical knowledge can never apprehend the laws of reality. Without grasping these laws, it is impossible to re-create and transform reality. Nondialectical knowledge thus results in a completely superficial classification of phenomena (pragmatism) or clings to subjective visions of utopia. Examples of this might include mechanical materialism and humanist reformism, but perhaps also modernism in its merely internal refinement of the movement of intellectual curiosity.

Knowledge that doesn't develop dialectically signifies the failure to arrive at any dialectical unity between reason and perception (Mao Zedong, "On Practice"). With respect to theoretical self-awareness, as we have mentioned, viewpoints that privilege methodology run counter to those who advocate practice as panacea, and yet they also represent mechanical applications of theory that remain unmediated by practice. As such, the more theory comes to be refined, the more it establishes an unprincipled relationship of dominance over perception, which thus falls into an unprincipled state of overflow. This is clearly contradictory to the principle of realism, which approaches its objects by virtue of transparency of expression through the self-awareness of knowledge. This contradiction gives rise to surrealism, for example, which adopts the laws of the subconscious as its method. Following World War I, there were major reevaluations of the naturalism that had reigned throughout Europe, particularly among the literary movements that privileged methodology. Surrealism was the most emblematic of these. Yet the surrealist subconscious only looked at "things." Since it had no way to discover those broader social laws existing outside "things," it could not produce works beyond its own creative methods. Through the external force of the resistance movement during World War II, however, surrealism's most brilliant artists acquired dialectical knowledge by means of that practice (Aragon, Picasso, etc.).

In fact, realism is sustained strictly by practice. Since it has forfeited practice, introverted naturalism is unable to produce works that adequately win over readers.

Hence these types of indirect knowledge and the advocates of practice as panacea that I mentioned earlier are emotionally opposed to one another. It is clear, furthermore, that this opposition actively reinforces the aversion to theory on the part of those who regard practice as panacea. These latter become even more convinced of practice's all-powerful effects and even more hardened against theory, and it would not be surprising if they came to be plagued by their own double, which argues in favor of the particular conditions in Japan that formed the I-novel. These two types have both lost the viewpoint of practice and are like homeless wanderers for whom body and shadow are severed. Realism can never emerge from either of these. For realism, as seen from the history of its emergence, is a form of real knowledge (alongside scientific knowledge) as considered from the perspective of practice in its transformation of reality. Contempt for theory never leads to an emphasis on practice; even if one emphasizes practice subjectively, that merely becomes part of its objective loss.

II

Once again, the basis of practice is productive practice, that is, the transformation of nature. In the class society established on this basis, social or class practice is necessarily inevitable. Under no conditions can man avoid these fundamental forms of practice. If he ultimately seeks to avoid them, his practice would consist in *transforming* the living self into a lifeless corpse, and this would result simply in his extinguishing himself.

Insofar as practice involves the transformation of reality, must it not naturally deepen just as knowledge deepens? This does not mean that one should move about recklessly. One must appeal to knowledge in order to extract the goal inherent in action (which may often be unconscious), endow that action with a program, and thus make it reasonable. Goals must be achieved through the deepening of practice.

The deepening of practice is possible only through the deepening of knowledge. And the deepening of knowledge can take place only on the basis of the deepening of practice. True human conditions, it can be said, lie in the unity between practice and knowledge. Stalin remarked that "writers are the engineers of the soul," but doesn't this truly mean that engineers transform the soul? As is clear from Pavlov's theory, the soul is subordinate to the flesh, it is nothing other than the movement of matter. As such, the transformation of the soul is of course not an end unto itself but rather something that must be part of the transformation of matter. As a transformation of subjective conditions necessary for external transformation, the transformation of the soul should be subordinate to the practice of transforming reality.

In other words, realism as a technique of the soul can be described as inherently based on transformative activity and the partisanship of knowledge.

"In terms of technique, one must thoroughly know the laws of the soul and control it. One mustn't gamble by relying on intuition and chance. An engineer's actions are a living concrete expression of practice and knowledge": by speaking only in these terms, you who scorn theory will immediately counterattack. And your counterattack will likely be half correct. No matter how much writers study the theory of conditioned response (and it is far better to do this than not) in order to theoretically learn the laws of the soul, this alone renders one absolutely incapable of writing anything. Writers must do more than simply know the physiological laws of the soul. Knowledge of the soul must be acquired perceptually and concretely.

To know the soul perceptually and concretely already implies knowing it through figurative expression. Thus we must once again problematize the difference between literature and science or theory. Here this is necessary in order to grasp their connectedness as well as distinction not on the basis of contempt for theory but rather in terms of forms of knowledge.

My thinking is as follows: scientific knowledge *formulates, through the aid of concepts*, direct contemplation so as to more deeply and fully grasp its *objective laws*.

Artistic knowledge *typifies, through the aid of perceptual expression*, direct contemplation (of course not as such, for this would mean not writing the word "pen" but rather setting an actual pen between typed lines) so as to more deeply and fully grasp its *subjective laws*.

Here so-called reality or sense of reality refers to the certainty of artistic abstraction. When this is raised to the level of universality, it becomes a type.

The difference between type and pattern is not simply quantitative. It is not the case that the former emerges when the latter is produced and thousands of its constitutive elements collected and averaged out. A *type must correspond to a formula in scientific knowledge*; it possesses a universality that is qualitatively different from average value.

It can be said that the aim of realist art consists precisely in the apprehension of such types.

While the differences between theory and literature corresponds to those between reason and perception, formula and type, and abstract abstractions and concrete abstractions, it nevertheless clearly runs counter to a dialectical deepening of knowledge to claim that subjective laws can be sought simply through perceptual knowledge. The experience of subjective laws (i.e., direct experience regarding the soul) is first formed as perceptual knowledge, from which rational knowledge is then created. This rational knowledge has a countereffect on perception, organizing and deepening it, and from this interaction types come to emerge. What mediates this interaction is expression or form. Of course expression is not fixed, since it changes with each interactive repetition. But perhaps such change is better described as typification. The type contains both the form and content of knowledge.

If expression or form moved toward formulas rather than types, interaction would naturally progress toward the former rather than latter, with the result that perception would cooperate with reason. Since expression develops and undergoes ideation simultaneously with knowledge, this is a very natural state of affairs. Expression can also be described as the hypothesis of ideas.

Literature is clearly something that should be felt rather than commented on. However, this does not mean that theory should be scorned. Theory has its own role, and if it is formed within knowledge through uniting with practice, then it should certainly combine with perception to aid in the creation of types. Also, perception without the aid of theory would be unable to create types.

If a writer seeks to occupy the standpoint of realism, he must adopt the viewpoint of practice in terms of transforming reality. His goal must be the liberation of mankind. This is not the psychological liberation offered by prison chaplains to condemned prisoners, but rather the real and concrete liberation provided by the liberation forces that opened the gates of the Nazi concentration camps. Theoretical liberation alone is not the conclusion here, for one must also desire subjective and perceptual liberation through emotion. In other words, one must be partisan.

But of course literary works cannot emerge immediately from partisanship. The writer would likely have to wait for a very long time. Or perhaps he would merely write pamphlets and reportage without ever arriving at the creation of types. But this is another problem in and of itself. Even if it is true that no answers are given without equations, this does not mean that answers exist for every equation. This situation doesn't provide the least excuse for scorning theory and making light of practice.

If a writer thus wishes to be a realist, he must adopt the viewpoint of practice while bravely and comprehensively destroying those elements of naturalism within himself. To repeat: practice is never in and of itself "absolute," for materialist action is formed only by combining with knowledge. Practice is neither a religion nor a moral imperative. Rather, it is a necessity that inheres within the subjective conditions of the self. Practice is the basic condition of the human structure: when it joins with theory, it becomes science; when it joins with perception, it creates types.

In terms of this tendency to deify practice, Lenin issues the following warning in his *Materialism and Empirio-Criticism*: "Of course, we must not forget that the criterion of practice can never, in the nature of things, either confirm or refute any idea *completely*. This criterion also is sufficiently 'indefinite' not to allow human knowledge to become 'absolute,' but at the same time it is sufficiently definite to wage a ruthless fight on all varieties of idealism and agnosticism."[9]

Finally, a literary theory from the standpoint of realism would not simply abandon the superficial listing of impressions and intuitions or the subjective inferences that derive therefrom. Nor would it issue public outcries in favor of the unity of knowledge and practice. Rather, it would necessarily make a clear stand of its partisanship, concretely support the advance of literature, that is, deepening and enriching the perceptual knowledge of writers, and utilize theory in concretely aiding in the creation of types. If possible, this literary theory should point out the inner necessity by which realism develops into socialist realism. The future path of literary theory consists in explaining how the laws governing the deepening of knowledge can be scientifically grasped as well as how types are created through perceptual knowledge. Dogmatic criticism based simply on forms and methods no longer adds to the development of literature.

THE HAND OF A CALCULATOR WITH THE HEART OF A BEAST: WHAT IS LITERATURE?

I

Under the title "How to Make Verse," Vladimir Mayakovsky wrote that there are no methods to make verse. Here I thought I would follow suit and write about how to write fiction when there are no methods to write fiction.

This might sound as if I were simply playing with paradoxes, but that is not the case. During the stage of handicraft production, all productive technologies were mysteries passed from hand to hand in the form of unspoken skills. Now, however, such mysteries have come to be exposed as the mere egoism of craftsmen as grounded on relations of production. To borrow the words of Mayakovsky once again, "You have the right to demand that poets should not take the secret of their craft to their graves."[1] There any many writers who believe that one should not write about how to write fiction, but these methods must by all means be widely liberated, given the importance of this essential question, "What is fiction?"

First published February 25, 1955, in *Iwanami kōza: Bungaku no sōzō to kanshō*, vol. 4.

Question: Why do you then speak so paradoxically as opposed to beginning in a more straightforward manner?

In order for you to understand that there are no paradoxes here, I have to first speak about writing manuals, which are popular but quite useless. In fact, a great many manuals have been written that respond to—or rather, that appear to respond to—the demand made by readers or aspiring writers to disclose the secrets of writing. Yet how many of these books offer knowledge that is actually useful to writing? One discovers upon reading them that few actually focus on how to write and that most appear to be handbooks on what constitutes *good* fiction. I use the word "appear" here since, as goes without saying, I haven't actually read these works but am simply imagining what they say. I have no desire to read such books, since I can figure out their content without reading them. Even if they seem academic and focus on plausible topics, most are fraudulent publications or what essentially amounts to the same thing. Devoted to such topics as moneymaking secrets, ways to become popular, how to write letters, or keys to becoming a better swimmer, such books take advantage of the misunderstandings on the part of unhappy people who do not grasp the real meaning of what they are looking for, thereby defrauding readers of two or three hundred yen. I am not the only person who feels this way; most serious writers say the same thing. George Bernard Shaw declared that such manuals on writing techniques do more harm than good for aspiring writers, while Mayakovsky maintained that no general law exists for writing since writers actively create these laws.

Question: Aren't your remarks becoming increasingly contradictory?

Please let me continue a bit more. Even from my own experience, in fact, the act of writing itself is a discovery of how to write: far from relying on anything lawlike, it is more or less an attempt to destroy anything lawlike. Even in the case of scenarios, which are considered to have more conventions than fiction, I wrote the original scenario *Kabe atsuki heya* [*The Room with Thick Walls*], which received rather good reviews, without having any prior knowledge of the genre and without even having read one previously. When I first wrote the play *Seifuku* [*Uniforms*], I made no use of any materials for dramatic composition and felt no need to do so. I wrote my second scenario, *Furyō shōnen* [*Juvenile Delinquents*], about the Matsukawa Incident that was then taking place, and it was because of these difficult conditions that I encountered so many obstacles that I wanted many times to abandon the manuscript. Things reached such an impasse that, feeling the need for some reference materials, I suddenly went out and bought two or three scenario-writing guides. In reading them, however, I realized deeply how unfortunate these aspiring writers are who are forced to buy such books. Yet one of these books was not at all like the fraudulent publications that appear under such headings as "How to Write Letters" or "How to Make Sketches." Rather, it was quite serious-minded and written at a high intellectual level. I read it with interest, thinking that it would certainly be useful for something. This book contained plenty of examples with sharp analyses, such that anyone would find themselves nodding in agreement. While reading it, someone might grow convinced of their own ability to write well. Of course this enticement of the reader's confidence is not entirely insignificant. Nonetheless, I would insist that feeling such confidence and actually being able to write are two very different things.

Even if such books are like sweet nectar for aspiring writers, they are in no way effective medicine.

Question: It sounds a bit as if you're boasting. Are you saying that writing is a question of talent?

Talent is important, but this has nothing to do with boasting. I simply wanted to stress that the commonsensical perception of technique is too simple. If one grasps its essence, then mastery of technique at this stage is so easy as to pose few problems. My point is that the techniques truly needed for writing are to be found elsewhere, but that these authentic-seeming manual writers set up a smoke screen around this essence. The (technicist) manner of writing that I am rejecting here might appear at first glance to be the revealing of a secret, but I want people to remember that it is actually something whose value is predicated on the preservation of a secret as secret, like an esoteric tract on Japanese fencing.

My point here is not that there are absolutely no methods of writing. Practice-based, and thus real, methods of writing overcome technicist notions of writing, and so we must come to an intellectual understanding of the act of writing—that is, we must return to the question of intellectual motive. This cannot be doubted. If for example Columbus's biography were entitled *Ways to Discover America*, and this title had no symbolic meaning, even a child would understand the humor involved. No matter how thoroughly one knew about the various plans and preparations behind Columbus's voyage, or how meticulously one knew about the circumstances behind the difficulties he encountered and how he overcame them, it is nonetheless impossible to speak about rediscovering an America that has already been discovered. All one can do is play at imitating Columbus in the same way. One can learn about Columbus's spirit of adventure from his biography (if the biography is excellent), but it is clear that one can never learn about the concrete techniques used to discover America.

Question: But isn't it enough to learn about this spirit of adventure?

That is exactly my point. This is why I excluded in advance those cases where the title *Ways to Discover America* could be conceived metaphorically. As a metaphor, a profound analysis of Columbus's adventure could play an important educational role. In other words, my point is not that an analysis of techniques in fictional expression would be of absolutely no use in writing fiction. Even if useful, this is not because such a book directly concerns the question of how to write, for it might be useful in the way that certain kinds of political essays or science books are useful. I don't deny this at all. However, it would be slightly false to title such essays "how to write."

If this were truly a book about how to write, then it would not simply be a technical manual but would naturally have to aim at a synthetic and practical grasp of fiction. And it would have to provide direction to aspiring writers by concretely circumventing the wall where they find themselves at an impasse. Speaking from my own experience and imagination, one of the major elements in this wall appears to be the technicist understanding of writing. Such overemphasis on technique actually prevents a true understanding of writing.

Consider, for example, how one rides a bicycle. In order to ride a bicycle, technique is certainly necessary. It would be a considerable academic accomplishment if one were to describe in writing the infrastructure of the technical acquisition involved in comfortably riding such an unsteady vehicle as a two-wheeler. Yet this would be less a book about riding than an essay on neurophysiology. One would still not know how to ride a bicycle even if one read this, just as one could still write this even if one were unable to ride a bicycle. But even if such knowledge were not directly useful in riding a bicycle, it would clearly be useful for something. Although such a work might not be useful in learning how to write, that is no reason to deny that it might be a brilliant book on literary theory.

In contrast, what about a book that minutely described the techniques needed to ride a bicycle from an external perspective? For example: "Hold on lightly yet firmly with both hands, keeping your wrists and arms at a 135-degree angle and your elbows at a 120-degree angle. Lean away from the frame of the bicycle and apply your body weight as variable to the following numerical formula. Rest your left foot on the pedal while using your right foot to strongly kick off from the ground three times, etc."

In terms of fiction, this would be the equivalent of a so-called writing manual. One might come to believe oneself capable of riding a bicycle in this way, but I guarantee that this would be impossible no matter how many times one tried. Yet this is not to say that there is no truly useful advice. Such advice turns out to be surprisingly brief and simple: Don't be afraid of the bicycle. When about to fall to the right, turn the handlebars to the left. Forget any habits associated with walking. It's easier to avoid falling by increasing speed. When practicing, find the largest open space possible. The most important thing above all is to practice repeatedly and with confidence. Any technical guidance more detailed than this will likely be more harmful than helpful.

Do you now understand that there was absolutely no paradox involved when, at the beginning of this essay, I called for a method of writing when there are no methods to write? As goes without saying, however, I do not agree with the conservative view that there are no teachers of fiction, that each person must learn about and create fiction by themselves. This might be fine in the case of bicycles, but fiction is more complex. Or rather, fiction has been made too complex through its corruption by various mistaken views. I would like to offer some advice in order to dispel these misunderstandings and arrive at a practical understanding of fiction.

Question: Is this a case of crying wine and selling vinegar?

No, for my original intent was to display this vinegar. My introductory remarks were slightly too long because I wanted to avoid misunderstanding and have you understand that it was in fact vinegar that was being sold under the heading of writing. The original error here consists in expecting wine from this heading.

In fact, many writers just getting under way have the same fault (as I did as well) in being too subjective in regard to their own creative activity. As a result, the two major elements of fiction, the "what" and "how," come to be separated. Doesn't everyone encounter difficulties here? What expressive techniques can be meaningful without discovering some unity between these two? Those who seek techniques strictly from the standpoint of the "what" are as if searching for ways to play ball without a ball, while those who seek techniques strictly from the standpoint of the "how" appear to be figuring out how to play with a ball from a picture. What is missing here? A practical understanding of ball playing. An awareness of the motives involved in what one is seeking. An ability to objectivize one's own demands. The original misstep here consists in expecting wine from a book on writing.

Isn't it true that unifying the "what" and "how" is the first step in writing, the way to overcome the technicist prejudice and discover the original meaning of technique? I believe that the only way to discover how to write lies in rejecting methods of how to write.

II

In order to unite the two basic elements of fiction, the "what" and "how," I would like to consider a third element, that of the "why." Even in detective fiction, isn't it true that the best way to deduce the identity of the criminal is to investigate the motives for the crime? Motives restore the abstraction of deduction to the level of the concrete. It provides real direction to the analysis of criminal methods. Must we not reconsider creative activity from the perspective of motive?

In fact, works that are well written and deal with important issues but provide absolutely no literary excitement generally have unclear motives. I am not suggesting that motives be openly expressed. Truly great works often conceal motives, rendering them obscure, but there is an enormous difference between obscure motives and a lack of motives. Even if obscure, motives must be present. Just as criminals who lack motives are generally mentally deranged, so too might we regard works that lack motives as unqualified as fiction.

One of the faults that derive from naturalist literature can be seen in most contemporary fiction in its obscuration, subjectivization, and individualization of creative motives, but this influence seems to have spread deeply through the respective methods of the "what" and "how" camps.

It is interesting that these two camps, which in so many ways appear to be like cats and dogs, unexpectedly coincide on this point of unclear motives. As to the circumstances surrounding this coincidence, despite terminological differences as well as discrepancies in what they value and reject, both camps more or less subscribe to a theory of instinct. Of course it is impossible to fully explain all motives. Yet it is strange to find cases where no motives can be explained.

Why do you write? Because I want to.

Why do you want to? I don't know why, but I simply must.

Clearly, one writes because one must. Yet no matter how spontaneous and impulsive this feeling, it cannot become an excuse justifying why motives cannot be explained. Here I would like to discover what is concealed behind such impulse.

Question: I am puzzled as to why you are being so pretentious. Isn't this simply a case of a writer reacting to an appeal from reality?

That is certainly the case. But there is more, since that alone cannot explain how a writer is able to hear the voice of reality.

Question: That is not so difficult. Quite simply, doesn't this represent the very content of a writer's daily life?

That's true. However, it is not only fiction that can be conceived as a reflection of daily life. Aren't most human actions both the reflection and content of daily life? I would like to consider the writer's particular motives in choosing fiction (or artistic expression) from among the numerous forms of reflection and their infinite possibilities. I suspect this might allow us to move one step closer to understanding the structure of fiction—that is, the secret of how to write—which is the main subject of this essay.

My thoughts on the clues to discovering a writer's motives are as follows. There must be a practical vehicle of mediation between the general knowledge of daily life and the particular knowledge of fictional expression that allows for a deepening of general knowledge through fiction, and this vehicle ensures the natural and easy transition from the particular to the general and the general to the particular. As goes without saying, this vehicle of mediation is the reader. It is the existence of the reader that holds the key to discovering motives, just as it is his mode of existence that determines the mode of fictional expression (or cognitive structure).

Some might claim that there is no need now to state the obvious. My remarks might well sound too pretentious, as you have said. Yet the fact is that this analysis of the reader's mode of existence has been overlooked precisely because it is so simple. One can find statistical tables about readerly phenomena, but does this really provide a true picture of the reader? Literature should be subservient to readers; the view that readers are subservient to literature is not real analysis. This view is harmful to literature as well. Neglecting the role of the reader produces a result that is, for example, preoccupied with internal observation as a particular law, a viewing of the structure of fiction strictly from the perspective of fiction. This also creates an unnecessarily complicated, fancy, and sterile theory of literature, as if one were using not graphics but rather words and circuitous and abstruse explanations in order to explain very simple geometrical proofs. By skipping over the reader's existence and mechanically linking reality and fiction, moreover, one distorts the essence of fiction and ends up promoting the clay work substitute for living fiction (such as putting the preaching remarks a burglar makes to his victim in the third person). Just as fiction cannot be discovered in a writer's head even with the use of X-rays, so too is it impossible to discover fiction by mobilizing detectives and searching all over town. The mediation of the reader immediately clarifies the identity of fiction just as it illuminates the writer's motives in choosing the expressive form of fiction.

Let's begin to consider things from the relation between writer and reader.

The general view here seems to be that writers exist and create works, from which readers are then formed. Hence many people say that writers should do what they want and write what they want, and that it is up to readers to decide whether to read these works or not. Of course there are also those who believe the opposite, claiming that writers must serve the reader. I agree with this latter theory, but I am troubled by the fact that many moral imperatives are given as reasons for it. However, the real question is which comes first: the writer or the reader?

This is reminiscent of the chicken and egg debate. It has been biologically demonstrated that the egg precedes the chicken, but this logic seems somewhat forced when directly applied to fiction (although I think it is likely the same). Yet I hope we can at least clarify in this relationship that the egg represents the reader and the chicken the writer. That is, just as the egg comes first in the context of the chicken's origin, so too in the case of human beings is it self-evident that childhood precedes old age (other than for characters in the Salacrou play). Here I hope to make clear that a writer must first be a reader before becoming a writer.

Is this point not clear to all? Any writer, in whatever form, must first pass through the stage of being a reader. It is unimaginable that someone could become a writer without first being a reader. Only a daydreamer who had fallen into an unhealthy idealism could exoticize the writer in this way. Such misperception is similar to believing that thought is possible without language.

As all concrete examples reveal, the writer must always develop from the reader.

Now the problem here is one of how the reader develops into a writer.

Question: Obviously. The reader at some time thinks of something and writes a work, thereby becoming a writer. What remains unclear is the relation between this self-evident point and the topic of "how to write." Don't you think that we are moving further away from the main topic? Don't you really intend to equivocate and avoid answering by speaking of a way to write in which nothing is written?

I very much understand your concern. It appears here that another kind of chicken and egg must be considered: which comes first, the writer or the work? It seems that your view is that the work makes the writer—that is, the work is the egg. In this view, the reader and writer are interrupted by a sudden mutation, or no essential difference exists between them apart from the unexpected result that is the work, hence making the motive for writing fiction something quite accidental or perhaps a common everyday occurrence. In other words, it is simply a waste of time to try to deepen one's practical knowledge of fiction writing and reveal the secrets of writing. Insofar as someone is forced to write these manuals and remain loyal to this theme, he can only disregard the question of what is useful and try to schematize what appear to be useful writing experiences. The overflow of useless writing guides is perhaps a philosophical phenomenon based on such resignation.

Yet is your view that the work precedes the writer actually correct?

This is a very difficult question. Cleary the opposing view that the writer precedes the work carries many dangers. By subordinating the work to the writer, one weakens the work's status as a product of society, overestimates the position of the writer and reinforces the notion that fiction is based on individualism. It is undeniable that this understanding has been one of the pillars of the I-novel view in Japan. Thus the work comes to be reduced to the writer's way of life. The issue of how to write is replaced by that of how to live. There is no easy answer to the question of whether this danger is greater than the art for art's sake and spirit of craftsmanship that derive from the notion that the work precedes the writer. Perhaps these two views are equally dangerous. If these are the only two paths available to fiction, then the fate that awaits it is invariably one of ruin.

Fortunately, however, the foregoing questions are seriously mistaken in their inception. Such unrealistic conclusions are created by confused discussions about the general (phylogenetic) and individual (ontogenetic) relations between work and writer. This relation is not so mechanical. It is a fact that writers become writers by creating works, just as works are created strictly by writers. It is not a question here of which is subservient to which. Let's cease all abstract discussions of this complex relationship. I would prefer to begin with concrete observations of the writer's origins.

I believe that, just as future chickens already exist within the embryo of eggs, so too do the germ of writers already exist within readers—that is, all readers, or all people insofar as they can become readers. Of course I am not saying that readers naturally develop into writers in continuous transition. Even plants develop dramatically, incrementally, and revolutionarily. The writer's development is also dramatic and revolutionary. However, the source of this energy must be understood as inherent within the reader.

Now I would like to clarify one part of this discussion on fictional techniques while examining such processes as concern how this energy inheres within the reader and in what order it develops.

III

I once received the following letter from a young man who wished to become a fiction writer. This was a long letter that was in part incomprehensible, so I shall note only the main points. This young man seemed to be convinced that he was a literary genius. Although he had not yet written anything, he suddenly realized his own talent and asked if there weren't anything I might be able to teach him. He stated the reasons for his confidence as follows: upon seeing a cloud, he would immediately think of such lines as "the thin cloud floated like my heart." While out walking, he would imagine himself as a character in a story and murmur, "He walked slowly, staring at his feet," and when blowing his nose, such phrases would pop out of his mouth as, "He noisily and annoyingly blew his nose." The young man insisted that these things or inspirations were clearly an appeal from the genie of fiction.

Up to a certain point, of course, most readers experience something like this, for it is entirely unrelated to literary genius. Fiction won't emerge no matter how many such phrases are lined up. Yet one of the achievements of modern fiction is that it very simply provokes in readers a desire to express themselves in any form possible. Regardless of how widely fiction opens its doors, it can never do so enough. Even though the young man's belief in his own genius was completely unfounded and an infinite distance separated him from writers, it was still clear that he had discovered how to plug the gap of his literary imagination and move one step closer to becoming a writer.

Now what are the motives behind this budding impulse? As goes without saying, it lies in the sense of excitement in discovering new forms of interest in reality. Schematically, this contains the following points of analysis. The young man: A. through his mediated form as reader; B. discovers, or rediscovers, reality; C. this motive leads him to experience the pleasure of reading; D. he then becomes perceptually or rationally aware that reading represents one form of knowing reality; E. yet he fails to realize that his excitement represents a knowledge of reality that is enabled by a certain hypothetical medium of fiction (or literary works in general); F. he conflates that knowledge with his own direct experience; G. and unconsciously begins to make gestures in imitation of the works that provided him with this clue to discovery.

This is a form of playing house, but I don't say this contemptuously. Who could have contempt for a child? Clearly only a dried-up, conservative snob could scorn the educational significance of playing house. Isn't it precisely the destructive spirit of playing house that represents the first call of humanity?

It is a perfectly natural desire to wish to give back the pleasure that one has been given. Due to the uneven distribution of property, it has become commonsensical to view these two things as contradictory or oppositional. As historical materialism reveals, however, such oppositionality is not decisive. Rather, it is essential to unify these two elements in the context of human practice, in which man transforms himself by struggling against nature through society. We can thus draw the following conclusions.

The desire for expression inheres within the desire for knowledge and becomes possible strictly as its development.

In other words, in order to see or feel reality with the desire to write about it, one must first have the experience of seeing or feeling reality through the written. This also represents the key to solving the problem of tradition vis-à-vis creation as well as the problem of how to evaluate the classics, but I won't go into details here.

The foregoing conclusions in turn lead to the following points.

The structure of fiction evolves and develops in such a way as to make it more convenient and useful for readers to discover reality through it. This structure represents the structure of knowledge in general, since there is no exceptional meaning or value about it. The structure of knowledge in general is the structure of language: just as language without structure cannot be called language, so too knowledge without structure is not knowledge, and there can be no fiction without structure. Even that fiction that lacks the clarity of structure that one finds in fixed verse or theatrical form, and that is occasionally called "unstructured," invariably contains structure in the proper sense of the term.

As for the origin of this structure (of fiction), it is not that writers devised this structure in order to create fiction or make it more fictionlike. Rather, one must say that writers extracted something that existed latently within knowledge in general, and that they did so with the help of existing traditions through the form of readers. Writers did not freely create this structure; rather, it was the structured quality of knowledge that produced the form of fiction. One must understand that the need to finally create this form lay concealed within the structure of knowledge.

As goes without saying, the question of how to write depends upon familiarity with the nature of this structure. Now how can we best understand this structure?

Here we must return to the question of the reader. The process in which the structure of general knowledge develops and evolves into the particular structure of fiction appears most vividly in the reactions provoked in readers when they encounter literary works. In fact, great writers create works based on their profound study of readers. Great writers are always conscious of another, inner self, the reader in themselves, and their fiction advances dialectically through that dialogue. I do not mean this in the narrow sense, of course, such that their writing takes the form of a conversational, oral, or first-person style of narration. Much less am I referring to how writers manipulate readers. Contempt for readers represents the fall of writers. Here let me introduce the following passage from Gorky's short story "The Reader," in which he brilliantly expresses the essence of the reader as crucial, powerful, and frightening. In these lines, the ghost of the reader addresses the writer:

> How do you justify your *rôle* of author? Loading people's memories with a rubbish of photographic stereotypes of their life, poor in events, you do not know how to present it in such form that the picture will incite in men a vengeful shame and a desire to create other forms of existence. Can you quicken the pulse of life? Can you breathe energy into it as others have done?

He then continues: "Man slumbers . . . and none rouses him. He needs the lash and the flaming caress of love after the blow of the lash. Do not be afraid to hurt him; if you love him as you strike, he will understand the blow and receive it as deserved. But when he shall feel the shame and when the blow stings—give him the caress of fire. . . . Do *you* know how to love men?"[2]

As you can see, the reader is a truly frightening disciple for the writer. The reader is both disciple and teacher. In other words, the writer must be someone who is able to hear such words from the reader. Although the writer is produced within and by the reader through his demand, the reader never allows the writer to become more or less similar to himself. Rather, the reader demands that the writer be a true expert.

Stalin described writers as technicians of the soul. Doesn't this aptly express what readers demand? Writers must be technicians of the soul rather than merely technicians of prose. Fictional techniques are techniques of the soul, and ways of writing must be understood as the substance of these techniques.

How then can one master these techniques of the soul? Concretely speaking, this question comes down to knowing the reader. For when one speaks of certain works affecting the soul, that soul of course refers to the reader.

The writer's first lesson can be described as battling the reader in order to know him. The writer's emergence from the reader takes place through the reader's self-mirroring—the surge of emotions provoked in him by the work—and objectification, and appears as the writerly part of the reader splitting off in opposition to itself. This opposition and conflict continue until the writer ceases being a writer. The struggle with the reader can thus be seen as the writer's alpha and omega.

It must be noted, however, that this notion of the reader is not to be understood in its narrow, commonsensical meaning. If the writer complies strictly with the phenomenal demands of the reader without listening to the latter's true voice (as for example described by Gorky), then the essential meaning of fiction as the knowledge and discovery of reality (realism) will be lost. To describe fiction as a technique of the soul signifies that it alters or transforms the reader's soul, providing him with the new vision needed to see reality, and thus Gorky's lash is absolutely necessary. The reader demands of the writer to awaken that which slumbers inside him.

As Lu Xun remarks, however, not all propaganda is literature: "just as all flowers have color . . . but not all colored things are flowers."[3] Here one must deeply understand the reader's historical and social meaning.

The reader is transformed upon reading fiction; it is not the case that he is transformed and simply thinks that he has read fiction. It is thus impossible to deceive the reader that what is not fiction actually is. The addition of theoretical commentary can become propaganda instead of fiction. Fiction doesn't provide such a conclusion, for it must change the soul and help the reader furnish a new conclusion. Now what are the criteria that make fiction fiction?

This question must be considered on the basis of the legacy of historically produced fiction. Man's soul is nothing other than the accumulation of this legacy. Through studying this legacy, writers can first acquire the techniques needed to appeal directly to the soul. Readers are situated within tradition but attempt to go beyond it and glimpse the future. They are the historical force that represents the junction between the past and reality.

The second lesson for writers consists in studying the past literature accumulated within readers. The writer's urge to write goes beyond the immediate impression he receives from reality and is invariably linked to the desire to express that reality in the form of fiction so as to convey it to the reader. Here the reader's surge of emotion as provoked by the work is already anticipated in advance within the writer's own mind. The writer anticipates a reality that has been reconstructed through the prism of the structure of fiction. For the writer emerges from the reader and still houses the reader within him. Through the writer's identification with the reader, or perhaps through invoking the reader within him, he is able to make the creation of fiction his own intrinsic demand. This is based on his experience of encountering and being moved by the works of the past (not necessarily in the sense of the classics).

Regardless of whether he is conscious of this or not, the writer cannot escape the relation in which he becomes motivated to create fiction as based on his own internal reader as well as those past works accumulated within that reader. If he fails to consciously grasp and pursue this point, his works will invariably become subjective and self-indulgent. This is why writers lapse into an excess of adjectives and abstract nouns. They are in a rush and so borrow a car without knowing how to drive, grabbing the wheel and noisily thrashing about. These writers see only half of the reader's demands.

When there is an excess of adjectives, one doesn't know what is being said. Essayistic fiction that contains many abstract nouns is all too easily understood, but it is utterly unexciting. These may appear to be contrary tendencies, but they are merely two sides of the same biased propensity that results from an inability to see fiction objectively as a social product. Together with his impulse (the readerly), the writer must be an engineer who regards these tendencies with detachment. Just as centrifugal and centripetal force are both required in order to draw the locus of a circle, so too does a work become effective only as a dialectical unity of the opposition between writer and reader. Just as speed is increased when one drives as rationally and accurately as possible, so too can accuracy and calmness of description convey great passion.

The writer must exist within the unity of hand and heart—that is, within the continued tension in his work between identifying with the reader and maintaining his own self. This is the writer's third lesson. The hand must restrain the impetuous heart while the heart urges on the faltering hand. The fall of the writer can be seen when he tries to escape from this pain and compromise these two forces by either leaving things to the heart or stifling the heart so as to save the hand's strength. The heart of a beast with the hand of a calculator: that is the writer's ideal.

As I near the end of this essay, it seems that I have finally approached the gateway to this problematic. I hope that you have somehow been able to follow the path in which the questions of "what" and "how" one writes emerge from the motive of "why." Motive lies at the point of separation between writer and reader, but it is the work that traverses this opposition and struggle and reunites them.

In other words, one must grasp through actual practice the structure and manner of writing fiction as well as the totality that these form. Just as reality is complex, so too are there vast differences in the form and content of fiction. Man and events, man and man, man's inside and outside; these matters seen in terms of individuality, human collectivity, in the context of investigating events, through man's actions, or perhaps mediated by psychology: it is quite impossible to determine a general way of writing shared by all of these. It may of course be possible to academically classify and compare such structures as those of the short story, full-length fiction, and psychological novel, but the results would be complicated and obscure and not very applicable in a technical sense. It is more important to read widely, objectively reorganize one's impressions and excitement from books, and learn the habit of constantly accumulating experience in the context of the dialogue between writer and reader. Fictional methods in the narrow sense are simpler than one imagines, and it is much more difficult to grasp the fundamentals of a writer whose methods appear simple. One's prose style will easily improve if one always remains self-conscious in the context of the tension between writer and reader. For that is a matter of discovery rather than of learning.

In the context of an amusing event, for example, if one barely writes about the event but merely lines up adjectives such as "amusing" or "pleasant," then one conveys to the reader nothing more than the nature of the event.

But if one concretely conveys the event's substance as figure, then the reader can experience the emotion of amusement on a perceptual level. And if one succeeds in uncovering the essence of that amusement, then the reader can even learn from it. These facts are intellectual issues and involve the discovery of types from within the event (such as Columbus discovering America), but the question of improving one's prose style is contained in the process of this search as a necessary result. Prose style is like the pin on a pair of binoculars that brings things into focus, for one must find out for oneself how to adjust to the object. The logic behind this may be difficult, but it is quite easy to accomplish when actually writing. For brilliant prose ultimately consists in describing types (which refers to the conclusions of perceptual knowledge, just as formulas are the conclusions of rational knowledge).

Now what is the nature of the emotions that these types evoke in readers? Even without any knowledge of the theories on types (it is of course better to know them), anyone can experience such emotions by reading great works. Writers can also experience them through their own internal reader. While experiencing such emotions, they can objectively review those experiences, transforming them into something more general or universal, which they then accumulate in their own inner cabinets. Writers undergo this process jointly with readers. Such cabinets grow full through repeated reading and come to be arranged by the act of writing. This arrangement corresponds to improvements in prose style and, more broadly, to the hand vis-à-vis the heart and the "how" vis-à-vis the "what." The presence of these cabinets control and objectify the writer's subjective impulses and centrifugal force, thereby allowing them to function as a centripetal force.

There is a great deal of suffering involved in actually writing: the writer finds himself at wits' end, muttering aloud, destroying what he writes, groaning over it. This is what happens when he ransacks his inner cabinet in consultation with his fellow supervisor, the reader. In this activity, thought and prose become virtually indistinguishable from each other. No writer can answer the question of whether he is writing while thinking or thinking while writing.

Let me cite here one of Mayakovsky's famous experiences. This is a passage found in "How to Make Verse":

About 1913, returning from Saratov to Moscow, I said to a woman traveling in the same carriage, in order to prove my respectability, that I was "not a man, but a cloud in trousers." Having said this, I realized at once that it might come in handy for a poem and what if it were spread by word of mouth and wasted to no purpose? Terribly anxious, I spent half an hour plying the girl with leading questions and was only reassured when I satisfied myself that my words had gone in one ear and out the other. Two years later "a cloud in trousers" came in handy as the title for a whole long poem.[+]

It is clear that Mayakovsky himself didn't even know if this "cloud in trousers" that he so valued and had stuffed into his inner cabinet was a thought or an extraordinary expression. Knowledge is supported by expression while expression is concretized by knowledge. It is impossible to formulate, in the manner of letter writing or an illustrated encyclopedia, the methods one might use to think of such a memorable phrase as "a cloud in trousers." For the efforts that a writer must accumulate in order to acquire an expression are not so simple. In order to walk, people must alternately use both their right and left legs. In order to walk ten steps, one cannot use only the right leg for five steps and the left leg for five steps. Here the "what" and "how" are the equivalent of these left and right legs.

Despite appearances, then, there are no secrets to be revealed about writing. The secret is that there are no secrets. To repeat: this is in no way paradoxical. Even if one can analyze the color red, such explanation cannot make someone feel this color. Likewise, there are limits to any commentary on writing.

Yet it is both possible and necessary to suggest to aspiring writers ways to study writing. This is because they have their own desire to write. For all buds are contained within this desire. As I have already written far too much, I will summarize my thoughts: the first step for aspiring writers is to objectify their desires so as to see them as the desires of another. The self-conscious separation from one's own inner reader begins at this point. If one succeeds here, then all that remains is to walk alternately using both legs within the context of the tension and struggle with the reader. For it is the reader who represents the infinite vein of creation.

"In general, I think that the sadness of disillusionment lies not in falsehood but rather in regarding falsehood as truth. . . . It is better to forget failure than to prevent it" (Lu Xun).[5]

No truth exists outside the reader, just as there can be no frightening collapse if one keeps the reader in sight. The greatest possible daring and adventure are permitted and demanded. The difficulty is to be found less in improving one's prose style than in the courage to continue battling with the reader.

DISCOVERING AMERICA

I

I don't know America very well. Needless to say, I've never set foot on American soil nor made a systematic study of American literature. All I know about it is from the several Americans with whom I've spoken, the section of America represented by the military bases, and the image of America as reflected inside of us through what I've seen on the film screen.

In sum, this is not America itself but a mere secretion made up of the country's existence and daily life. Yet I feel I must write about certain things regarding America that have not often been discussed. I fully understand from my trip to Czechoslovakia last year how foolhardy this is. A discovery does not depart from conclusions that are already glimpsed, but rather must always be based on the inexpressible details that lead up to them. It is not necessarily the case that one understands what one sees, but one understands less what one doesn't see.

First published November 1, 1957, in *Chūō kōron*.

Nevertheless, Franz Kafka wrote the novel *Amerika* without seeing America. Among Kafka's works, which dwell constantly on rejection and protest, this is the one book filled with light and hope. While this is not so-called "America," it is a resource that cannot be overlooked when thinking about America. In the novel, America begins on a ship, which is an artificial maze made of iron. As always, the protagonist fears becoming forever lost on the ship—it is, after all, America—but he is able to safely disembark. Next he meets the *successful* uncle who lives in a skyscraper. This uncle's behavior is informed by the principle of absolute freedom. The uncle, who embodies the unity of these two incompatible principles of freedom and the absolute, is a kind of god of contradiction, and the two characters do not get along at all. Finally the protagonist is mercilessly, but certainly not maliciously, thrown out. (Although one senses that this heartless contradiction is a reflection of the ancient city of Prague, Kafka's birthplace, most Europeans who come in contact with America seem to be bewildered by it. Graham Greene refers to this in his remark that "innocence is a kind of insanity.")[1]

Many Europeans seem to be bewildered by America. In many cases, its contradictions appear as confusion and are thus seen as strictly negative. As one might expect, however, Kafka foresaw what lay ahead. Of course this remained a prediction: although he tried to depict a shining world, the light of that world remained strangely empty and even carried a scent of death. Light could be found but this was a world without substance, and so nothing existed to receive this light and shine. The novel was discontinued prior to completion. Perhaps this was because Kafka lacked the necessary details to use as a stepping-stone to discovery.

During our respective journeys of six weeks, I deeply experienced the importance of detail while traveling through Kafka's native Prague, whereas Sartre discovered the virtual absence of detail in his trip to America, which contrasted with the wealth of detail to be found in the Old World. Even if Kafka had gone to America, then, would he still have been unable to complete *Amerika*? Precisely because Sartre saw the reality of America despite the fact that he found no details there, he reached the same point that Kafka had previously. Sartre explains very implicitly that the conformism of America symbolized by its roads and the individualism symbolized by its skyscrapers are only superficially incompatible, since they coexist three-dimensionally. Yet he cleverly avoids mentioning anything further. Or rather, actually, he refuses to do so: "New York moves Europeans in spite of its austerity. . . . Yet, for Frenchmen of my generation, it already possesses a melancholy of the past. . . . [Skyscrapers] were the architecture of the future, just as . . . jazz

[was] the music of the future. . . . [Yet jazz is] in a process of slow decline. Jazz is outliving its day."[2]

If Kafka had gone to America, would the conclusion of his novel have been, as always, one of eternal rejection? It seems that Sartre, at least, would reply "yes." Yet this question remains for me a troubling mystery. What could America be concealing behind its contradictions?

II

Sartre's point concerning the absence of detail in America is unsettling and yet familiar. If the reader lacks the ambition to write the conclusion to Kafka's novel—in other words, if he wishes to stop at the level of the problematic raised by Sartre—then ignorance of detail might not be such an obstacle.

That is fine, as far as I'm concerned. For what I want to, and indeed must, write about is not America itself but rather my own discovery of America as a problematic—specifically America as a kind of "criminal" vis-à-vis Japan. Concerning such matters as the trial, attending to the family left behind, helping find work upon release from prison, etc., it is best to leave these to the various interested parties. Like a detective in a mystery novel, it is quite possible that I'll achieve my goal simply by deducing things from the criminal's footprints and items left behind at the scene of the crime. Even if that is the only evidence I have, the present situation compels me to do this.

In Japan, fortunately, the criminal's—or what appear to be the criminal's—footprints and items left behind at the crime scene can be found everywhere. For example, the Czech writer Adolf Hoffmeister visited Japan the other day as a representative of the PEN Club. When I asked him if Japan was actually as he had expected it to be, he replied evasively that he wasn't sure yet, but that there was something about Tokyo that at least superficially reminded him of an American city, particularly one on the West Coast.

Of course the experts will regard this remark as based merely on trivial customs, and that regardless of whether one supports or rejects America, it does not provide a clue to this debate. But I wonder if it is not precisely such narrow-minded fastidiousness that lies behind the confusion and vulgarization that characterizes the manner in which intellectuals view America. A clever criminal has a trick of scattering about many false clues as a way of concealing the real ones. Yet these real clues can be discovered only by first examining the false ones. I, for one, find such matters of custom to be of considerable interest.

In terms of a nation's customs having such mass influence on other nations, no example really comes to mind except that of America. Purely on this basis alone, can't we say that customs are important in thinking about America? It was for this reason, no doubt, that old-fashioned intellectuals found this topic too much to handle and ended up vigorously ignoring it. American culture has clearly been ignored. It is seen as a nuisance for both the left and right.

In his essay "Nihon chishikijin no Amerika zō" [The Image of America on the Part of Japanese Intellectuals], Tsurumi Shunsuke writes the following: "Apart from the very brief years at the end of the Edo period and the immediate postdefeat, Japanese intellectuals have been slightly embarrassed to go against fashion and view America as a topic of intellectual seriousness. Even at present, we are invariably influenced by America in our daily life through deep entanglements of interests, and yet we intellectually ignore America as much as possible. This pose of being attached in the lower body while forcing oneself to turn away with the upper body is common among Japanese intellectuals."[3]

Tsurumi explains that this attitude is due to the inner workings of a sense of inferiority on the part of these intellectuals. I certainly agree with his assessment, but is that really the only reason? Although this may well amount to the same thing, my sense is that the style of thinking on the part of Japanese intellectuals is hardened by European thought, or a commonplace form thereof. These intellectuals readily agree with the phrase about "Chaplin, who couldn't become Americanized even after forty years," but they don't ask whether it is not precisely this Chaplin that is most American. According to Sartre, however, it is also characteristic of American intellectuals to openly criticize their own country, something which Europeans find difficult to understand. Nevertheless, "Do not imagine that any of them . . . believe that they are speaking ill of America. For a Frenchman to denounce an injustice is to speak ill of France, for he sees France in terms of the past and as unchangeable. For an American, this is to prepare a reform."[4]

In other words, American intellectuals have not yet lost their transformational thought. Can we not then say that the Chaplin who was driven out of America is at least as, if not more, American than the America that drove him out?

Yet Sartre also writes of those people who constantly ask themselves if they are irreproachably American. As he points out, however, these people are not necessarily of a different type than those who wish to escape from Americanism. Doesn't this ambivalence—the "antinomy of anguish"— somewhat resemble the attitude of Japanese intellectuals toward Japan? Japan and America are seen as extreme contrasts, situated in a crude opposi- tional relation, but common elements may actually exist between them. It seems to me that the tendency on the part of Japanese intellectuals to neglect America is connected, at a deeper level, to their tendency to neglect Japan.

Seen in this way, one could list numerous commonalities between Japan and America. For example, what do you imagine when you read the follow- ing passage? "The striking thing is the lightness, the fragility of these build- ings. The village has no weight. . . . Then [the European] is struck by the lightness of the materials used. In the United States stone is less frequently used than in Europe. . . . Even in the richest cities and the smartest sections, one often finds frame houses. . . . Everywhere you find groups of frame houses crushed between two twenty-storied buildings. . . . The result is that in the States a city is a moving landscape for its inhabitants, whereas our cities are our shells."[5]

Although this appears to be a description of Japanese cities, it is actu- ally a passage from Sartre's travel account in America. Of course one can regard this as a rhetorical or actual coincidence. In the case of Japan, this problem is typically attributed to poverty and lack of planning. In wealthy America, however, other reasons must be sought. These reasons have less to do with lack of planning than the fact that future planning has become too much a part of everyday life—in negative terms, Americans remain stuck in their own dreams. As a result, buildings forever end up as merely comfort- able campsites. Don't the Japanese also harbor within themselves this same overly functionalist notion of buildings?

Countless other commonalities between Japan and America can be listed here as well. But I will have to address this problem later. Now I would like to return to the discussion at hand and reconsider these infamous American customs.

III

"There are good things even in America": Following Khrushchev's critique of Stalin, these words have often come to be heard among so-called "leftist intellectuals." Of course this is not a bad thing. Compared with the intellectual brokers, who discuss the relation between western art and Japanese conditions or preach at great length about man while nevertheless pretending to see neither anticommunism nor economic subjugation, these words are sensible and smart. It must be said, however, that the substance of these *good things* remains extremely dubious. There seems to be no discernible difference here with the views of Nakaya Ken'ichi, who could not in any way be called a leftist. Nakaya makes the following remark in the roundtable discussion "Chibeishugi no teishō" [A Call for Americanology]: "Ultimately, Japanese people know about America only through such trivial and partial phenomena as film and jazz. Because of the scarcity of solid empirical research, there is no true knowledge of America. . . . There has been a clear tendency to look down upon the extremely empirical methods of England and America, although recently things have gradually improved."[6]

In other words, the good things about America include, for example, a pragmatic way of thinking, and this is treated as clearly distinct from the country's *trivial* customs. Otherwise one would gradually go back to the America of automation and cybernetics, or perhaps that of Faulkner, Hemingway, and Melville, and then slightly more leftist to the America of the New Deal and Whitman, until finally one ended up at the words "Reminiscing of the past and the woven banner of American independence."[7]

This song about bamboo spears and woven banners is of course refreshing and memorable. And it must certainly be the point from which we think about America. Insofar as we grasp the substance of this woven banner merely impressionistically or conceptually, however, it is in no way linked to the America of chewing gum and Superman. "Oh America, where art thou?"

Even anticommunists cannot directly oppose customs. They can only politically fight back by introducing such neologisms as "capitalism of the people." Yet Americanism comes to be forgotten in the shadow of this debate. It appears to friend and foe alike as nothing more than a frivolous, superficial form of popular culture. Tsurumi Shunsuke's reference to the "pose of being attached in the lower body while forcing oneself to turn away with the upper body" is much less conspicuous among intellectuals than among those unintellectual bureaucrats who have begun calling for a revival of moral education.

Must we then link Kafka's novel with a sense of disillusionment and grow used to such descriptions of the Statue of Liberty as that offered by the protagonist of *The Quiet American*: "an emblematic statue of all I thought I hated in America—as ill-designed as the Statue of Liberty?"[8]

My view is slightly different.

America permeates everything from the woven banner to chewing gum, from Poe to Hollywood and television, from Eugene O'Neill to slapstick and musicals, from Whitman and Jack London to Mickey Spillane and King Kong. Unless we understand how deeply America permeates every-thing, it will be impossible to conceive of the real America — and even of the America-like shadow that infests everything around us.

Regardless of their leftist or rightist tendencies, the inability on the part of intellectuals to link together the woven banner and chewing gum is due simply to the fact that they are bound by certain fixed ideas. Even our Amer-icanologist Nakaya Ken'ichi (I do not refer to him as pro-American since he lacks the courage to recognize American customs) attempts to deceive us by replacing Americanism with something Anglo-Saxon in speaking of the country's good points with reference to England and America. In other words, the cause of this prejudice is the narrow-mindedness that I warned of earlier, for Japanese intellectuals associate the rational spirit strictly with the logic of the Old World. That sounds nice, but in fact the basic reason is the status consciousness of intellectuals. They simply accept as a priori such value judgments as the distinction between classy and vulgar, refined and coarse. Or rather, their inability to question this produces a kind of blind optimism.

Even the parallel lines that never intersect in Euclidean space freely touch and separate in non-Euclidean space. The two things seen by a cer-tain system of thought can become one thing when seen by another system of thought. Of course the reverse is true as well. Thus we can be fairly sure that a site exists in which the notion that the woven banner is tied to chew-ing gum exists alongside another notion in which Superman is not necessar-ily tied to American imperialism. Wouldn't this site precisely be called the infrastructure of Americanism?

IV

There exists one myth in America: a unique kind of legend of a liberated and free "people." This myth seems to be fundamentally different from the image of democracy in the Old World. Of course present-day America is the world's most powerful imperial nation, it has deported Chaplin as well as lynched a black minister over the issue of mixed schooling, and even Americanologists are forced to offer pained excuses: "Apart from the question of whether this is good or bad, the fact is that America is currently establishing a semiwartime framework, and Japanese people should know this. While the Japanese believe that this is a time of peace, the Americans believe they are in a semiwartime framework. A major discrepancy can be seen here."[9] For these reasons, America has been taken to task by progressive intellectuals, who argue that imperialism has even distorted its concept of freedom, but it seems that this concept contains other discrepancies as well.

These discrepancies perhaps derive from its origins. Democracy in the Old World was revolutionary in weakening power, but in the New World it has had the opposite meaning: "Very generally, the absence of a European class system, vast and plentiful nature, and thus relatively easy possibilities for independent farmers. On the other hand, the need for cooperation among people in order to found a 'society' in the wilderness, and then the demand for voluntary participation in power in order to secure that cooperation. Or rather: not simply voluntary participation, for even compulsory participation was necessary. Attendance at town meetings was obligatory, as was attendance at general (colonial) meetings."[10]

Seen as a laboratory event, this really must be described as a perfect democracy. Rather than a moral ideal, the principle of equality in political participation appears as an actual means of livelihood. Yet I add the disclaimer about this as a laboratory event because, despite the fact that success was perfect microscopically at the level of livelihood, a correspondingly macroscopic worldview was utterly lacking. Ultimately, a powerful capitalist class rose up, weaving its way around this excessively optimistic blind spot in which "society" was equated with "government." Interestingly, this capitalist class did not attempt to destroy the budding local system of direct democracy; rather, it sought to concentrate power by means of a "pseudo-communalization of the Union," which made a show of strengthening that direct democracy. Thus it worked to extend the microscopic sense of unity between "society" and "government" to the level of the central government while preserving the myth of the people.

This situation created within Americans an innocent or naïve sense of democracy as well as a fatal weakness, for as long as they were protected on a microscopic level (or given the illusion thereof), they remained unaware on a macroscopic level of how they were being led around by the nose. Intellectually, for example, Americans achieve fine results at a microscopic level, but these results are ultimately flawed: "[Pragmatism] possessed many good qualities that were overlooked by European socialism, which derived from German idealism and was clearly systematized by Marxism. At the same time, however, it shared the particular blind spots of American socialism in failing to grasp both the development stages of world history and the economic forces that drive history independently of individual will."[11]

These facts might appear to signify the ingenuity of the ruling class and the stupidity of the masses—and such aspect certainly exists—but one can also say that the "myth of the people" is so strong and deeply rooted among the American masses that it has not been controlled by even the world's largest monopoly capitalist. Even if this myth is appropriated by imperialism or takes the form of an isolated and suffocating democracy, it unquestionably remains a myth of the people and is in no way a myth of the ruling class. Here one also finds the foundation that produces the apparently grotesque new amalgam of "capitalism of the people."

The "myth of the people" lives on and reaches full bloom in American customs as well. Even in Hollywood films, all the American heroes are "nameless people": a jazz star's success story, the expert gunslinger in westerns or the reformed juvenile delinquent. The French avant-garde painter and self-proclaimed elitist Georges Mathieu visited Japan the other day and pretentiously remarked, "Americans, I am a *reactionary* like you!" This was a serious miscalculation on the part of someone who only had a European notion of reactionism. Such manner of speaking would not be accepted by Americans. Things won't go well unless one speaks like the protagonist Lonesome in the film *A Face in the Crowd*: "Shucks, I'm just a country boy."[12]

There may be critics who contend that such matters are merely part of the drug culture created by the media. I don't necessarily disagree: "In the process of communicating, each person is transformed into a receptor of the messages transmitted by the media, and the opportunities for response are remarkably limited."[13] At the same time, however, as Tsurumi Shunsuke states, "The media does not necessarily cause the masses to become more passive."[14] If the media contains an objective law, then it must not be forgotten that the masses also have such a law. The film *Celui qui doit mourir* [*He Who Must Die*], directed by Jules Dassin after he left America, is interesting in its hinting of this relationship. Common villagers are selected by the village elders as characters in the Passion play, to be performed on festival day. These villagers are ordered by the priest to identify with their various characters, such as Christ and his apostles. While trying to do so, they become leaders of a rebellion and soon find themselves aiming their guns at the village elders.

Nevertheless, I have no intention of becoming a believer in this "myth of the people" and singing praises to the good health of Americanism. One can certainly see here the projection of the media. There is an overflow of myths that have lost their creativity and become mere shells of themselves. At the same time, however, it should not be forgotten that the will of the people is also reflected in the media. American imperialism contains in its pocket a sleeping lion. This lion is in no way lulled to sleep by chewing gum or westerns, for these things are themselves the very form of the lion. It is not the case that revolution in America can begin only by renouncing chewing gum and westerns, as liberals imagine. On the contrary, revolution will begin precisely through a revolt on the part of these things themselves.

V

It is thus utterly impossible to endorse Sartre's remark that "jazz is outliving its day." One might conceivably understand these words as expressing a general view that everything produced by Americans will become a mere shell of itself. As an assessment of jazz itself, however, this view seems all too liberal, which is unlike Sartre.

It seems to me that nothing displays so fully as jazz the contradictions and energy concealed within the "myth of the people." However, my point is not that it is the wild primitivism of black culture that excites those who are drained by the city. Such a situation was extremely popular even among European modernists following World War I. This phenomenon is significant in and of itself, but it seems that the question of jazz is more deeply rooted in the infrastructure of the masses.

First, jazz is now a custom. The masses took this new form that derived from no mother country and rapidly made it into a custom, and one can appreciate the efforts involved here in breaking with the past and bonding with the present. These efforts correspond with the will to create a unified America: "*He* is an American, who, leaving behind him all his ancient prejudices and manners, receives new ones from the new mode of life he has embraced, the new government he obeys, and the new rank he holds" (Crèvecoeur).[15] Americans don't originally exist, they are created. And the people themselves must subjectively participate in that creation.

Second, this new form was, of all things, taken from the black slaves. It seems unnecessary to explain what blacks signified to Americans in the past. They were merely putty in sealing up the gaps in this cracked "myth of the people." This reveals a horrible contradiction, and also functions as powerful evidence behind the theory that this myth was a sham. Leaving this point aside for the moment, however, how did these *dirty* Negro songs become popular songs among whites? The active rhythm of this music, of course, perfectly fit white sensibility. But it was more than that. Although this might seem contradictory, whites did not actually feel a sense of superiority as the dominant race. There is no better example of a subject race culture being embraced and fully assimilated with so little resistance. It is here that one finds the populist expression "myth of the people" as the basic trait of American culture. This expression is exactly the same as Lonesome's laugh as he dashes down the path toward becoming a television star while pretending, "I'm just a country boy."

While whipping blacks in reality, America raised the world of jazz into a magnificent art. I happened to see a performance of African dance by the Katherine Dunham Dance Company and felt that it was much more intense and melodically creative than the Bolshoi Ballet, which retains something of the patrician about it. A comparison between Dunham and Bolshoi is interesting in several ways. In the Soviet Union, people receive things from an exalted past and attempt to breathe new energy into them. In America, by contrast, people receive things from a lowly past and assimilate them into themselves. Although both countries actively seek out new energy, Soviet culture remains at a very human (in a conceptual sense, and thus very psychologistic) level, whereas America breaks down and reconstructs that energy more mechanically. (Even in the Soviet Union, however, there are of course exceptions such as Eisenstein and Mayakovsky.)

In sum, everything about American culture emerges from its roots in the "myth of the people," and this culture is so fundamentally populist that it has become fully assimilated to American customs. While it is easy to define American culture as "imperialist decadence," such definition loses sight of everything about America. Of course it is the decision of each individual whether they wish to neglect America, just as it is the decision of each whether they wish to ignore the Soviet Union. Yet if one recognizes that the Soviet revolution was not limited to the single nation of Russia but rather signified a revolt against world capitalism, then the particularity of American culture (i.e., populism) must also be openly seen as one hint or prediction of the world's future, even if it is limited by being a laboratory event. This is unrelated to the question of whether one is procommunist or anticommunist. Socialism and capitalism are at war, not Russians and Americans.

Numerous other examples can be cited that reveal the populism of American culture. For example, the roughness and humor of its literature; the technocratic leanings and craftsmanship of its writers as well as the diversity of their backgrounds; the immediacy of expression; the extreme ups and downs in status. The populism of American culture is clearly inscribed in both its positive and negative aspects.

Even in the context of the works, there is the hard-boiled issue in mystery novels and the semidocumentary issue in film. Fields that were traditionally undervalued in realist art theory have come to emerge with the support of American traits. I have, for example, already mentioned Jules Dassin. With his films *The Naked City* and *Brute Force*, Dassin was regarded as a writer with merely an excellent eye but no real thought—in other words, as someone who did not escape the limits of Americanism. Yet in contrast to the directors of Italian realism, who also sought a new form of immediacy and were considered artistically superior but whose works lost their theme and so devolved into melodrama, Dassin unearthed new themes from the site where Italian realism had lost theirs. In this way, he was able to make the groundbreaking work *Celui qui doit mourir*. One must resist the conventional view that good work cannot be done in America. Dassin would still be a brilliant American no matter where in the world he works. What is important to note is that one could read the birth of *Celui qui doit mourir* as anticipated by the semidocumentary techniques that emerged out of Americanism. These techniques embodied new critical methods. They represented new evaluative criteria that could foretell the energy of the American people, even in gangster films.

Finally, I shall end with just one more typical case—the musicals that have achieved popularity even in Japan these days (I too have gotten in on this). As goes without saying, this uncertain new art has its origins in pure spectacle. In this sense, it is somewhat similar to the emergence of Chaplin. In his book *Gendai Amerika bungaku shuchō* [*Major Currents in Contemporary American Literature*], Donald Richie describes musicals as "an important compromised success," but they have certainly been an *important* compromise.[16] This is because musicals represent a compromise with popular sensibility, as they are broken down to the mechanical level (i.e., the level of universality) that I discussed earlier. Musicals do not always center on music, as the name suggests, since they are based on the actions of everyday life. Given that they represent a very universal sensibility, characters have come to include not only individuals but crowds and neighborhoods as well. Thanks to George S. Kaufman and Morrie Ryskind's *Of Thee I Sing*, musicals suddenly broke free of melodrama and became art. Here as well it is noteworthy that success was achieved not by escaping popular or mass appeal but rather by making inroads into the universality of the masses.

The proximity between creativity and the popular in American art might be a weakness, but it is even more a source of infinite possibility.

Yet it seems that Americans themselves are not necessarily aware of this point. This no doubt is one of the self-contradictions of the "myth of the people." The other day I met John Dos Passos, whose bargain basement anticommunist convictions I found quite irritating, if entirely predictable. It finally got to the point where I wanted to say, along with Graham Greene's protagonist, that "innocence is a kind of insanity." But let's not engage in simple judgments here. While such insanity is of the utmost danger, it also conceals a positive energy that can be understood only through the criterion of Americanism. For the time being, though, let's leave Americans to the Americans.

The more serious problem concerns the American presence that permeates throughout Japan. Many thoughtful people have described this presence as the result of America's imperialist policies as well as the workings of Japanese comprador politicians, but are there really no other reasons? Might it be possible to conceive not only of external factors but also of corresponding elements that already existed latently within Japan, and which were triggered by American proximity?

Surprisingly, one can cite numerous concrete similarities between Japan and America. Differences, of course, are plentiful and easier to see. I won't compare individual instances here, but it is not necessarily the case that differences outnumber similarities. We can imagine this simply by considering the speed and depth with which Americanism spreads throughout Japan today. Just as western European liberalism proves to be an impediment in assessing American culture, isn't there a risk that a simple criticism of this culture might result in suppressing the energy that one has now finally begun developing within oneself?

Let's abandon ready-made concepts and confront reality directly. Without trying to fully explain the formative process of Meiji authority by the concept of European-style democratization, we should ask whether new discoveries can be made by relating it to American particularity. It is entirely possible that what appears positive might actually be insignificant, and that what appears insignificant might actually conceal valuable energy.

It is said that the CIA is happily applauding the Americanization of Japan. To be sure, this is a bit worrying. Yet matters concerning the Japanese people should be left to Japan, and it is not worth discussing the CIA's assessments and judgments. It is not only Mephistopheles who "would do ever evil, and does ever good."[17] It may be that those CIA officials are Europeanized and haven't noticed the populism contained within Americanism.

DOES THE VISUAL IMAGE DESTROY
THE WALLS OF LANGUAGE?

I

It is difficult to convey one's intentions, but it is easy to be misunderstood. While I certainly don't believe in literature for literature's sake, I also have no desire to become a leader of audiovisual culture. My point here is quite simple: the linguistic arts and audiovisual arts must not be mechanically opposed to each other, for it is only by discovering their shared task that one can reveal their respective identities.

In his novel *La nausée* [*Nausea*, or *Ōto*] (which, more accurately, should be translated by the word *mukatsuki*), Sartre described the shock and anguish that is given to man by something that is not yet named (i.e., existence). By naming something, or transferring it to the order of language, man was able to subjugate, neutralize, and domesticate it. For example, by giving a stick the name "stick," he was able to know it as a stick and thereby obtain not individual sticks but rather abstract sticks in general (an infinite

First published March 1, 1960, in *Gunzō*.

number of sticks). In other words, it became possible for man to use the stick as a tool. Monkeys also use sticks, but they are not sticks in general. Hence monkeys cannot use tools.

Man has named almost all of existence. And he has not simply named it; he has also used the framework of words to express the relations between things. The evolution of grammar is nothing other than the evolution in man's knowledge of nature. This relation can clearly be understood if one examines the process of language acquisition from infancy to adulthood. In addition, patients suffering from aphasia gradually experience a regression in grammatical structure from the level of childhood to that of infancy, and this occurs alongside a corresponding breakdown in the cognition of spatial relations. Those patients who are severely afflicted lose the concept of angles and apparently cannot even use a ruler to cut a board at a right angle. There is something unimaginable about the permeation of language within reality.

Our solid everyday world is constructed in this fashion. Pavlov referred to this as a stereotypical and stabilized conditioned response. Pavlov was not a romantic, however, and so did not necessarily use the term "stereotype" in a negative sense. Rather, he valued this as a faculty that was extremely effective in preserving the individual organism. For clearly aphasic patients who are stripped of their linguistic armor are rendered as defenseless as infants. In other words, things that appear in all their nakedness without the mediation of language represent a kind of demon territory. Such things have no meaning. They have no causal relations, logical connections, or evocation and association of concepts. The strange appearance of these naked things can only be compared to the world of the infant, whose reality consists solely of lonely, impressionistic fragments that are grasped as an extension of oral sensations, or perhaps to the fragmentary and deformed world of the schizophrenic, who has lost sight of the logical connections between things. I suspect that this situation is like the head of Medusa, which turns everything it sees to stone. Words are the mirrored shield that protects itself from Medusa's sorcery.

However, so-called advocates of the visual image seem to subscribe to a very naïve theory of reflection in which everything appears the same to dogs, monkeys, or babies—anything with eyes. These advocates casually make the following claim: "Visual images are unlike words in having their own unique methods to express and convey various types of abstract content, etc." Unfortunately, however, I cannot imagine that wordless animals— dogs, monkeys, pigs, etc.—are capable of arriving at some type of abstract thought. Aren't such things possible only in fairy tales? These advocates of the visual image seem not only to underestimate the function of language; they also do injustice to the images they advocate by regarding them strictly through analogy with language.

Of course visual images in and of themselves address viewers. Yet they can achieve their effects only by prompting the reproduction and construction of language, since viewers are already endowed with language. One can speak of a pure visual image only when images say nothing, projecting a fragment of grotesque images. If visual images say anything, they immediately become a medium that elicits language. In fact, don't even advocates of the visual image need language in order to speak of the wonder of this concept of the image? If by some chance one could use visual images alone to express the capacity such images have for abstract thought—but let me put an end to this snide speculation.

II

Nevertheless, I am not trying to dismiss the significance of visual images. On the contrary, I wish to place even greater value on their contemporary significance than do their advocates. So-called advocates of the visual image are merely patients suffering from a language complex, for while they might seem to grasp visual images and language in oppositional terms, the fact is that they are desperate to raise this image to equal status with language. The value of the visual image can in no way be guaranteed by its equal status with language. Rather its raison d'être must be discovered precisely in its antagonism and destruction of all linguistic elements—stability, universalization, meaning, communication, interpretation, association, etc., all of which are achieved through abstraction.

Discourse on the visual image originally constituted one branch of the antiliterature movement that appeared throughout all genres in the first half of the twentieth century. This discourse arose as an opportunity to establish its own identity and purity in each genre as a declaration of independence from the prose art then dominating all genres, which had reached its golden age during the nineteenth century following the invention and popularization of the printing press. (Some writers seem to grasp the claims of audiovisual culture simply in terms of the relation between literature and mass media, but this vulgar understanding must itself be described as redolent of mass media.) The influence of prose art is surprisingly powerful, however, and other genres have made little headway in their independence movements.

I am not opposed to this trend of independence movements in and of itself. On the contrary, I even think that I am leading the way forward. However, I cannot endure these so-called advocates of the visual image in the *tepidity* of their knowledge of bare external reality. All they are attempting are the antitheses of picture-story films; because illustrated explanations of fiction are quite dull, they simply emphasize the uniqueness of the image and create images that support the restructuring of language.

As I showed in my example of the patient suffering from aphasia, the operation of language lies concealed even in the case of a board being cut at a right angle. This is to say nothing of film, since the function of language operates even in an eight-millimeter film on insect behavior, despite the absence of sound, orator, or subtitles. Even in the completely abstract films of Norman McLaren, one becomes aware of the internal movement of language in its struggle to overcome that abstraction. Those who aren't aware of this movement are no longer human but rather a monkey or perhaps a yeti.

Such is the relation between language and visual image. Man encounters things that immediately give rise to the movement of language, and mental activity consists in the subjugation of these things. Even dreams are said to be a restructuring of language. And the strange mental pictures of schizophrenics must be described less as naked reality than as the afterimages of language as it collapses and disappears.

The true significance of visual images must be rethought after thoroughly examining the thickness of the walls of language. Upon encountering the visual image in all its destructiveness as the ahistorical, accidental, and violent pure object that refuses all established language, dogs and monkeys would simply yelp in alarm and turn tail. Man, however, would begin fighting back through the force of his linguistic impulse, which matches up to the image. Man would try to invent or create a new system capable of absorbing and taming that unknown image.

The value of the visual image is not to be found in this image itself. Rather, it can be seen in its challenge to the established system of language, for it powerfully stimulates and revitalizes language.

Thus literature and the audiovisual arts can no longer simply be opposites. Regardless of genre, artistic creation naturally takes a scalpel to the extremely close relationship between language and reality—the safety zone of stereotypes enclosed by the walls of language—thereby creating a fundamentally different linguistic system (which of course also leads to a new discovery of reality). As might be expected, this point also directly applies to prose art. In order for fiction to shock language (i.e., consciousness) and recover the energy needed to revitalize it, one must first depart from the framework of fiction and experience the shared task of art. In this sense, I am certainly an *ultra*visual imagist in comparison with other visual imagists, and that is also how I regard myself. At the same time, however, the present state of audiovisual culture does not make use of the visual image's destructive capacity. On the contrary, it is similar to fiction in remaining shackled by the walls of language and requires an even more powerful methodological consciousness in order to break through this deadlock. In this sense, I am rather a proponent of literature (in the broad sense, including for example my own prose as well).

Methods cannot speak through visual images. And the walls of language are more solid than one imagines. Novelists also have an obligation to participate in the making of dynamite so as to ensure the destruction of language.

ARTISTIC REVOLUTION:
THEORY OF THE ART MOVEMENT

I

Let me formulate a bold hypothesis: "Art is perception generated by logic."

In other words, while I tentatively acknowledge the well-known classical definition that science represents rational knowledge and art represents perceptual knowledge, this perception is in no way spontaneous or intuitive. Rather, it is a case here of secondary perception, which first becomes possible only through the mediation of reason, understood as the opposite of perception.

Of course perception preexists reason and is fully capable of standing alone even without that mediation. Dogs and monkeys lack reason, but perception undoubtedly exists in both. (This is the first system of conditioned response.)

Such perception is of course partially shared by man, who possesses reason (the second system of conditioned response). Although mutual

First published March 10, 1960, in *Kōza gendai geijutsu IV: Gendai geijutsu no riron.*

understanding between man and animals is to some degree an anthropo-
morphic misunderstanding, one can nonetheless imagine that it is partly
based on this shared perception. Yet even if such perception were the same
in a physiological sense, it already exists in man in a qualitatively different
form than it does in animals. This is what I mean by secondary perception,
which is influenced and altered by the appearance of reason.

Take, for example, the apparently instinctive habit of walking. Jean-Marc
Gaspard Itard, the author of *The Wild Boy of Aveyron*, refers to the education of this wolf-boy to brilliantly describe how walking is by no means
entirely instinctive but rather a habit that is only first acquired in the context
of human society (society is formed through the mediation of reason). The
wolf-boy had lived outside society and could move backward and forward
only by leaping, despite the fact that his limbs were more than adequately
developed. Also of interest is how difficult it was to train the boy to fix his
gaze. Having built a bulwark against the contingencies of nature through
the formation of society, man gained the freedom to gaze and concentrate
on individual things. Wild animals are constantly exposed to contingent
dangers, however, and so it is much more natural for them to pay close
attention to all that takes place around them. It is only from the perspective
of man that things appear free to seek new relations or agreements outside
the immediate relation of friend or enemy.

This is, in a word, so-called "human sensibility," and while this topic
might not be worth taking up, it is nevertheless the case that the descriptive
term "characteristically human" is excessively vague and somewhat difficult to use. Generally, this description remains fixed as an intuitive expression based on moral criteria. As goes without saying, however, my notion
of human sensibility here is quite unrelated to moral law. This is precisely
why I am rejecting the familiar term "characteristically human" and have
chosen the slightly pedantic expression "secondary perception."

There is also the danger that this term "characteristically human" will
be understood in merely a popular sense as advanced through cultural
refinement. Far from a process of simple, continuous refinement, properly
human perception is accompanied by leaps and interruptions as based on
the influence and transformation of "reason." I have no intention to present
here a discourse on human perception, but I would at least like to clarify
the following point: the alteration of "perception" through the intervention
of "reason" is dramatic and dialectical. In other words, the fact that changes
in "perception" reveal the decisive influence of "reason" has already been
proven materially (physiologically).

We can virtually declare as a scientific fact that all perceptual knowledge contains the hidden intervention of rational knowledge, without which it could not be formed. This can be seen, for example, in the deformation of spatial cognition (warped perception through damage to reason) that accompanies aphasia; or, conversely, in the parallel relation in infants between language acquisition and sensory differentiation; and also in the various relations between lower and higher responses as set forth in the theory of conditioned response.

II

The reason that I have started this essay with a long abstract discussion about the relation between reason and perception despite the fact that my theme here concerns artistic revolution is not due to any ulterior motive to endow my discourse with an academic style. Rather, it is because it seems easiest to judge both the properly revolutionary claims in art and that antirevolutionary activity that poses itself as revolutionary by seeing the understanding of perception as key.

Take, for example, one major trend in contemporary art: the claim for independence from literature. This claim is oriented toward artistic purification and has appeared in genres ranging from the fine arts, which was established prior to modernity, to such new forms as cinema. Such claim pretends to be new, but it is extremely doubtful whether it is new in any essential sense.

It is perhaps understandable why the ancient genre of the fine arts would wish to restore its independence and identity vis-à-vis the relatively (i.e., relative to fine arts) newer genre of literature. Insofar as it easily falls back on literary themes, the fine arts is no match for the more modern media that is the printed expression of literature. The fine arts thus surely requires an expression unique to it. The object to be sought in pictorial expression is strictly that which is irreplaceable by language.

Of course I am not completely disparaging of this orientation. On the contrary, I believe that the results produced by the pursuit of this antiliterary object are irreplaceably valuable. Efforts to pursue things more concretely and practically by isolating them from meaning have also been immensely stimulating for the literary world, which resides in the collusion between meaning and object. In its illumination of the world of the subconscious, for example, the surrealist movement has been the most successful in the genre of the fine arts.

One also finds an attempt to manipulate pure sensation in a purely sensory manner. Unlike surrealism, which in its aim to disrupt meaning revealed its attachment to the world of meaning, the path of the abstractionists can be described as more concrete and committed to the antiliterature movement in the sense that this group takes as its point of departure the rupture with meaning.

It might sound contradictory to describe the abstractionists as concrete, but my meaning is as follows. In terms of why the abstractionists are referred to as *abstract*ionists, this abstraction appears in the sense that what is expressed (the painting) is detached not from the concrete "things" it expresses that exist behind it but rather from everything "on the other side." This group is also abstract in the sense that the expressive materials it employs possess an abstract existence in, for example, color, line and *matière*. Yet such abstraction is slightly different in character from abstraction in a rigorous sense. If concrete entities are signs vis-à-vis human sensibility, then abstraction generally refers to the signs of those signs (as represented by language), which are unable to stimulate the senses directly. It is possible to act on the senses only by following an indirect course in which one evokes the first sign by eliciting sensory stimulation. However, the abstraction of abstract painting in no way aims for the sign of a sign. Rather, it very much takes as its primary goal the direct elicitation of the senses. That is to say, it does not stimulate the senses by recalling an actual "something"; rather, it seeks to create new signs by appealing more directly to the senses through those signs themselves. In other words, it artificially creates concrete things. In this sense, even the paradox that abstract painting is the most concrete appears fully viable.

Now this tendency is pushed to the extreme by the claims of Informel painting, which is regarded as the champion of the contemporary revolution in the fine arts. For me, however, such new claims are less important than the fact that Informel painting occupies the site at which one necessarily arrives by following the purification of the fine arts to its logical conclusion. It is clear that Informel painting was formed through a virtually complete rupture with literature. One can no longer discover any meaning or form that is organized by language and can be stored somewhere in an existing "cupboard of signs." It seems that Informel painting can be described as one of the symbols of the antiliterature movement.

However, I by no means regard the claims of Informel painting as a revolutionary event in the context of contemporary art. The antiliterature movement was able to play a revolutionary role for a certain time because of the dialectical opposition it maintained in its tension with literature. By exceeding and severing that tension, this movement becomes unrelated to literature, exactly like the coelacanth, which endures a living death in being trapped in an evolutionary dead end. Informel painting is merely the reverse of the notion of literature for literature's sake, and absolutely no actuality vis-à-vis the present can be expected of it.

III

The positive meaning of the antiliterature movement derives wholly from its challenge to the empiricism (i.e., the loss of any dialectic between meaning and thing) of literature for literature's sake. If this movement simply remains content with the genre of antiliterature and lapses into a position of nonliterature, then it clearly will do nothing except fall into aestheticism.

As I wrote at the beginning of this essay, human perception is established by reason. The relation between reason and perception is not one of contradiction and conflict, as is generally believed, such that the expansion of one leads to the suppression or contraction of the other. Rather, it is easy to create a certain state of stability between them in which each supports the other. This balance appears in the stereotype of so-called "everyday sensibility." Moreover, one often hears reference to the suffering caused by the conflict between reason and perception, but the truth is that conflict is not the substance of suffering. Rather, there are many cases in which suffering results from the urge to restore the balance that has been destroyed between reason and perception.

In other words, perception cannot be expanded by the contraction of reason, just as reason cannot be expanded by the contraction of perception. Balance itself is neither conservative nor progressive. But it is conservative to wish to avoid expansion on the part of either perception or reason so as to maintain balance, whereas a progressive function is introduced when one attempts to maintain equilibrium by expanding one of these in conjunction with the other. One might say that the task of art consists in temporarily disturbing this balance so as to make use of its restorative force in a progressive manner in order to expand and develop knowledge as a whole.

When one conceives of art in this manner, one realizes that literature is both extremely advantageous and disadvantageous.

The special characteristic of literature, in a word, is that it is an art that is expressed through language. Language is constituted by the signs of signs and is essentially abstract. Hence it was able to fully develop its abilities through the spread of print technology. Prose art reached its golden age through the mass production of signs of signs.

Insofar as prose art is art, however, it must appeal to perception. Yet the direct encoding of signs of signs would at most lead to calligraphy while the meaning of print media would be lost. Signs of signs strictly in and of themselves attempt to reproduce the stimulation of signs. From another perspective, this appears to be a very cumbersome detour. Simply because of this, some people feel that it is only natural to make way for such emerging arts as film and television. This is one of the grounds behind the discourse on the death of fiction.

Of course this is nothing more than a superficial discourse based on ignorance of literature. As a historical genre, the fine arts preexists literature, and I regard with some sympathy its fall into a nonliterary stance as an unfortunate instinct for self-preservation. Yet the fact that even such new media as television and film regard literature as a threat strikes me as delusional and a slight overestimation of literature. This is truly a senseless case of "literaphobia." For even if one remains silent and leaves it alone, literature has already announced the end of its reign.

I regard the new claims on the part of "literature for literature's sake" as themselves a verdict of literature's bankruptcy. Of course the new proponents of literature for literature's sake do not display any old-fashioned aestheticism. The principle of supremacy is similar, but it is articulated differently.

The proponents of literature for literature's sake make the following case. Thought can be expressed only by language, and thus the art form most endowed with thought is language-based literature. Media such as film that treat language as subordinate are merely a secondary art form.

To be sure, thought can be expressed only by language. One can even say that thought is language itself. No one can deny this because thought is systematic reason and reason is structured by "signs of signs." The only person who would deny this point is an unscientific idealist who divorces thought from language and makes no distinction between parrot talk and human words.

However, the present era is a time when men are desperately seeking thought or ideas. In this sense, even the notion of "literature for literature's sake" seems to have a point.

Even when newly dressed up in the form of thought for thought's sake, however, literature for literature's sake is in the end nothing but a principle of supremacy. Just as proponents of nonliterature misunderstood the relation between reason and perception, so too does literature for literature's sake completely overlook the dialectical relation between these two. One might regard this as ignorance of literature on the part of the proliterature advocates, for it mistakes the meaning of language (reason) in art in the same way as do proponents of the dead-end antiliterature movement. Even if one group underestimates literature while the other group overestimates it, the reverse side of a glove is still a glove.

"Existence" cannot be spoken of only through language, but neither can it be spoken of without language. It is only through the tension and dialectic between these two that "existence" first appears and becomes an object for human action and knowledge.

IV

The balance between reason and perception (everyday sensibility) contains the same powerful restorative force as a gyroscope. Expansion or damage on one side leads to an attempt to restore equilibrium as the other side immediately (if painfully) readjusts as a counterbalance. For example, the death of one's father or lover destroys one's everyday balance as based on their existence, and one must shed tears in order to offset that instability until finally creating a balance that takes their absence into account. Yet a new equilibrium is finally restored. If not, that is a sign of neurosis or mental illness.

Art can be described as a work that, so to speak, deliberately plots the murder of one's father or lover. Of course this is true not only of art, for pure theory also shocks one's everyday sense of balance. Marxism and the theory of evolution would be representative examples here. In these cases, the disruption of balance is triggered from the domain of reason. That explains why anticommunism is more emotional than rational.

Art, however, destroys one's equilibrium strictly from the standpoint of perception. Or rather, the destruction or perhaps proliferation of perception is lumped together and called art. Unsurprisingly, then, one recognizes in art a clear effectiveness and sense of purpose. One example here would be the overcoming of an older balance for a new balance, while another consists of tempering and reinforcing the restorative force of balance itself.

The demand for such effectiveness in art rests less on the artist's subjectivity or the recipient's desire for self-improvement than it does on the much more powerful social situation. For despite individual differences, a person's inner balance between reason and perception (knowledge is precisely the internal dialogue brought about by external reality) goes beyond these and involves a social and historical background, one that can certainly be categorized by such common factors as period, class, and ethnic-national characteristics.

The other day I saw Sugawara Takashi's adaptation of Michael V. Gazzo's play *A Hatful of Rain* (under the adapted title of *Yoru no kisetsu* [*Night's Seasons*]). Not only were the lines and names changed to Japanese, but everything from customs to social background was replaced by an unmistakably Japanese reality. The words "A Work by Sugawara Takashi" appeared on the pamphlets, so it is likely that even the play's story and plot underwent considerable changes. On the surface, at least, it was a completely Japanese play. Nevertheless, my experience at the theater was very strange. While watching the piece, America seemed to inadvertently ooze from the background onstage, and I suddenly felt as if I were watching an American play. Finally, I had to make great efforts to convince myself that this was a play set in Japan.

This goes to show that the ethnic-national characteristics that sustain an artwork—that is, the work's proper social background—of course not only go beyond language, customs, and geographical conditions but even go beyond phenomenal events. Perhaps one must not simply acknowledge reality here but also consider the deeper question of form (i.e., the equation that represents the balance between reason and perception).

I am straying from my topic, but one often hears about the debate between theme and style. These terms are generally understood as opposites, with theme identified as content and style as vessel. In considering the common denominator of the ethnic-nation, however, it appears that the form of the theme itself must be reexamined. Isn't it the case that abstract themes that depart from form lose even their actuality as theme? When one thinks about it, even works that are criticized as formalistic possess their own themes. If these works must be criticized, it is less because of form than of errors in theme. If it is true that there is no theme without form and no form without theme, then we must be bold enough to discontinue such confused assessments of a work as "formalistic."

Yet to say that art is of its time—the notion of "ethnic-national characteristics" is another way of describing something as proper to its time—does not necessarily mean that art is unilaterally subordinate or adaptable to its time. Rather, it would be more correct to describe it as untimely in the sense that it takes as its goal the destruction of balance. Generally, however, this is fundamentally different from a supratemporality that negates its time. Art is based fully on affirming its time, and so one can indeed describe it as "of its time" since it intends to change that time. Virtually every time or period contains within itself a self-destructive dynamic, and this is constitutive of the period itself.

Just as a time or period contains aspects of both self-preservation and self-destruction, so too of course does art appear with these two corresponding tendencies. If one were to classify these formally, they would appear as conservative art and progressive art. It is no longer possible to ignore politics when trying to grasp the present in all its increasing enormity and complexity. Balzac depicted the necessity of his time despite remaining very conservative in his ideas, but such a situation no longer prevails today. Nevertheless, I do not believe that one can judge the conservative or progressive nature of art simply from the political perspective that appears in the work. Of course I have no intention to use as evaluative criteria such moods as conscientiousness, Establishment sensibility, or spirit of resistance. If one is interested in such things, then it seems more straightforward to use such stamped or formulaic criticism as, for example, how often the term "revolution" is used, how often the word "strike" appears, or how many workers appear.

I believe that the criteria for judging the progressiveness of art can be found entirely in the work's ability to bring shock, excitement, and pain to the balance between reason and perception, thereby destabilizing and revitalizing that balance. In terms of the "image versus language debate" in film, the criteria can be found in the degree of disturbance caused by driving a wedge (or new image) between image and language in the context of their collusion and free exchange. (Thus I cannot agree either with those theorists who regard the camera as a fountain pen in believing that images alone can express thought nor with those theorists who view film as a secondary art form in claiming that the subordinate treatment of language renders it difficult to express thought. All images invariably possess a corresponding language as their counterbalance. New images destroy that balance and immediately develop a correspondingly new linguistic realm. Thus images can think in the sense that they must invariably give rise to linguistic activity.)

As goes without saying, however, this determination of the progressiveness of art is simply what I have repeatedly described as the function of art in general. I am hardly unbiased here, but I do believe that art must inherently be progressive in order to be art. Even if one doesn't specifically speak of artistic revolution, true artistic creation is nothing other than artistic revolution. I am more or less indifferent to art that is not part of this artistic revolution, and I do not even regard such works as art — or at least I have omitted such works from the object of my criticism.

V

This role of artistic revolution was once played by the antiliterature movement, as represented by the avant-garde. This is not to say, of course, that the avant-garde as such was antiliterature. In their discovery of the subconscious and pursuit of the *objet*, etc., the avant-garde embodied an attitude of rejecting any collusion between perception (image) and reason (language) so as to challenge unknown perceptions. This attitude appeared most powerfully in the form of antiliterature, and it is certainly no accident that the avant-garde movement left its most substantial marks less in literature than in the fine arts, film, and theater. Even though it risked losing its oppositional tension with literature and so becoming trapped in a dead end, it is an undeniable fact that this antiliterature movement fulfilled the inherent role of art in *revitalizing* the relation between man and reality.

But I believe that the role played by the antiliterature movement is now over, or at least art can no longer be revolutionized according to its formulations. Antiliterature could become artistically revolutionary only in a nineteenth-century-type situation when prose fully reigned over all the other artistic genres. Today, however, literature has already been ousted from its throne, and this movement is being used as an excuse for aestheticism.

The work of artistic patricide as represented by destroying the balance between reason and perception cannot be replaced by the simple slogan of "antiliterature." The antiliterature movement could be effective only as artistic revolution when literature visibly appeared as a powerful antithesis. If, however, there was a weakening in the earth's gravitational pull and the moon's rotational speed increased, the moon would stray from its orbit and cease being a satellite. In its neglect and abandonment of literature, the antiliterature movement has necessarily lost its critical spirit and ceased being art.

The revolution in culture brought about by print is already a thing of the past. Following the discovery of film, one sees in radio and television the beginning of a revolution brought about by the airwaves. This is not simply an issue of old and new. As with print at the time of its invention, this trend represents the proliferation of mass production and popularization through new media. Expansion in quantity is invariably converted to quality. Like those religious authorities who once denounced print as the invention of the devil, those who disdain the airwaves in their belief in the superiority of print will soon become but a distant memory.

One basic difference from the time of print's invention, however, can be seen in the fact that airwave culture has from the beginning been supported and developed by vast amounts of capital. Might makes right. Although the situation today has not yet gotten to the point as to cause any qualitative changes, nonetheless one does see even university professors spout thoughtless, conventional views about literature's uselessness.

In such circumstances, the role played by the antiliterature movement can be only a very strange one. These children of beggars have overnight come to be seen as the hidden progeny of kings. The popular notion regarding the purification of genres might appear as if art were defending its isolated outpost against the force of mass communication, but the antiliterature movement's posture of resistance against their past beggary during the reign of literature is now nothing more than a fossilized relic. Although the notion of literary superiority would also form part of this purification of genres, the champions of such purification still speak of their antiliterary views, which makes me suspect that they have not yet forgotten their past resentments against literature.

If the goal of art is to revitalize the tension between reason and percep-tion, I believe that today's slogan for artistic revolution would be less "antilit-erature" than, indeed, "a reevaluation of the spirit of literature."

There are those who will reply, "Yes, but . . ." Of course cinema still hovers at the level of literary adaptations and literary films. I have repeat-edly protested this trend, and my views remain unchanged today. I have not changed my mind on this point.

My notion of a reevaluation of the spirit of literature is essentially differ-ent from introducing literature to other genres. Literary films are of course merely abridged popularizations that save on their promotional funds by exploiting the titles of well-known works. These films don't even introduce literary qualities, but I would reject them even if they did. I am calling for literature as an opposition in order to awaken tension. For that matter, this might also be referred to as "critical spirit," which is the most prosaic of all prose.

In the past, the antiliterature movement was always intensely conscious of literature. Artistic revolution was thus possible. It is not that counter-revolutionary elements were found in literature itself. Literature of course cannot deny its own guilt in failing to duly criticize its own weakness as a linguistic art (its indirectness or abstraction consists in necessarily reexpress-ing the perceptual world through the mediation of language understood as reason or signs of signs), compliantly taking advantage of its reign to straddle the everyday balance (or stereotype) between reason and perception, and uncritically conflating meaning and existence. Nevertheless, it has worked to turn its weakness to good use and develop and expand perception.

Yet this ability to turn its own weakness to good use is by no means limit-ed to already existing literature, for such function already exists in language itself. Just as man expanded his range of objects through the use of tools, language's power of abstraction has provided important wings of imagina-tion to the concrete world. Take for example the invention of the Invis-ible Man: it was the power of language that linked together the otherwise concretely incompatible entities of invisibility and man. Another example would be the Cheshire Cat that leaves behind its own "grin" in *Alice in Wonderland*, for such a figure cannot appear through any other method. It is hardly unusual to find examples in which literature has turned its indi-rectness to good use and successfully discovered new forms of concreteness. (Nevertheless, literature must be faulted for its inability to make such inven-tions part of the literary mainstream.)

I even suspect that it might be literature itself that was the arsonist responsible for lighting the fire of the antiliterature movement in the other genres. Since antiliterature is a conscious method, it is preceded by language and criticism, so such possibility cannot be discounted. Isn't it correct that the substance of the antiliterature movement lies less in the search for genre propriety than in the shared task of art, which in revitalizing the tension between reason and perception goes beyond genre? This is precisely the meaning I refer to when speaking of a reevaluation of literature.

Discovering the shared task of art that goes beyond genre and revitalizing stereotypes through patricide—these are not simply ideals, for they must necessarily be reflected in concrete artistic creation. This requires an orientation toward synthesis rather than purification. Rather than a mere mechanical synthesis that integrates genres, however, this is an operation that animates the spirit of dialectical synthesis as found in the tension between reason (abstraction) and perception (the concrete) within all genres. My call for musicals of course relates to this point. The same is true of Brecht's notion of *Verfremdungseffekt*, or "defamiliarization effect." Brecht often brings print onstage, but his aim is very much conflict rather than harmony or explanation.

Artistic revolution today is thus beginning to move toward synthesis in its departure from the one-dimensional attempts at purification on the part of the antiliterature movement. When art joins together with the quantitative revolution taking place in the new mass media of airwave culture, it will invariably discover new relations with the masses. Establishing such new relations with the masses is precisely the ultimate goal of artistic revolution.

POSSIBILITIES FOR EDUCATION TODAY:
ON THE ESSENCE OF HUMAN EXISTENCE

I. MAN AND EDUCATION

My remarks represent my own amateur views on education, and I am afraid that they might be somewhat off target. As someone who is completely non-educational, I am quite unable to speak about the technical aspects of education in any concrete and specific manner.

In what sense is education possible or perhaps impossible? Like all of you, I have been educated in a certain way, and it seems to me that there must be some commonalities in the experiences of those who have been educated. I would like to speak now on the basis of these commonalities.

When I think about education, I am actually a bit skeptical about whether something like a good or excellent education exists. There are certainly cases of bad education, but I wonder if there is really something like good education. I am somewhat doubtful. I write fiction, for example, but I don't think it is possible to arrive at true fiction without going beyond its limits or one's despair over it. I am not alone in feeling this way, as such sentiment is

Lecture given August 8, 1965, and first published in the October 1965 issue of *Seikatsu kyōiku*.

quite common among writers. In terms of education as well, when one feels overly zealous about education, regarding it as unquestionably containing vast possibilities, that is often the sign of subjective bias, one less revealing of actual results than of the complacency of educators themselves. That is fine, and my remarks will return to this point at the end, but let me now explain what I mean by this.

My generation came slightly after the so-called "postwar" writers. We received a completely militarist education. As far back as I can remember, socialist thought had been eradicated: there were no books about it and no one alluded to it.

Ōe Kenzaburō, who is about ten years younger than I am, is seen as a postwar writer, and he received a strictly postwar democratic education. Ōe was a child of an age of pure democracy prior to the reaction against this system. Thus he very much trusts his own sensibility.

When I met Ōe and began regularly speaking and associating with him, however, I didn't feel that there was such a big gap between us. Yet I did feel a gap with those who were ten years older, who in a sense were quite knowledgeable about socialism and were very discouraged during the war.

This shows that I in fact wasn't so influenced by the militarist education I received.

In recalling that time, no one trusted any of the teachers. That is, distrust of teachers was something of a common practice.

In truth, this attitude was quite strange. Our distrust of teachers did not spring from any antithetical convictions against militarist education. Rather, we middle school students were taught in a strictly militarist way, and yet it had become common practice for us to distrust our teachers.

For example, there was the ceremony of the imperial portrait, which required us to bow. Our teachers would all bow their heads at the command "Bow!" and so had no idea what we students were doing. It was popular among us to see who could remain the longest without bowing. In that environment of pure militarist education, this trend actually became a common practice for us. Such behavior can be said to reveal the force of intuition or resistance in children. Yet it can also be considered an immunity to a kind of foreign sickness, an immunity that exists fundamentally in man and latently in children. It is because of the emergence of this immunity that we are able to live among bacteria.

It is a major question for education to consider whether this latent force of resistance could have been developed.

In looking back at that period, I have asked myself whether education was unhelpful or if it was perhaps best if I hadn't graduated. But this is a very difficult question.

For example, there are those who didn't attend school at all. Yet their sense of judgment about various things was not worse than those who graduated.

Thus it is a fundamentally difficult question to know to what degree education is helpful.

II. POSSIBILITIES FOR EDUCATION

Education is possible even for animals. In the case of animals, conditioned response can be made more complicated by various conditions. Yet that is the extent of it, and this differs from our notion of education. In contrast to animals, what does it mean to say that man can be educated?

For example, the case of Helen Keller has been described as miraculous, since even someone who is deaf, dumb, and blind was able to communicate as a human being.

On a medical basis, I long believed that the Helen Keller case was a lie. That is to say, it was a show: I was unsure about her response since she responded with specific signs rather than with words, in the manner of an animal's conditioned response. Perhaps she was trained in the way that one teaches a monkey, and this involves interpreting hand signals. I was convinced that her case was fake, since the interpreter could arbitrarily make up things based on her hand signals. I even considered writing an essay about Helen Keller as a phony.

But I was mistaken in this. I realized my error when I happened to judge a commercial broadcast competition. I agreed to do this because of the opportunity to see documentaries that were generally inaccessible. One documentary concerned a deaf, dumb, and blind child whose case was studied at a certain university; footage of that child was taken until the age of twenty. While watching this footage, I understood that Helen Keller's story was real.

There was some basis to my suspicion that the Helen Keller case was fake.

Human beings can in no way be formed without the mediation of language. As is well known, Pavlov formulated the theory of conditioned response. His theory of language builds on this but is surprisingly not well-known. I studied in the Medical Department at Tokyo University, but even there the physiology textbooks we used contained no more than two pages of explanation about conditioned response. This shows how much Pavlov has been denigrated or ignored in Japan, even among experts.

What is known about the theory of conditioned response, for example, is simply that food is offered when a bell is rung, and that a dog begins salivating merely at the sound of the bell. Yet Pavlov's theory builds on this, leading to something very different in its unveiling of a revolution in thought comparable to the change from a geocentric or Ptolemaic system to a heliocentric or Copernican one.

An unconditioned response can be seen when salivating is caused by the stimulus of placing something sour in the mouth. A conditioned response occurs when this sour object is placed in the mouth at the same time that one rings a bell. The next step involves salivating merely at the sound of the bell: this is a conditioned response. In order for such a response to be formed, a brain is required that combines these two things. This is called the first conditioned response.

Let's say we then pronounce the phrase "summer orange." Physically, this involves nothing more than a vibration of air. The phrase contains a certain wavelength and stimulates the tympanic membrane. In order for this word to signify, there must be something higher than a conditioned response. I would like you to understand that this requires a different level, just as two lines create a surface and two surfaces create a space.

An unconditioned response is a line, whereas a conditioned response is a surface. When two surfaces unite, the second (second system) conditioned response appears. This is language.

Pavlov reached the conclusion that language represents the second system of conditioned response.

However, there are various theories about language. According to both pragmatism and American behavioral psychology, for example, language is a means to communicate thought.

Thus language picks up and conveys human thought, which means that thoughts can be formed even without language.

According to Pavlov's theory, this notion is completely wrong. Language is not the means to transport thought, but rather thought itself. In other words, the question of whether a given phenomenon is to be understood as thought or as language is entirely a matter of perspective.

Pavlov's achievement was massive, since he was the first to understand language physiologically or materially.

Subsequent research about Pavlov's theory remained undeveloped, and there was often a tendency to use the phrase "conditioned response" when referring to something as uninteresting or unsophisticated.

When someone was described with the phrase "conditioned response," this generally meant that he was a bit simple.

Far from being simple, however, conditioned response is today more elaborate than even the most sophisticated machinery. Elaborate computer systems barely reach the elementary stages of this theory.

The human brain contains both an old cortex and a new cortex. The latter makes language acquisition possible while also helping to distinguish man from other animals.

A dog will sit when told "Sit!" This represents the first conditioned response from the old cortex and involves no understanding of language whatsoever.

In terms of what it means to understand language, a monkey will use a stick (tool) in order to reach objects above it. Yet a monkey cannot make a stick (tool). Monkeys use sticks (tools) only when sticks happen to be lying around in their field of vision.

The same is true of throwing stones. It is not the case that monkeys think, "Oh, I believe there are some stones behind the house," and then go off in search of them. In other words, tools are understood strictly as an extension of the senses. For monkeys, a stick (tool) is practical and empirical as opposed to conceptual. When man needs a stick, however, he makes one by breaking off the leg of a chair. For man, sticks have an infinite existence. This is because he has acquired the concept of "stick."

The monkey's stick is strictly visible, an extension of experience.

We can see here the fundamental difference in the brain between the old cortex and the new cortex.

It was through the acquisition of language that man first distinguished himself from the other animals. My suspicion of the Helen Keller case derived from this blind spot in my understanding.

Helen Keller can neither hear nor see: how can she acquire language? How was language acquisition possible for her? I considered this question in various ways but could find no such possibility. Aha! Helen Keller is a mere impresario, I thought! She does good business traveling around earning money. It was only when I saw that television program, however, that I realized that she was authentic.

Even if human beings are deaf, dumb, and blind, they still possess a new cortex. But this cortex remains inaccessible to them. For such people who cannot see or hear and are locked in a world without those images, sense is limited to the skin. How could they develop their new cortex? This was a major question and concern for me.

When I watched the television program, I learned that education for these children consisted of something entirely different than for those with fully functioning senses.

These children acquired fairly advanced knowledge, equivalent to the first year of middle school. But they were unable to jump. They could not do things that children generally do without thinking.

The word "jump" combines two meanings: to raise oneself off the ground and to move in a certain direction. For those whose senses are not fully functioning, the combination of these two things can be surprisingly frightening. Leaving a fixed position involves a momentary departure into the void, and it is hard to understand the sense of direction accompanying it.

In order to teach these children to jump, one first introduces the concepts of distance and direction by throwing a ball. One then walks with the child in that direction. Next the child attempts to jump, which he or she is now finally able to do. In other words, these children can now leave the ground with both feet.

When I saw this, I felt enlightened by the fact that the educational sequence was so different from what it is generally. At the same time, I learned that there was enormous potential to educate people, and that infinite possibilities were available if one could just find the right methods to unlock that potential.

This closely resembles Pavlov's formulation of the second system of conditioned response. That is to say, it is related to the material understanding of human thought.

III. DEVELOPING THE TALENT TO MAKE LEAPS

I have discussed the question of how to draw out man's inherent qualities, those that make him human. If these methods are elucidated, then man's educational potential is unlimited.

Now I would like to speak about my ideas on the importance of these methods in the context of the education received by most people, that is, those with fully functioning senses.

I feel skeptical about the necessity of educating children in a way that puts substantial focus on memorization—and I am not saying this merely because my own grades at school were so lopsided.

In considering Chinese characters, for example, there has been a movement these days to limit their usage. Some people claim that it is now impossible to write, since the number of characters has been excessively reduced. Indeed, I too would find it difficult to write if I had to do so without using any characters. Nonetheless, I believe that fewer Chinese characters would be best.

Kamei Katsuichirō says that when the word "Kyōto" is written in katakana rather than in Chinese characters, the sense of the word is lost. He adds that such linguistic confusion represents a confusion in the spirit of the Japanese people, and that this will gradually lower the level of the Japanese. This claim is utterly preposterous. I can assure you that it is false.

While it is true that parts of man's thinking derive from accumulated habits, one can nevertheless always learn things when one is forced to do so after having graduated from school.

Drills involving the writing of Chinese characters in place of hiragana were quite popular long ago, and one's ability to study was primarily measured by this skill.

But such drills are completely useless.

I write fiction and so know people who believe that these drills are useful, but that is incorrect.

There is also the question of reading. It is quite stupid to have a student read and interpret something. Students can interpret if you leave them alone; this is not something that can be taught.

There is absolutely no need to memorize such things as correct Chinese characters and correct interpretations.

What is needed is the talent to make leaps. The ability to make leaps in thought involves leaping away from certain kinds of thinking. This alone should be taught.

I am referring here to the ability to recognize different ways of thinking. If this can be taught, then I believe that students will go quite far. Thus I am asking how meaningful it is to educate students in an excessively complicated manner.

This notion of leaps in thought can be seen in geometry in the drawing of auxiliary lines. When one cannot draw these lines, one tries various things within the framework of the original diagram. But the problem is suddenly solved as soon as these lines are drawn. That is the trick.

This is a trick of leaping. If one understands the trick, then math becomes truly enjoyable, a kind of recreation. Thus the question concerns how it is possible to develop the talent to make leaps. In the case of math, one quickly figures things out by oneself as soon as one grasps the fundamentals. It seems to me that very few things can be taught here.

Thus I don't believe that man's knowledge arises from an accumulation or extension of experience.

IV. THE MEANING OF "ENRICHING EXPRESSION".

One often hears people speak of enriching expression. While expression should certainly be enriched, this nevertheless represents a misunderstanding of the notion of power of expression. For example, this notion is mistaken to mean power of description. In Japan, "power of expression" is generally understood to refer to imaginatively describing something. Such force of description might be helpful in writing tanka poetry, but not much more.

The most important factor here concerns the manner in which content is drawn forth from things or observation. This involves, in other words, the construction of theories based on facts. Japanese people are very poor at this. Although they can construct theories on the basis of concepts, they have difficulties constructing theories from facts.

An example of this can be found in reportage. Much reportage in Japan merely scratches the surface. I have gone to some of these sites and found things that completely contradicted this reportage. Most of this reportage, in other words, is utterly false. This is due to the poor powers of observation on the part of reportage writers. It is well-known throughout the world that Japanese reportage writers are not very observant: they are unable to deploy a distinct perspective in observing things from a distinctly comprehensive field of vision. This is due to deficiencies in Japanese school education. One must go beyond the view that sees the accumulation of experience as leading somewhere.

V. CULTIVATING ORIGINALITY

Because education is so individual and experimental, it seems to me that each teacher should teach according to those methods that they find to be the most enjoyable. This wouldn't represent such a big difference and the results would be neither good nor bad. But perhaps there might be some difference. What is most important, then, is the teacher's enthusiasm. Such enthusiasm should be understood not in terms of a sense of mission but rather as enjoyment. I can even see no harm in treating the students as guinea pigs. For people are extremely strong regardless of how much they are treated in this manner. Even if one twists them a little, they never become as twisted as one thinks. People are quite resilient and will survive even if one leaves them alone.

One thus needs to fearlessly engage in educational experiments. Since the materials here are so durable, one can experiment with peace of mind.

Without such experiments, both children and teachers become bored. This would be horrible. In order to reach this ideal goal, improvement of teachers' labor conditions — including its social and financial aspects — must be a precondition.

I discovered only much later that our math teacher was a socialist. He was persecuted for this and seemed to have pent-up feelings. The students immediately understood. In one year of high school, we studied the equivalent of three years of math by ourselves.

As for why we did this, there must have been something there. In terms of what that something was, I suspect that the teacher's role was fundamental.

How then can one give children the chance to leap? And how can one elicit a different and original sense of judgment from within real life? It thus seems to me that the logic of a continuously looping series of cause and effects is unnecessary for education. It is more important to ask: how can one escape such chains of thought? In other words, emphasizing the importance of identifying exceptions and developing ways of thinking that can release one from these chains will lead to the cultivation of resistance, defense, and discernment vis-à-vis those forms of control that emerge together with the increases in social hardship that are sure to come. Such resistance, defense, and discernment are intuitive in nature and cannot be taught by language. The point is how to cultivate these things.

BEYOND THE NEIGHBOR

I

Apparently many people believe that it is only natural to problematize the notion of "tradition" in an a priori fashion. This is a bit difficult for me to understand, since I don't feel this way at all. Of course "tradition" exists. But does its presence mean that we must always problematize it, like alpinists who climb mountains simply because they are there? Perhaps not. Why then problematize "tradition"? The notion of "tradition" can be divided into two main categories. The first consists of artworks. These represent "tradition," those visible traces that appear on the surface of history. In classical performing art, for example, apprentices are taken in and indoctrinated until they are finally initiated into some mysterious secrets. It seems that certain kinds of traditionalists conceive of "tradition" as a finished work to be transferred from writer to writer. The other kind of "tradition" is the history inscribed within us as invisible traces. This is the domain that I would

First published December 25, 1966, in *Gendai geijutsu to dentō*.

like to consider. I don't mind if those who feel an urgent need to problematize "tradition" do so by regarding it as a finished work. It seems baseless, however, to problematize "tradition" a priori when there is no need to do so. Apart from village folk art, it was certainly possible to establish a fixed course of "tradition" as passed down from writer to writer and performer to performer in those cases where the transmitter held a clearly determined social position, as in the professional, refined art cultures of the past. But we no longer live in an age where writers (in the broad sense of the term, including performers) occupy such fixed positions. Following modernity, writers have no social rank or position. The course of transmission from writer to writer has thus collapsed. The true medium of transmission is now the general reader or spectator.

Writers are never writers from the beginning. One is a reader before becoming a writer: only after reaching a certain stage of maturity as a reader does one then jump to the level of writer. Letters from literary youths often contain the following: "I simply think up sentences while walking down the street. These sentences instantly take shape, such as 'The tree is standing there, with white clouds hanging from its upper branches.' It seems that I have all the makings of a novelist." Such talk is of course outrageous, but there are many people who think of literature in this way. They regard literature as a kind of amateur performance in which writers and readers are separate from one another. Yet all professional writers have invariably passed through a stage where they were hungry, avid readers. Nevertheless, one finds oneself in the following exchanges: "I am not so interested in conventional literature, for I want to write something uniquely expressive of myself." "Really? Well, what have you read?" "I have not read so much." "That's why I am asking: what have you read?" "Actually, I have not read anything." Nothing can come of such an attitude. It is utterly impossible to create something when all one has read is one's primary school Japanese language textbook. If people who enjoy reading typically read eight books, for example, then one should read at least sixteen. In other words, one first makes the leap to being a writer when one feels the need to read materials that are only rarely read.

Of course reading many books is no guarantee that one will become a writer. There are always people who cannot write no matter how many books they read. But reading gives rise to something within one, and writing provokes the desire to share this urgent spontaneous feeling with others. Who is this other? In fact, this other is oneself. Here an internal split first appears between writer and reader. Like a process of cellular division, the writer emerges inside when one feels the need to give something new and original to oneself as other. This of course represents a leap to another level. Yet real writers do not seek to establish readers outside themselves. Only craftsmen who have lost all creativity unwaveringly consider the reader as a pure other. Real writers should understand that the other is simultaneously themselves. It is thus false to say that one writes for oneself or for the masses; one writes for neither. The self is divided between reader and writer, and the true process of literary creation consists of a dialogue between these two.

Regardless of whether one says, "I would be satisfied if ten people read my work" or "I have one hundred thousand readers," such statements are mere word games. The reader within oneself signifies infinite readers or the concept of mankind in general. One represents the reader oneself, and this fact exposes the writer to a certain danger. In other words, a poor internal reader means that one will become a poor writer. This notion of internal reader—a reader among readers—does not refer to the reader who buys many books, thereby profiting the writer. Rather, it suggests that ideal existence that possesses the most all-encompassing sensitivity vis-à-vis the mode of historically produced fiction and its works. It was from the "tradition" inherited by readers and spectators at this level that modern art, in stark contrast to the classical performing arts, began to freely develop. Even in those cases where we adopted something from the classical arts, that was made possible by the presence of readers and spectators, who prepared the way for the transition to the level of writer. Transmission through indoctrination in the style of the temple schools of the past is now no longer possible. What thus seems to me to be the most contemporary route of inheriting tradition consists of making the work a milestone to be passed down from reader to reader in such a way that writers will necessarily emerge from this flow.

As such, the reader's simple appreciation for the finished work has become more important than the criterion of value employed by the critic. Here, however, the reader refers not to the average reader but rather to the chosen reader whose maturity is one step away from transformation into a writer. Far more significant than "tradition" in the sense of those traces that lie exposed on the surface of history is the invisible image of "tradition" that flows among readers. As soon as one says this, however, people immediately appear who attempt to revitalize tradition with a contemporary sheen by dramatizing folktales with moral lessons culled from the present day. Many people appear to be delighted by such plays. Those who quickly say, "After all, tradition is important!" possess a mentality that is similar to those juvenile delinquents who wear badges in the hope of maintaining their pseudo form of solidarity. They might be lonely. Those who speak so frivolously about "tradition" seem to be psychologically desolate. Why can't we look inside ourselves and honestly ask, "Why do we lack the task of tradition?"

Yet it is possible that such people authoritatively possess this task. I don't have this—although I must say that this absence has never bothered me. I have gone hungry several times in my life. That bothered me quite a lot. But my own lack of "tradition" has never compelled me to go out and borrow it somewhere or made me so dizzy that I could no longer walk. In any case, this is what culture means. Regardless of whether or not we problematize "tradition," it is impossible to escape from it. "Tradition" is precisely that from which one can never escape. No matter how much I might claim to lack "tradition," I am nevertheless forced, for example, to think within the linguistic structure of the Japanese language. Even if I say to myself, "Today I am going to speak such and such language" and then use a private language that no one else understands, that could no longer be called language. For language presupposes a universality based on commonality with others. The same is true in the case of money. Even if someone begins printing their own money by declaring, "I don't like yen, for yen don't really seem to come my way. I have thus decided as of today to use a different monetary unit," such money will never become valid. Even if we secretly print money at home, there will still remain something too late in the context of our thinking and daily life. It is this aspect that I would like to problematize. And I would like to do so not because it is important. Rather, I want to problematize it as a borderline case, for my desire to crush this thing that fetters me would, if realized, likely result in my own negation. One can thus begin to understand that the "tradition" that flows from reader to reader can become a major issue even for us today. This issue differs from that of folktales and famous classical texts.

II

I understand the tactical meaning why "tradition" must be problematized. In such expressions as "ethnic-national feeling" or "national character," the concept of ethnos or nation is very weakly constructed. These expressions are similar to the topic of sex in that they represent a kind of taboo that one hesitates to speak about frankly. Taking advantage of such flinching, conservative thought has introduced these terms by transforming them into catchwords. These terms could weaken anyone. Many people feel weakness, cowardice, fear, and anxiety when faced with such expressions as "ethnos" and "national character." And this situation is in no way resolved by an intellectual pronouncement of these expressions as "Rubbish!" There are those interested in raising ethnic-national questions who insist on the need to take advantage of this popular fear. Such tendency can also be seen to some degree in the Communist Party. The Communist Party uses the term "ethnos" to initially frighten people, and upon sensing this fear, it then introduces the word "class." To begin with the word "class" would not be frightening, and it would quickly be defeated by powerful conservatives. The term "anti–ethnic-national" contains something menacing about it and resembles in nuance the wartime expression "unpatriotic." This term evokes a sense of psychological fear, making people feel as if they have done something terribly wrong. Tactically, such expressions are certainly effective, but it seems to me that they pose a great danger.

For example, one hears talk these days about the "corruption of the Japanese language." Such a statement comes not only from conservatives but even from those who are considered progressive. Upon hearing this expression, one somehow believes it to be true. However, the question of whether the Japanese language has really been corrupted must be considered academically. What exactly does it mean to speak about language as corrupt? Some people point to the heavy influx of abbreviated words from English: "Just visit the ladies' wear section in department stores, for it's impossible to know what's what there!" But language is structure, not words and vocabulary. Words are just a small part of language. Thus even if one tries to destroy language, it cannot be broken so easily. Of course young people today use a strange language, but even that is grammatically consistent. They are merely making slight alterations in language as based on their knowledge of grammatical rules. This is similar to the case of juvenile delinquents and their badges, for all these young people are doing is creating a kind of solidarity through their knowledge of the nuances produced by such changes. Artisans also have their own particular way of speaking among themselves, while farmers use a mountain language—one perhaps laced with superstitions—when going off to work in the winter mountains. In speaking about these linguistic changes, however, it is important to note that only words change, not grammar. This involves the appearance of minor differences in the small links between words.

When language is thus understood as a total structure required for communication, it becomes impossible to speak so easily about linguistic corruption. Hence criticism of such corruption on the part of traditionalists is truly comical, revealing nothing so much as their own ignorance of language. In terms of the issue regarding old and new kana orthography, for example, it is hardly possible for someone to speak in one or another of these ways. There is only one way to speak. In other words, regardless of whether we proceed with the new kana or adopt the old kana, their basic structure remains identical. Of course those who support the old kana system have some grounds for their argument. They say, for instance, "This is a matter of structure and so there should be rules. Take inflections, for example. One uses *tsu* without the voiced sound and *zu* when voiced: because there is no rule here, isn't it actually more troublesome? People speak about how orthography now follows pronunciation, but this really involves a neglect of structure." Such an argument is correct in its focus on this single aspect. When considering the question of language, however, we must not begin with writing. Rather, we must begin by understanding the structure of language as a whole, prior to writing or even spoken language. To repeat: there is nothing more traditional or harder to change and corrupt than language. Debates about language must be informed by a scientific grasp of its structure.

One often hears people speak of "Japanese modes of thinking." Of course different modes of thinking do exist in reality. In primitive societies, linguistic structure is itself different. For example, one finds in such societies many nouns but few particles or auxiliary verbs. We have the common noun "bird," which seems obvious. Yet this noun is very rare among hunting peoples. To use an extreme example, two completely different nouns are used to describe a bird that is resting upon a tree branch and one that is flying in the sky. We are able to understand these two birds structurally, thereby universalizing them. Hunting peoples, however, cannot do this. In such cases, one would have to admit that there are modes of thinking specific to certain peoples. Let's say, for example, that a Frenchman lived among the Eskimos and gradually learned their language. He would nevertheless be unable to translate that language. Eskimos do not have myths, for they grasp time in strictly spatial terms. Rather than myths or heroic epics, therefore, the stories that they tell are limited to such quotidian matters as hunting methods. In other words, Eskimos possess a different mode of thinking; their linguistic structure is completely different.

Despite grammatical differences, however, it is possible to conduct a circuit of translation from Japanese to English, English to French, French to Russian, and then Russian back to Japanese. Through the mediation of an intermediary language, it is even possible to make computers translate. Yet even with such an intermediary language, the computer would likely be unable to translate Eskimo.

Now how have our languages evolved to the level of translatability? With their separate departure points, how did they arrive at shared characteristics? It seems likely that these languages became fixed during the transition from hunting to agriculture. Hunting peoples prioritize space over time, and so our sense of history, linguistic structure, and methods of abstraction and universalization came into being only after we had embarked upon an agricultural lifestyle dominated by time. In other words, despite differences in the shapes of plows, the very system of using plows to till soil is identical, and it was on this basis that man's language first reached the state of translatability. Even if there does exist something like "Japanese sensibility," therefore, its existence can be explained grammatically, despite differences in individual words. As such, it is less important for us to consider any uniquely Japanese ways of thinking than it is to grasp that we stand on the side of universality. Man has now reached the stage where economic principles go beyond the framework of state or ethnic-nation and demand to be conceived internationally. We live in an age where frameworks are increasingly being eliminated, thereby privileging an internationally shared problem consciousness.

In thus considering in its total structure not only language but also tradition in general, it becomes apparent that we can no longer regard tradition merely as those branches that appear on the surface. Failure to heed this point would result in the dominance of the following logic: "Currently the struggle for ethnic-national liberation has become part of the mainstream of world politics. It is thus imperative that we rediscover the ethnos, for otherwise we risk becoming a stateless people." Such talk leads to the popularization of folk theater. The ethnic-national fear that resides within our unconscious is in fact a fear of being forced out of the solidarity of the ethnos. It is thus extremely frightening to become aphasic. The punishment of "banishment" also existed in the past; "banishment from Edo," for example, meant that one was exiled from Tokyo to the Izu region. This is the fear of being forced out of a frame or border. Such latent fear is reawakened within us when we are referred to as "anti–ethnic-national." Within this fear, we become attentive to "tradition" in its visible form, understood as something that flows from writer to writer as opposed to from reader to reader. Such "tradition" is a pardon: people are forgiven if they speak about "tradition." In its reliance upon a structure in which the mediation of the ethnos functions as a pardon, the Communist Party, for example, raises an ethnic-national question in its attempt to become the party of the masses. Yet we must turn a cold eye to this structure itself.

III

In response to my novel *Enomoto Buyō*, people commented that "Abe Kōbō has now converted to historical fiction." Of course such comments were made from the perspective of a negation of tradition, but the very notion of posing the traditional and nontraditional in oppositional terms is still nonsense, for this represents a mere reversal of traditionalism. Enomoto Buyō spent the turbulent years of the Meiji Restoration in Europe, which was then experiencing its own turbulence, and there he witnessed the final stages of the defeat of feudalism at the hands of the bourgeoisie. In Meiji Japan, Enomoto saw no opposition between the forces loyal to the Tokugawa and those who wished to restore power to the imperial court. The very notion that these forces were oppositional would likely have been incomprehensible to him. Enomoto had witnessed the process in which the collapse of the feudal system in Europe had given way to the formation and achievement of the modern state. He thus recognized the need to return to Japan and destroy the notion of loyalty, which is akin to the desire to climb a mountain simply because it is there. Such was my hypothesis when writing this novel. I tried to show through this hypothesis that the notion of loyalty is extremely relative, and that it might be possible for us to form organizations even without the mediation of loyalty. In other words, I sought to criticize the notion of loyalty that is brought forth as the all-purpose adhesive required for solidarity. I wondered if it were possible for organizations to exist that could incorporate antiloyalty, betrayal, and even ideological conversion—or even that negated and incapacitated the notion of ideological conversion itself.

As I wrote in my novel *Tanin no kao* [*The Face of Another*], the notions of "other" and "neighbor" coexist within us. We regard those people within the community as "neighbors" and those outside as "others." The "other" is the enemy and the "neighbor" an ally. In declaring that "the other is also a neighbor," Christianity allows the notion of the "neighbor" to impact the "other," destroying its barriers. This is quite similar to the techniques employed by the Meiji emperor and government following the upheaval. In other words, what one sees here is the attitude of "Well done, my enemy. I've got to congratulate you." The notion of loyalty to emperor and state came into being during the Meiji period, for until that time loyalty was restricted to one's feudal lord. In the journal *Shisō no kagaku* [*The Science of Thought*], I found a fascinating account of something that had been over-heard. Apparently there were still people in the Kyushu countryside who not only had never heard of the emperor but even could not imagine the existence of anyone in Japan more illustrious than the feudal lord of Shima-zu. According to this view, "The great lord of Tokugawa also exists, but he rules over an area that is quite far away. Around here, of course, the lord of Shimazu is still the most illustrious." From within these circumstances, the Meiji government was forced to create the notion of the state in a single stroke. The government had to artificially produce an image of the Meiji emperor, since nobody knew anything about him. What was then required for this project? Previously men pledged loyalty to their respective feudal lords, but particularly when such loyalty came to be divided between the Tokugawa forces and those who wished to restore power to the imperial court, these same men became sworn enemies who violently hated one another. In order to unite them, there needed to be forgiveness through the pledging of loyalty, even if this object of loyalty was the enemy feudal lord. In other words, what was required was the attitude of "Well done, my ene-my. I've got to congratulate you." It was in this sprit that Fukuzawa Yukichi wrote *Yasegaman no setsu* [*Spirit of Manly Defiance*]. Crucial here is the principle of fidelity as found in the maxim of "not serving two masters," for a buffer zone was created in which all would be forgiven if one practiced such fidelity. To this end, the Meiji emperor began issuing all sorts of medals and decorations. The insurgent Saigō Takamori even received one, despite the fact that he had attempted a coup d'état. Saigō had clearly planned treason. According to the policy of these imperial decorations, however, such trea-son was acceptable since it was conducted with a great deal of sincerity.

A labor union delegation visited a certain socialist country. I traveled to this country soon thereafter and heard the following story. Apparently the members of this delegation began drinking in the morning, declaring bois-terously, "Japan is a capitalist country. It's a wretched situation. In com-parison, your country is just wonderful. We must turn Japan into a socialist country as soon as possible." Becoming increasingly drunk, they shouted,

"Off to our next stop!" And with that the group filed into the street and set off walking. "Please wait a moment, since we'll prepare car service." "Who needs cars? We shall walk!" "But it's much too far." "No! We said we will walk!" "That is ridiculous!" "We are the sons of Kyushu! When the sons of Kyushu say something, there is no turning back!" The hosts were quite upset by this behavior but followed behind in their cars, picking these men up one by one as they collapsed. Having finished telling me this story, these hosts then asked about the meaning of this term "Kyushu sons." I was at a loss to explain. They were members of the Japan Coal Miners Union, and so I suspect that they felt quite a bit of class consciousness. When they got drunk, however, they suddenly turned into the sons of Kyushu. This incident reveals how widely the aims of the Meiji government have spread. The image of the Kyushu sons has come to be directly tied to the image of the Yamato people. This structure is not necessarily unique to the Japanese, for it can be found in all countries. The invisible traces of certain eras are more deeply rooted within us than one thinks.

Unlike Christianity, we shall not expand the notion of the neighbor to the point where it impacts the other. On the contrary, we must attempt to communicate directly with the other by effacing the idea of the neighbor that exists within us. This might throw people into a state of extreme solitude. One often hears people speak these days of the "solitude of crowded trains." In truth, no neighbors are to be found on such trains: everyone is an other. Yet the unavoidable skin contact between strangers is in no way limited to crowded trains. There are still many people who believe that cities are to be rejected given the richness of village communities where one is surrounded by neighbors. In ten or twenty years' time, however, even villages will become like cities. How can we overcome this image of the neighbor—that is, the sense of solitude we feel when surrounded by others? Solitude is not so important, for it is merely a sentiment. Indeed, nothing can be done if one doesn't accept the solitude of this situation while seeking to restore direct communication with the other. We are already at a stage in which nothing can be resolved by mediation through a kind of national interest, in which one attempts to engender good relations between neighbors within the framework of the neighbor. Even labor unions in Japan still operate on the basis of the neighbor. Despite the fact that American pacifists and warmongers are neighbors, they cannot collaborate with one another. Moreover, conflicts between neighbors in the same country will quickly and inevitably spill over to others. Internal adjustments among neighbors are impossible.

The great popularity of gangster films in Japan is a manifestation of the crisis this country is facing, a situation that can no longer be dealt with through the framework of the neighbor. Those who have been forced out of neighbor-based relations create these same relations with others who have been similarly forced out. These are gangsters. It is the yearning for such antineighbor and yet neighbor-based associations that generates the great interest in gangster films. Those people who have moved to the suburbs and become integrated within neighbor-based networks typically stop watching films. Those who watch films most frequently are people who have moved from the countryside and find themselves unemployed or in a position where they could be fired at any time; they are without neighbors and feel extremely alienated, living in cheap apartments in the center of the city. What attracts such people are the antineighbor and yet neighbor-based associations that one finds in gangster films. It is for this reason that gangster films have become so popular. However, there is no point in turning to such negative phenomena. Even the student movement will be torn apart by regarding people as either neighbors or enemies. Ours is a period in which everything will be torn apart. There seems to be no way to go beyond the notion of the neighbor. Yet the objective world outside us forcefully demands that we overcome this notion. It is this gap, I believe, that drives us to solitude. Precisely because of this, the situation can change only if we strike back by welcoming solitude and effacing the notion of the neighbor.

IV

Insofar as labor unions and the peace movement continue to remain organized on the basis of a neighbor consciousness, they will become similar to today's Communist Party in Yoyogi. If these are to be modern organizations as opposed to neighborhood associations, they must directly organize the other. As I have mentioned, an organization centered on the other is one in which no loyalty is required. As we have seen, loyalty and ideological conversion have come to be used relative to each other in the context of real politics. Thus insofar as we use the notion of loyalty as an adhesive, there will invariably come a time when it is strangely torn off.

As was the case with fascism, most of the courageous supporters of the Tokugawa forces originally came from farming backgrounds, as for example Hijikata Toshizō. If this era had been dominated by a rigid social class system, these farmers could never have become warriors. At a certain point in the Edo period, however, merchants began saving money and buying shares of samurai stock for their children—in other words, it became common among merchants to adopt one's children out to samurai households in exchange for economic assistance. Yet with the decisive defeat of the Tokugawa shogunate during the war over restoration, poor farmers who could not afford this arrangement suddenly seized their chance to destroy the framework of the social class system. Real samurai, disguising their identity, turned tail and fled, thereby depleting samurai registration. Into this gap leaped the second and third sons of farmers. Hijikata Toshizō may have been homosexual. He seemed to possess the same pathological energy as the Nazis, who reversed their sense of humiliation by arming themselves and gaining control over the state. The Shinsengumi itself was first led by men from samurai backgrounds. Yet Hijikata soon created the first rule that "One must not violate the samurai code," and this led to the assassination of all leaders with samurai origins. Thus only two men from farming backgrounds remained: Kondō Isami and Hijikata himself.

The Communist Party in Yoyogi hates revisionism even more than America does. For it also uses the notion of loyalty as an adhesive. In the context of the party's thought system, there is no greater evil than ideological conversion, since converts are even worse than imperialists. Such *distortion*, which also led to the emergence of Stalinism, appeared in such a way as to link our notion of loyalty with unconscious (in a negative sense) community traditions, taboos, and security instincts. It is the same in America, where despite its liberalism it is considered taboo to violate the principle of "loyalty to America." Sex has been made into a taboo, but it too continues to exist regardless of whether it is considered a taboo or not. In those places requiring loyalty to the state, everyone feels unhappy with the high taxes but considers this issue to be an impossible taboo. Lucian of Samosata tells the following story in his work *A True Story*. A man travels to a shrine construction site and asks, "Why are you building a shrine when we Greeks no longer believe in the gods?" The reply came, "Savage tribes from the provinces come here as tourists, and shrines make the best tourist attractions." "I see," said the man. In ancient Greece, apparently, shrine construction had already become part of the tourist industry. Lucian clearly composed this dialogue as a form of resistance. Here we can see just how long we have been constrained by such taboos.

One speaks about the tradition of revolution. What is required, however, is not tradition but methods. Our need to introduce the notion of tradition even in the context of revolution reveals just how firmly we are gripped by this disease of tradition. We must revolt regardless of whether or not such tradition exists, and so methods are what are required. From long ago in Japan, there were no methods in those things that were overtly referred to as "tradition." It is from this absence of methods that the idea of inherited tradition emerges. Once methods appear, therefore, the notion of tradition becomes redundant. In the jungle fighting of the Vietcong, for example, no one uses bamboo spears despite the presence of such a tradition. This is of course a question of method, not tradition. Methods can also be transmitted in different ways than tradition. Existing traditions had no system of transmission, and their value was generated in this fashion. Such value would disappear with the emergence of these systems. This is why traditionalists despise modernity and become conservative. According to Mishima Yukio, there can be no tradition in the natural sciences because facts change and errors disappear when they are discovered. I disagree with this point. Methods remain even when techniques are rejected. Tradition in the natural sciences can be described as independent from the consciousness of tradition, which makes it unlike cultural tradition.

Lu Xun writes that soldiers stand at the forefront of revolution while writers arrive at the end. It is easy to feel that writers must stand at the forefront, since they are so cowardly. This, however, would represent a misunderstanding of the relation between a writer's life and work. In this view, the function of life comes to be replaced by the transformation of life into a work. To imagine that a revolutionary life produces revolutionary works points to a confusion in this relation, for what appears here is the extremely direct idea that those writers who do not write revolutionary fiction thus reveal their inability to participate in revolutions.

Such a notion is incorrect. For example, one must write incisively even about how harmful and false neighbor-based relations are. It is thus perfectly fine for writers to pursue what can only be achieved by literature.

Katsu Kaishū believed that men must erase their own traces upon completing their work. He said that all vestiges of one's name and past must be erased. This attitude is very rare. Upon completing work A, most people wish to leave behind their own name and traces in the form of A', for they consider this to be their just reward. For Katsu Kaishū, however, a great man is defined by the understanding that his footprints cannot be traced back through his work, that nothing of him will remain to be commemorated. It is this spirit that is needed. Such was also the gist of Katsu's criticism of Enomoto Buyō.

The I-novel represents the transformation of the writer's own life into his work. The I-novel writer generally appears in his work as a character. This very much resembles the situation of so-called "leftist writers." Although these two contexts might appear to be opposed, commonalities can be seen in the creative attitude that seeks to render the life in the work. If one leaves behind a work, it is more difficult and yet more necessary to efface oneself and one's life within it, in the manner of Katsu Kaishū.

The words I just quoted from Lu Xun are quite significant. No doubt their sarcasm was directed to China's leftist literary establishment at the time.

Nevertheless, my point is not that all classical texts are worthless. Of course there is much that is fascinating here. Yet this fascinating quality does not derive from the fact that these works represent tradition. They are fascinating because they are fascinating, and nothing more needs to be added to this. Otherwise our efforts to focus on the premodern in order to negate the various contradictions of modernity and its unclear, oppositional relations between surface and interior might soon become bound up with a straightforward problematization of "tradition." I believe that the most contemporary and effective way for us to view "tradition" is as a trap, something dangerous and likely to drag us inside it.

THE MILITARY LOOK

I don't necessarily believe that all military uniforms are linked to fascism.

Throughout the history of military uniforms, however, it is rare to find a masterpiece that so closely approaches the quintessence of military uniforms as those of Nazi Germany: the ominously stiff silhouette; the rhyming verse refrain of menace and death; the full satisfaction of aesthetic demands without the slightest loss of combat functionality.

Yet the military is fundamentally the backbone of state power, so it is hardly surprising if its aesthetics make a zealous display of its power. In the case of the modern military, however, the rapid development of firearms has led to the disappearance of uniforms with the classic warning coloration and a concomitant advance in the design of combat-based protective coloration. In aesthetic terms as well, what is now sought is a truly prosaic style that goes hand in hand with the hypocrisy of the modern state. Whereas ostentatious and exaggerated uniforms were suited to the "king's" army, practical uniforms are better suited to the "modern state." In fact, compared with the magnificent regalia of the guards of the Vatican, whose military strength is

First published August 1, 1968, in *Chūō kōron*.

nonexistent, even the uniforms of the American military, which boasts of being the strongest in the world, are so plain as to remind one of fatigues. The trend of making military uniforms increasingly prosaic has now become so general that I am tempted to set forth a principle regarding the inverse proportionality between the evolution of contemporary uniforms and their aesthetic perfection.

Now in the case of Nazi uniforms, exactly what kind of ingenuity was required in order to achieve such a brilliant effect of power? Was it the lion's mane or the swelling of the rattlesnake's tail? In any event, these uniforms were mass-produced, thereby restricting any waste or exaggeration intended solely for dramatic effect. They could not be like the uniforms of the Vatican guards, who number but a hundred men, apparently still clad today in the same regalia designed by Michelangelo. In terms of the emphasis on functionality, Nazi uniforms were perhaps even the equal of recent American uniforms. While certain Prussian-style traces can be perceived at the base of the steel helmet, these did not impair visibility and were quite rationally shaped so as to offer protection to the head.

Nevertheless, it would be immediately clear to anyone how different these Nazi uniforms were from the American fatigues style. Yet it is difficult to express this difference in quantitative terms. It would be easier to do so with warning coloration-type dress that allows one to emphasize the expression of attributes rather than essence, as with the feathered headdresses worn by warriors of the Kenyan plains, but it is not so easy with function-based uniforms (and, more broadly, manufactured objects in general), as these repel all existing adjectives in the same way that oil repels water. For example, it is impossible for adjectives to properly describe the design of the latest supersonic aircraft as determined by wind-tunnel experiments. This represents an entirely new prototype of adjectives, for such things could not be described in any way other than by themselves. In terms of the Nazi uniforms as well, there seem to be no suitable expressions apart from saying that they appear in the Nazi style.

Even though the context would be identical if we described American uniforms as appearing in the American style, however, there seems to be a slight difference in nuance here.

As I mentioned, the prosaic quality of American-style design as representative of contemporary military uniforms derives from its functionalism, for these uniforms appear to call to mind fatigues. If one were to ungraciously cast suspicion on such design, however, there seems to be something intentional in the fact that these uniforms *"appear to* call to mind fatigues." In comparison with Nazi uniforms, which are indifferent to appearances in their pure status as uniforms, the American design conspicuously overemphasizes its quality of everydayness.

The definition of fatigues here is simple: generally speaking, they must be thoroughly practical. Yet today there are many different types of jobs, and so there must be various designs appropriate to each. If fatigues are efficient, safe, and low priced, then there is no real need to conceive of a specific design for them. Rather, taste and habit are much more important in shaping their image. Ultimately, they represent a kind of everyday sensibility. They embody an image of labor as projected onto a screen of everyday sensibility.

In other words, American military uniforms can be seen as very shrewdly designed in terms of smuggling in the everyday sensibility of Americans under the name of functionalism. They are masked uniforms that are truly suited to the hypocrisy of the "modern state." Their meaning is the very reverse of the feathered headdresses worn by Kenyan warriors, for their prosaic nature reveals less the essence of military uniforms than those attributes needed to conceal that essence. Such uniforms resemble a certain kind of singer who deliberately sings in a hoarse, guttural voice so as to exaggerate his folk qualities.

In comparison with these American military uniforms, the Nazis can be said to have had pure uniforms that did away with all such hypocrisy. Indeed the design of those uniforms was characterized by the negation of everydayness. Today all reality is produced and consumed in accordance with the structure of the state. If therefore it is the state that guarantees everydayness to the individual, then it is also the state that can confiscate and repossess that everydayness. In principle, democratic states reject identifying the destiny of individuals with the state, but military matters are considered an exception. Soldiers are treated differently from civilians, as even stipulated by law. In other words, good soldiers are placed under the direct control of the state, to which they are forced to surrender their civil everyday life. As such, it is only natural that military uniforms that truly appear as military uniforms are severed from everydayness, and there is nothing strange if they shamelessly gesture toward state power. Just as the results of aircraft experiments in wind tunnels typically provoke interest in aesthetics, it stands to reason that the pure uniforms of the Nazis also produced a kind of aesthetic effect. Those were truly the uniforms of men who were one hundred percent soldiers.

I am now holding two photographs in my hand. One is of several Nazi soldiers immediately before they storm into Stalingrad. A soldier aims his automatic rifle while kneeling on one knee as another is seen with his upper body floating as he appears to throw a grenade into the crack of a partially destroyed building. Faint winter sunlight shines dully on their steel helmets and drably emphasizes the wrinkles in their dust-covered uniforms. They are no doubt utterly exhausted, but they are unmistakably soldiers of Nazi Germany. Like seasoned actors, they appear in the photograph to be intently performing the role suited to their Nazi uniforms.

The other photograph was perhaps taken several months later. The place is different, but this too is of two Nazi soldiers who are walking toward the camera away from a gap between destroyed buildings. One soldier has his hands folded on top of his head while the other, several steps behind, approaches the camera with a fearful gait holding a white handkerchief in front of his face. There are perhaps Red Army soldiers behind the camera. In other words, they are surrendering Nazi soldiers. Or more accurately, they are two Germans who have just ceased being Nazi soldiers.

However, what stands between these two photographs is not simply a span of several months. The change these soldiers underwent is quite striking. It is like an actor's face, vivid and real, after he has returned to his dressing room and washed off his role together with his makeup. This real face takes me by surprise. More than fear or exhaustion, it is actually this face that strips the Nazi soldier of his status as soldier. One of the soldiers looks like an honest youth who was perhaps the son of a farmer in some remote German village. It is difficult to see the face of the other soldier, but he might be an apprentice. Their real, everyday faces have suddenly returned, and it is the uniforms that appear perplexed and confused. This is similar to the actor who has removed his makeup, making his Hamlet costume now appear false.

At the same time, this also proves how perfectly their Nazi uniforms erased their real faces and eliminated the everyday. Defeat robbed these soldiers of more than the will to fight. It also stripped them of the meaning and idea behind their uniforms as well as deprived them of the state itself, which gave those uniforms their own identity as uniforms.

These two photographs must be described as a valuable record of the death of a certain military uniform. They also document the death of a state. Just as the signs of an animal's death first appear in its heart, so too might the signs of a state's death first appear in its uniforms.

This relation between the state and military uniforms is doubtless not limited to the particular circumstances of Nazi Germany. Even if only a question of degree, this relation contains a certain universal principle. Just as buildings are buildings regardless of whether they are made of wood or ferroconcrete, or whether they are prisons or palaces, the state's function as a state, regardless of differences in social system and national conditions, means that there must be certain commonalities. If we consider the military as an armed group that is forced by state power to remain isolated from everydayness, then all military uniforms (apart from those worn by militias and guerilla clans) will in any case certainly die out in the manner of the second photograph. Otherwise they might continue living in the manner of the first photograph. And if they live, their aesthetic impulse will remain more or less dormant.

No matter how much the military pretends to indulge everydayness with its fatigues style, one never hears about their recognition of unions or abolition of medals and decorations. Insofar as the state functions as a state, what is ultimately desired of military uniforms is that they become better uniforms. In all armies, therefore, the fastidious inspection of soldiers' uniforms and gear remains one of a sergeant's major duties.

It was several years ago when I first heard rumors about the military-look fad. Frankly, I was unable to hide my sense of bitterness at this news. According to articles in the glossy weekly magazines, exclusive military-look corners had been set up in certain sections of department stores, and such items as Nazi swastika armbands had become popular. Following the eradication of the Nazis, of course, military uniforms of such pure beauty had completely disappeared. Military power itself had greatly expanded, but uniforms in general had become much more modest, perhaps out of political concerns. It was perhaps in revolt against such hypocrisy that restless youths had been driven toward uniforms of greater purity.

I am well aware that youths often rebel. Rather than claiming that such rebellions arise from their dissatisfactions, one might even say that youths seek out those dissatisfactions in order to rebel. This tendency no doubt derives from a kind of dropout mentality that is particular to adolescence. This phrase "dropout mentality" might sound bad, but there is no negative implication here. Rather it refers to the sense of fear one gradually grows conscious of in the relation between oneself and the world, and this reveals a sensitivity that is essential for objectifying and expanding one's own potential. Such a dropout mentality appears as suspicion and discomfort with the established order, which otherwise presents itself as perfect and complete. By focusing its antennae on the heretical rather than the orthodox, this dropout mentality also functions as an auxiliary fuel tank for society. As long as these youths have an indefinite future, there is nothing particularly strange about such rebellion, even if it appears to be "without a cause."

My sense of bitterness is thus not at all directed to the military-look fad itself. Rather, it is directed to the world that implants the foolish illusion that aesthetic military uniforms, as represented by the swastika armband, can become present-day heresies and function as an emblem that satisfies the rebellious spirit of these youths. As long as the military look remains a fad, peace will appear in the eyes of these angry youths as an orthodoxy that rules over most of the contemporary world.

In this sense, of course, one can certainly see in the recent discourse of so-called "progressives" a tendency to rest on the laurels of their peace-based orthodoxy. As if in response, conservative commentators howl back by adopting a tragic, faux-minority pose. These two groups make a perfect picture when matched up together—a cartoon in which the majority forces for peace support the status quo while several lean, hungry wolves bide their time, waiting for their opportunity.

If this were true, then the military look would be perfectly fine. No matter what, one must unsettle any orthodoxy that rests on its laurels. Besides, youths are rebelling against the concept of "peace" rather than peace itself. Rebellion is inherently an awareness of one's own powerlessness and ends up attacking concepts at most. Just as conservative forces regard left-wing rebellion as harmless, so too is right-wing rebellion more or less unthreatening.

But today how much orthodoxy has been promised for peace? Of course affirmation of war itself seems to be over. If someone advocated war for the purpose of war, that might certainly deserve to be called heretical. But the idea of war as a necessary evil has now been consumed as our daily bread for a disgustingly long period of time. Japan merely happens to be one of those exceptional countries where people don't need to directly smell the scent of gunpowder. War for peace. Using war as an excuse to maintain the orthodoxy of peace. A suspicious-looking long-term bill of high face value for which there appears no date of payment. Ironically, the reality of this situation is such that the peace orthodoxy also supports the war orthodoxy.

Even if the Vietnamese War were to end tomorrow and the day came when people would no longer die in battle, such peace would ultimately be but another name for a cease-fire. Even if that peace were to last ten years, that would be nothing more than a long cease-fire. Unfortunately, the conditions under which the military look could become an actual rebellion are nowhere to be found.

Perhaps for this reason, the military look disappeared without becoming a major fad. According to one theory, it was forced in Japan to make way for the sensation of the Twiggy miniskirt, thereby missing out on its chance to become a real fad. That was a fad for women, however, whereas I am interested here in fads for men. Yet trendsetters these days are not overly concerned about this distinction between men and women. It seems that the trend now is to develop unisex strategies, so it might be naïve to think of fads as separate for men and women. In any event, without causing any great fuss, the military-look fad quickly disappeared with barely a shout of encouragement.

Just recently, however, I unexpectedly had a chance to see the real military look, despite the fact that it is now quite out of season. The place was Shinjuku, at a corner of a very crowded underground shopping area. Let me begin by introducing the style: the coat of course had a stand-up collar and the color was navy blue with ocher embroidery around the ribs. Its shape resembled an eighteenth-century European military uniform, but the actual impression was that of something handed down from a cabaret doorman. All manner of crests and badges were affixed everywhere. Gold braid fell from the left shoulder. On the right arm, shamelessly, there appeared a Nazi swastika armband. The trousers were made of black woolen cloth with red embroidery on the sides. On the feet, moreover, rubber *zōri* sandals were worn instead of shoes. The hair was very long, in the style of hippies.

I instantly felt ashamed by my lack of foresight. It seems that I had seriously mistaken the military-look fad, or perhaps the fad's meaning. If that outfit were what is meant by the military look—or if that were its parody— then I could fully understand it and make sense of it. The outfit mostly didn't match, but one could detect some expression precisely in that mismatched quality. If someone were showing off a pure military uniform in this manner, he could only be a schizophrenic patient who had escaped from a mental hospital. However, it would be quite impossible for a schizophrenic patient to offer such comment. If I were to arrange strictly from memory the crests and badges worn in place of military decorations on the outfit, there was for example a ski tournament memorial award, a woman's large red lips holding a cigarette, a clipping from a department store brand, and a membership badge from the Japan Automobile Association, etc. I suspect that those rubber *zōri* sandals might actually have been intended as part of the Vietcong look.

It was truly an insolent farce. As someone who seriously turns his head merely upon hearing the phrase "Nazi swastika," I myself was unwittingly part of the group being mocked.

When one considers this style, which cannot be mass-produced, one realizes that it cannot easily become a fad in the manner of changing skirt lengths or tie widths. Fads begin by insinuating themselves into people's desire to assert themselves by appearing different from others; these fads then incite people's desire to remain current by joining a group that asserts itself until, finally, the fads completely sell themselves to the point of obsolescence. A masterful cocktail of rebellion and sycophancy provides a chance for trendsetters to show their skill, and while this cocktail makes one drowsy, it has virtually no stimulating effects. As can moreover be seen in the fate of Nazi uniforms, those uniforms that are divorced from the state no longer even retain the form of uniforms. In particular, since military uniforms began to assume a mask of hypocrisy, they barely appear as real uniforms, and those that do *appear as* uniforms can exist only as parodies. In the past when military uniforms still existed in Japan, I used to see such soldier doll figures as toy soldiers made of lead, but even these were imitations of an earlier era of soldiers with warning coloration-type uniforms. Parody can't even be seen in dolls. Parody fads are a parody of fads themselves, which is not logically possible. Rather than attributing the decay of the military look to its defeat to Twiggy, must we not regard it as a defeat to itself?

Ultimately, the outfit that I saw was perhaps not a fad at all but simply an irregular blooming of the military look that appeared slightly out of season. There would be nothing odd about it being a parody if it were such an irregular blooming.

But then how are we to consider the Beatles? One theory claims that it was the Beatles who pioneered the military look. Twiggy, who is said to have killed off the military look in Japan, vanished all too soon while the Beatles' name still lives on even today.

In, for example, their record *Sgt. Pepper's Lonely Hearts Club Band*, the title, of course, and even the album jacket are the very epitome of the military look. In the center of the jacket are the Beatles, looking quite serious in military uniform. Yet this uniform is a gaudy affair with all the frills from the era of uniforms of protective coloration. The Beatles' serious expressions naturally produce a comic effect. In front of them is a flower bed adorned with marijuana flowers, while gathered behind them stands a sculptured group of such contemporary heroes as Marx, Marilyn Monroe, Edgar Allen Poe, Marlon Brando, Che Guevara, and Al Capone. This is quite an insolent design.

The content of the album is no less ingeniously devised than its jacket. Come on, everyone, please listen! "It was twenty years ago today that Sergeant Pepper—i.e., the hot-tempered sergeant—carefully taught our 'Lonely Hearts Club' band to play. So let me introduce to you a song by the famous Mr. 'Castration Knife.'"[1] Through these very funny lyrics, ultimately, the dreams and ideals of a lonely and hard-hearted sergeant are fully transformed into parody.

In other words, the military look did not first become parody after it had drifted to the town of Shinjuku. Such parodying was clearly prepared by the Beatles, who pioneered the military look. If we consider parody as an awakening, the very opposite of fads, then this look seems to be an antifad fad. What had been impossible for conventional theories actually began in this manner. Of course the military look could not become a major fad. As an antifad fad, it could only be a flower that blooms out of season. Even for comic actors, however, knowingly wearing a parody is an advanced technique that requires a great deal of experience.

Among contemporary youths, has a new premonition thus come about that already allows them to understand this era as comedy? The concept of a parodied military look goes beyond a mere farcifying of military uniforms and even touches upon a farcifying of the state itself in its attempt to preserve the orthodoxy of military uniforms in exchange for the orthodoxy of peace. But this is in any case a rebellion, so it's no big deal. No doubt the Beatles were presented with medals because it's not such a big deal. Nevertheless, one can detect in their prank a poison that even medals cannot dilute. I might simply be imagining things, but I do believe that in this parodying of heresy there exists a daring kind of wisdom that might also parody the grounds of orthodoxy.

In any event, the era of anguished heresy seems to have already disappeared. Genuine heresy will perhaps come wearing a clown costume.

PASSPORT OF HERESY

Several million years ago there appeared the bipedal *Australopithecus*, who was clearly distinguishable from other anthropoids. Walking upright allowed their brain to develop and provided freedom of motion to both their hands and arms. The *australopithecines* were already using stone tools. Among our ancestors, they were the first prehominids.

According to Robert Broom, however, there also lived a different species of bipedal creature known as *Paranthropus*, who appeared one million years after *Australopithecus*. It seems that *Australopithecus* and *Paranthropus* coexisted for nearly one million years. For some reason, however, *Paranthropus* died out rapidly thereafter. The surviving *Australopithecus* continued to evolve and finally achieved the status of *Homo*, the same as man, under the name of *Homo erectus* some five hundred thousand years ago.

What were the major reasons that one of these two similar species of ape-men perished while the other was given a chance to evolve? Excavated fossils reveal that the difference between the two was mainly the following: first, *Paranthropus* was considerably larger than *Australopithecus*; and

First published September 1, 1968, in *Chūō kōron*.

second, the skull and jaw of *Paranthropus* were well developed, resembling those of a gorilla.

In terms of this first point, *Australopithecus* also changed over time and eventually came to grow nearly as large as *Paranthropus*, which suggests that the latter's robust size was not necessarily a handicap. As for the second point, to assume that *Paranthropus* represented a lower life-form based simply on their gorilla-like appearance would be to fall into the trap of personification. Such characterization refers strictly to their anatomical features, as for example the well-developed jaw muscles and large molars. These features merely signify that *Paranthropus* was herbivorous.

Strangely enough, however, the gorillas that appear in horror stories and science fiction are routinely depicted with bared fangs and fresh blood dripping from their mouths. This is a good example of how self-centered man is regarding the notions of evolution and advancement. It is man himself, not the gorilla, who prefers eating meat. Among all primates, in fact, only man is a meat eater. If one views meat eating as a sign of a savage, lower life-form and plant eating as more refined and noble, then the beast dripping fresh blood from his mouth would be none other than man himself. Creatures with a gorilla-like appearance might in fact be considerably more gentle and noble.

According to the general criteria for primates, in fact, it would be difficult to see *Paranthropus*'s herbivorous appearance as regressive. Indeed, the fact that they walked upright reveals that they had unmistakably evolved. If anything, we can see signs of partial regression in the jaw and molars of *australopithecines* as a result of their sudden modification as meat eaters.

If we were to distinguish these two creatures on the basis of legitimacy and heresy, then the extinct *Paranthropus* would be the legitimate descendant from primitive anthropoids, while our ancestral *Australopithecus* would represent a grievous heresy in its taste for raw flesh, which was something unknown to its brethren.

One finds the term "lone monkey." While this expression carries a ring of authenticity and otherworldliness, it actually refers to an outcast monkey that has been forced out of its tribe. Just as for man prison is in and of itself punishment, so too do confinement and isolation cause the greatest neuroses in monkeys. In terms of the instinct for tribal formation, there appears to be no real difference between the descendants of carnivores and herbivores.

Nevertheless, a considerable difference must be said to exist in the character or substance of these tribes. The carnivorous *Australopithecus* preyed on animals and so must have naturally formed small groups that were extremely mobile. In contrast, the herbivorous *Paranthropus* must have been more settled, forming groups that were as large as could possibly be sustained by available resources in order to maintain and protect their territory. Since group structure becomes more complex with greater size, the gorilla-like *Paranthropus* was perhaps also slightly more advanced in terms of socialization.

And yet *Paranthropus* died out. For one million years it changed little while living in the bounteous forest and simply disappeared from history. How did that happen? It is not a particularly pleasant image, but there is no proof to suggest that it did not finally end up in the stomachs of our ancestors the *australopithecines*. It is worth imagining what would have happened had these two groups come across each other. One would view the other simply as a nuisance to be chased away, while the other would react as if spotting an unexpected meal. Clearly the contest would be over from the very beginning.

(In the case of animals of similar size and shape, of course, carnivores are not necessarily stronger than herbivores. The latter can use their superior teamwork to resist the former's aggression. Also, ape-men who walked upright were already using stone tools. These tools were certainly much more valuable when used to confront wild beasts than to pick fruit and dig up tree roots. As hunters, *australopithecines* would have more readily learned the skills necessary for using stone tools, and this would have stimulated the cerebral cortex, allowing them to outwit their enemies and develop into skillful and dangerous tacticians.)

In order to avoid misunderstanding, however, let me state that I am not generalizing this example of *Paranthropus*'s defeat in order to claim that man's true nature lies in the destruction of peace through violence and the conquest of sociality by brutality. Rather, I am simply emphasizing the fact of our ancestor's canines in contrast to the molars of *Paranthropus* as an antidote to a glaringly humanist prejudice, in which, for example, the use of the name "Killer Gorilla" for the play villains in pro wrestling is met with little skepticism. In order for the ape-man *Australopithecus* to radically evolve into primitive man in the form of *Homo erectus*, in fact, he had to discover fire as well as use stone tools. I suspect that this discovery of fire was used less to improve the flavor of meat than to overcome the greatest difficulty of meat eating, that is, its rapid spoilage. When it became possible to preserve meat, even our hunters were permitted a brief respite. They escaped the fate of carnivorous animals—those eternal wanderers—and were able to enjoy the convenience and leisure that are part of a settled existence. Such an existence allowed them to develop traps, and the need for large amounts of prey hastened the unification and expansion of the group. Rules governing exchange and distribution were necessarily created, and a form of socialization incompatible with the nature of hunters—which for this reason alone, perhaps, was much more fluid and conscious than that of the spontaneous *Paranthropus*—came to be promoted.

Actually, fossil evidence clearly points to the remarkable evolution and transformation of *Australopithecus* in comparison with *Paranthropus*, which barely changed over one million years. Elements that facilitated change and evolution (e.g., a diverse gene pool) might have existed intrinsically in this heretical group, which abruptly broke with the primate tradition of a plant-based diet that had continued for tens of millions of years. An open history always prepares the way for diversity over uniformity, mobility over fixity, progress over conservatism, and heresy over legitimacy. History simply closes the curtain on any futile order or refuge. When the final *Paranthropus* thus perished on the outskirts of a warm and blessed forest, our heretical sons were, in the form of *Homo erectus*, already expanding their hunting range to everywhere in the world outside of the glaciers.

It wasn't simply sociality and nonviolence that disappeared together with *Paranthropus*; an excessively conservative society that knew only a fixed or settled existence died out as well. Only the heretical group that developed out of that society would embark upon the radical advance toward human history. It is precisely this heresy and instinct for mobility that have so deeply inscribed themselves on our hearts, and these may be the passport to the future.

With a few exceptions, however, what seems to resonate in the hearts of people in both East and West is the phrase or concept of "mother earth." Pygmies, who are experts at hunting, apparently even now scorn and disdain the nearby black farmers, but no one bothers about this. It's quite natural. Farmers have enjoyed a long history of agriculture, which might be only a fraction of the time represented by the age of *Homo erectus* but still numbers over five thousand years, which is dazzling on the scale of experience. The native myth that views farmers as the foundation of society has imbued man's heart to the core.

In this world, fixity is consistently seen as a virtue or commandment. Solidarity and collaboration are indispensable, and so when the comparatively tolerant concept of law as existing within a certain territory is directed outside it, its brutality comes to be exposed without compunction. Even in the case of primitive agricultural peoples, "The fundamental rule, that peace within the community must be upheld, does not always permit the law of equivalent retribution, a *lex talionis* ('An eye for an eye, and a tooth for a tooth')—often not even in the most serious of all crimes, murder within the group. . . . [There occurs] a duel of the conflicting parties, which, however, never ends in death."[1] Nevertheless, immediate death awaited those who crossed borders without permission. Such was the undisguised nature of farmer mentality, which stood in contrast to those herding peoples who made zealous use of the death penalty, since these latter had no real consciousness of borders and lacked any kind of punishment for border incursions. Such fixed morality was handed down in Japan even in the Edo period, to cite a more familiar example. Itinerant craftsmen were regarded as the very lowest form of life, while drifters and vagrants were treated as criminals. There even existed the punishment of "exile," all of which suggests that the abandonment of a fixed or settled life was tantamount to relinquishing one's right to live.

Can one thus say that the passport of heresy has already exceeded its statute of limitations and lost its validity? Are we to believe that now, when the earth is everywhere divided by disparate territories in the form of states, mankind has finally completed its journey and reached the Promised Land? Is it the case that heresy and mobility have already played their part, and all that awaits us now is to return to the pre-*Paranthropus* repose of the gorilla?

Unfortunately, I cannot agree with these sentiments. It is impossible for me to so tamely accept the validity of "mother earth," since this notion may yet turn out to be counterfeit. Regionalism, hatred of cities, arguments against standardized language, advocates of folk stories, prefectural associations, restaurants specializing in regional cuisine, dialectology research groups, patriotic education, and finally a "Festival Plaza" considered so important as to be made part of the World's Fair: these are all ultraideological brigades that gather to defend "mother earth" while waving around them a slightly orthodox coat of arms. These brigades even attempt to poke their nose into the principles of literature, inquiring into the presence of a work's umbilical cord. It seems to me, however, that an umbilical cord helps to determine only whether something is born live or hatched from an egg.

In the case of primitive agricultural peoples, I can certainly imagine the reason and necessity behind the appeal to "mother earth." The fixed existence of these peoples was a result of their own choosing. Yet that choice was also a battle, one which was no doubt fought both externally and internally. It is an often-reported fact that the nomadic underdeveloped tribes that still exist today despise farming. While traveling around Slovakia, I heard of Gypsies who were offered splendid apartments and guaranteed steady employment and yet repeatedly tried to flee, much to the consternation of government officials. The transition from migrancy to a settled existence is perhaps not as easy as we, who are already settled, might imagine. The roaming nature of hunting peoples was not something passive, as for example a necessary means to obtain food. Rather, it represented a basic way of life that had become so normalized that other forms of behavior simply could not be imagined. Just as we fear such eternal wandering, seeing it as a kind of "death," so too do hunting peoples presumably conceive of a fixed or settled existence in the same terms.

Yet some of these people have overcome that fear and settled down. Various theories have been put forth explaining their reasons behind that decision, but no one knows exactly. A "three-stage theory," in which mankind progressively developed from hunting to animal husbandry to agriculture, was accepted as common sense from ancient Greece to the nineteenth century. Yet this theory was gradually discredited on the basis of subsequent empirical research. Numerous cases began to reveal that migratory peoples display a surprisingly strong psychological resistance to settling down. It seems that the error of the classical "three-stage theory" lay in measuring the inner lives of migratory peoples strictly on the basis of those peoples whose lives were more fixed or settled. It is hardly the case that hunting peoples would immediately transform themselves into agricultural peoples if they could simply learn how to farm.

Julius E. Lips has proposed the following theory concerning this point. Hunting peoples did not begin their transition to a fixed existence as a result of the discovery of agricultural techniques, as is traditionally believed. Rather, as Lips argues, certain preexisting conditions for such fixed existence were already present, and these allowed for the emergence of agriculture and animal husbandry. Lips also introduces the concept of *harvest peoples* to refer to the intermediate stage leading to a fixed existence. Harvest peoples were a group situated between hunting and agriculture: they neither cultivated fields in the manner of agricultural peoples nor immediately consumed food in the fashion of hunters and gatherers, but rather made provisions against shortage by storing food for a period of time. When harvesting food that is to be stored rather than eaten immediately, one becomes more concerned about land that can be used for large-scale harvesting. Next there is a need for storage sites. Stability of existence was accompanied by an increase in family size as well as the organization of group work required for large-scale harvesting. Furthermore, in order to guarantee possession of the harvested areas, there was a strengthening of tribal unity. All these things gradually led to a deepening attachment to the land. As Lips argues, only the final step of planting seeds remained in order to complete the transformation into agricultural peoples, but these harvest peoples had already internally prepared the way for a fixed existence.

I accept this theory. By virtue of eating meat, our ancestral *australopithecines* split from the settled primates and journeyed off as eternal wanderers toward a much more unknown history. At the same time, they did not simply wander out of the dark forest or plains and become bloodthirsty beasts. When, as I have mentioned, it became possible to preserve meat through the invention of fire, these most powerful hunters, armed with secondary fangs in the form of stone tools, were forced to cooperate with several tribes in order to obtain larger prey. Although they had once been destroyers of society, *australopithecines* now found themselves again on the road to socialization. Yet this was not the closed society that had previously existed in the age of herbivorous primates but rather a divisional reorganization that was bound together by a clear consciousness of purpose. Measured strictly on the basis of its associative force, such a society was perhaps more fragile than the social bonds found in monkey tribes. What was crucial, however, was that this society was open, flexible, and based on conscious choice. While there is no evidence to support this, I wonder if such a process of secondary social formation was not also the process in which language was first formed.

Such socialization required a high level of intelligence in that it expanded the possibilities of hunting by provisionally adopting and utilizing a fixity of existence that was essentially contradictory to the hunting instinct. The balance between the nomadic instinct and the desire for fixity was dictated strictly by the amount of food needed to be stored and the length of time required for storage. Even during the Ice Age, when many animals died off, only mankind evolved and increased in number. This was due not simply to man's expertise in hunting but also to the fact that freezing conditions provided him with an opportunity to preserve meat for longer periods.

I thus agree with Lips's theory that the "harvest peoples" were a radical springboard in the history of mankind. Dried edible plants—such as grains and potatoes—can be preserved much longer than cooked meat, but they are unsuitable for immediate consumption. They require such advanced processing techniques as being ground into flour or boiled with water. Once these techniques are mastered, however, the ability to preserve food is dramatically increased. It would hardly be surprising if the balance between mobility and fixity were at some point reversed. Yet these harvest peoples did not then abandon the heresy of *Australopithecus* to return to the orthodoxy of *Paranthropus*. Such a reversal would be only that, a reversal, signifying nothing beyond itself. No matter how much the signal of fixity as transmitted by the brain overrides the rhythm of mobility as beaten out by the heart, it is still the heart that supplies blood to the brain. If the heart stops beating, then all cerebral activity must cease.

As the primitive farmers stood motionless on the rich soil and rested their plows, murmuring the words "mother earth" and fighting the violent tension within them, they must have gazed out at the distant horizon feeling both dread and longing for those elements of the "father" that lay beyond.

Several years ago I saw an interesting western film from the United States. I have forgotten the title, but it was not the typical plot in which cowboys battle the Indians. Rather, it added a new wrinkle in focusing on the actual practice of frontier economics: several pioneer farmers appear one day among a group of cowboys who have already settled down, and these white people with different interests clash with one another over the land. Naturally the cowboys were all dashing and clever, with very open views about the land. In contrast, the farmers were stubborn and provincial, thinking about the land in an extremely egotistical and possessive manner. The farmers also seemed to have a slightly better grasp of economics. A kind of Romeo and Juliet–styled romance appeared as well, but the film was mainly about the fundamental difference between U.S. law and the perception of law out West. It was an undeniable fact that national law, as it pertained to the land, was on the side of the much more narrow-minded farmers. The cowboys were defeated by justice, since the farmers had already paid for and registered the land. The drama did not end there, however, as an unforeseen catastrophe had duly been prepared. When the farmers dug their spades into the sweeping pasture land and turned it into long, furrowed rows, there intervened a natural justice that exceeded even the justice set forth by national law. The roots of the grass that covered nearly the entire expanse of the land were ripped out, resulting in the rapid desertification of the plain. The farmers could only stand dumbfounded among the blowing clouds of dust, as if frozen in place.

Although the film was of course made in the twentieth century, this frontier drama of conflict has been repeated in one form or another for thousands of years, since the first primitive farmers stood on "mother earth" and gazed off beyond the distant horizon. For medieval farmers, however, this drama appeared in the form of severe inner turmoil. They were forced to worry about preventing the desertion of family and companions while also protecting themselves from the lure of the horizon. No doubt they reassured themselves of the virtues of a fixed existence by speaking of the blessings of "mother earth" and contrasting these with the hardships of wandering. Finally they developed within themselves the specter of fear, convinced that what lay beyond the horizon was a land of ghosts and demons.

Turning the page of history, however, one discovers that the merely spectral ghosts and demons that lay beyond the horizon began to show themselves in the form of actually existing enemies.

For example, one finds the nomadic Altai peoples from the frontiers of China, the Scythians from the frontiers of Mesopotamia, and the Germanic peoples from the frontiers of the Roman Empire. I cite these examples with little regard to their historical eras, but what I am trying to problematize here is the general law of the frontier—that is, the broad dynamics of how frontiers were formed as well as how the opposition between mobility and fixity played out in the context of their formation—and so I would like to tentatively ignore the question of chronology.

Now when, where, and how did nomadic peoples first appear? We have already mentioned that the three-stage theory of "hunting to animal husbandry to agriculture" is factually inaccurate. In order to consider animals that could be consumed directly as livestock to be consumed indirectly, storage had to be conceptualized in such a way that was psychologically and materially possible. A surplus of feed and water was itself proof of an advanced stage of agriculture. These nomadic peoples must have focused a great deal on their livestock, as they were able to recover in their fixed existence the flavor of meat that had initially been lost when adapting themselves to this new way of life. At the same time, however, an inevitable contradiction exists between animal husbandry and agriculture regarding the use of land. Were there any ideas about how to increase the number of livestock without sacrificing available farmland? The grazing of animals outside of farmland perhaps emerged as a new technique designed to resolve that contradiction. The division of labor then followed, with people specializing in animal husbandry. Increases in the number of livestock led to an expanded radius for nomadic activities. Here we can see the birth of a secondary type of migratory peoples.

Initially, however, these new migratory peoples almost certainly did not have antagonistic relations with farmers. Herders must have been regarded as members of the same community, a kind of detached force of farmers. Yet at a certain point in time these two groups for some reason severed relations, gradually forming societies that were independent of one another. I do not know what that reason was, but such separation was a general phenomenon, so it must have been quite common. If I were to let my imagination run, I would say for example that agricultural society had reached a certain stage of development and begun establishing class divisions. The principle of rule in agricultural society operates strictly on the basis of private ownership of land, and this would not apply to nomadic peoples who abandon farmland. Even if these nomadic peoples rejected servitude and proclaimed their independence due to a sense of conflict over economic interests, the agricultural nobility would probably not have done more than reinforced territorial boundaries and erected a wall of *law* between the two groups. Separation from the nomads, the formation of the frontier, and the establishment of borders: it seems that these three events took place in virtually parallel fashion.

Hence nomadic peoples were also antiterritorial heretics whose emergence coincided with the territorial claims of agricultural peoples (the state-like formation of fixed existence).

For a time, no doubt, these two groups sullenly and reluctantly continued trading with each other. Although they certainly were not poor, the nomadic peoples were unable to support themselves due to the simplicity of their products and thus were forced to rely on trade with agricultural society. For its own part, agricultural society in its conservatism had no reason to refuse trade with the nomadic peoples, providing that its borders were kept inviolate.

But this situation would suddenly change around 1000 B.C. when the nomadic peoples of the plains of central Asia developed the skill to ride horses. With this skill, their status underwent a drastic change. The expanded radius of their activities led to greater tribal organization as well as significant advances in their capacity to domesticate animals: they could no longer be ignored as a social entity. For example, it seems that by 800 B.C. the nomadic Scythians had already abandoned the tribal system and adopted a state system ruled by a king. (A nomadic state, however, contains no borders. The area where today its horses run free is, in other words, a territory. Depending upon how one defines the concept, this area should perhaps not be called a state. At the same time, it might well be the case that accepting the state and the presence of borders as equivalent is itself one of the blind spots inherent to a form of thinking based on fixed existence.) Horse riding also led to increased military power. Superb mobility combined with the tactic of shooting arrows from horseback transformed the nomadic peoples as a whole into a fearsome army. The first nomadic empire of Scythia was no exception as it held sway from the plains of southern Russia to all of eastern Europe, and the famed "Scythian metal implements" excavated throughout the Eurasian continent are widely believed to be tributes taken from Greek colonial cities. Thereafter a series of powerful cavalries appeared one after the other, laying waste to all areas from China in the east to the heart of Europe in the west. Nomadic empires reached their peak in the thirteenth century with the Mongolian empire of Genghis Khan but were displaced from history in both name and substance when thirty thousand Tekke Turk-men warriors, who were descendants of the last nomadic emperor, Nader Shah (assassinated in 1747), were defeated by a Russian army equipped with cannons and machine guns. Thus we see that the drama between migratory and more settled peoples ceaselessly continued on the frontier as recently as one hundred years ago.

In the twentieth century, however, frontiers no longer exist. With the exception of the South Pole, the earth has everywhere come to be divided by fixed states, and beyond their borders lay only other, similar fixed states. Have all hearts now lost the need for migrant, mobile rhythms? Does not even one awkward person remain who finds himself confused by the fact that his heart beats out of rhythm?

> They stagger and roam about throughout the year with their friends. They eat and drink outside, and appear to lack homes to which to return. They do have their own territory, however, and one knows where to find people through word of mouth. They enjoy fighting and quickly form cliques, but they will run for their lives if they lose and aren't ashamed to flee. While they are particular about matters of personal interest, they lack all etiquette. Upon receiving gifts or earning money, the young people who are still active will take the best share for themselves, leaving what remains to the old dotards. Above all else, this is a world in which the strong rule. They will unblinkingly take for themselves the women who have only recently been widowed, even if these women were married to men from their own families.

I am not referring here to the *fūten-zoku* hippies in Shinjuku, nor am I exaggerating the character of contemporary youths. In fact, these lines, which I have slightly reworked, are taken from a passage about the Xiongnu peoples in Sima Qian's *Records of the Grand Historian*.

The Xiongnu were the first great Altaic nomadic peoples. They appeared around 300 B.C. from the highlands of Mongolia: their presence in the east forced Emperor Qin Shi Huang to build the Great Wall, while in the west they controlled half of Turkistan. The Xiongnu, according to one theory, were of the same tribe as the infamous Huns, who in A.D. 400 descended on Hungary from the Russian plains and later threatened Papal Rome, making people's blood run cold.

In any case, I found Sima Qian's introduction of these Altaic nomads to be extremely suggestive. Simply by omitting proper nouns, hunting terminology, and the names of livestock, the passage was suddenly transformed into a critique of contemporary customs. The *fūten-zoku* hippies who roam around Shinjuku might just be the reincarnation of the Xiongnu. That seems plausible enough to me. I'm not quite sure about chasing rainbows rather than livestock, but they very much resemble a migratory people in terms of ignoring social boundaries and wandering about. If this is the case, however, can we then say that the frontier that properly exists outside borders has actually moved to the center of the city? This is hardly surprising and indeed quite likely. If one thinks about it, cities have long possessed something of the inner frontier about them; they are the preferred hideout for runaways and criminals. Even in the case of donuts, for example, inside and outside are connected by a surface that is perfectly continuous. By running toward the outside, one will eventually come roundabout and end up on the inside.

However, this is not to say that I expect from these *fūten-zoku* hippies a historically transformative type of heresy. The naïve era in which one could accomplish something merely by posing as the simple antithesis of fixed existence is now long gone. Even if we were to bring back Genghis Khan and place him in the center of all the hustle and bustle of Shinjuku, he would at best end up as a purchasing director of redeemable prizes at a pachinko parlor. And in the case of mountain guerillas, who are experts in mobility, there is absolutely no chance of victory without first building ties with farmers, the very symbol of fixed existence.

Even during the period of the Mongol Empire, when their invincible cavalry from the plains swept with gale force across the continent, these nomadic peoples left behind them nothing but death and destruction. For all their brilliant victories on the battlefield, their influence on history was surprisingly minor. But perhaps that is simply the fate of those who reject a fixed existence. Ruins of the destroyed castles still remain in the kingdoms they conquered, and yet the nomads themselves, victorious, disappeared without leaving behind even a single tent.

And yet it seems that even these horse-riding warriors bent on destruction accomplished one major feat that no one else had ever achieved: they never built borders in the areas they occupied. Unlike the occupations on the part of fixed states, these nomadic peoples did not see the need to redraw borders; rather they allowed the destroyed borders to remain destroyed. Those peoples living a settled existence had hitherto believed that the borders of their land marked the ends of the earth, but now the real horizon suddenly appeared before them, stretching off infinitely into the distance. Long convinced that the time and space within their borders had existed and flowed on the basis of laws that were strictly unique to that area, they now discovered that the same time flowed outside. This discovery must have been a thoroughly shocking experience, outweighing even the trading of goods and the exchange of knowledge.

The nomadic peoples acquired victory and treasure, whereas those settled peoples obtained defeat and the knowledge of time. With the concept of time, the settled peoples took the first half step toward universality and, as the chains that had previously bound them to spatial particularity gradually loosened, then took another half step toward universality in feeling love for this same time that was now certainly flowing in other worlds.

Today in the metropolises in which we live, this shared sense of time has already become quite commonplace, perhaps because the simultaneous resonance permeating all space in the form of the two world wars still echoes among us. It seems that even the *fūten-zoku* hippies have quickly befriended the U.S. war deserters who fled to Shinjuku. When students in cities around the world take concerted action, no one is surprised by this spatial contingency. This is because everyone at some point has unconsciously acquired a sense of contemporaneity. Borders in their overdevelopment appear to have hatched the eggs of the frontier within their own internal space.

THE FRONTIER WITHIN

It is not the aim of this chapter to discuss the Jewish question. Nor is it my aim to raise the issue of discrimination or prejudice on the basis of race or social position. Rather, it seems that something like a thought of the "frontier within," which is currently my main theme, receives sustained expression in the work of many Jewish writers.

In writing this, I have in mind, for example, someone like Franz Kafka. Of course it is a bit of a stretch to interpret Kafka's work solely from the perspective of its Jewish characteristics. There is an argument one sees recently that focuses on the notion of the "father" in Kafka—that is, its Jewish characteristics—and while it may appear that this reading shows high regard for Kafka, it actually reduces the contemporary universality of his work to its particular Jewish qualities. There is something ineffaceably sectarian about this. Here we find an impractical attitude that is tantamount to seeing Marcel Proust, Charlie Chaplin, and Henri Bergson simply in terms of their Jewish traits.

First published November 1–December 1, 1968, in *Chūō kōron*.

Yet it would be similarly impractical to deny Kafka's status as a Jew. Kafka clearly wrote in his diary that he was conscious of himself as a Jew and that he tried to come to terms with this consciousness. The question is whether there exists some link or absolutely no link between his status as Jewish and the contemporary meaning of his work, and for this we must put aside literary tastes and our own particular agendas and reexamine without bias the subtle implications contained in the label "Jewish writer."

The easiest solution to this question would be to find a happy medium between these two choices. This would produce the following: "Despite being largely bound by his particular Jewish qualities, Kafka was finally able to achieve a contemporary universal form of expression thanks to his talent, which transcended these limitations." Now I don't completely reject this interpretation. Depending on the context, it is an undeniable fact that a rainy day means that we're having bad weather.

However, when this apparently irrefutable compromise is applied to and compared with other writers of a strong ethnic hue (non-Jewish writers), one immediately recognizes a very different resonance. Compare: "Kafka wrote with the heart of a Jew, and yet he rose above that to appeal to the soul of all humanity" and "Tolstoy wrote with the heart of a Russian, and yet he rose above that to appeal to the soul of all humanity."

Here I am not intentionally using a Russian as the counterpart of the Jew. There would be no real difference if I were to refer to a Frenchman, German, Arab, or Japanese. Rather, I simply happen to choose Tolstoy as a representative non-Jewish writer based on such things as his ethnic character, ideas, and global reputation, and I don't think there can be any complaints about this choice.

What then is the nature of the subtle division between the above two twinlike statements? To further summarize these statements, we ultimately arrive at the standard formula "universality through the particular" (this is the cherished mantra of literary critics), and perhaps Kafka and Tolstoy are qualitatively different with regard to the content expressed by this word "particular."

Even we Japanese are to a large extent capable of understanding the Russian particularity of Tolstoy. Of course perfect understanding is impossible but, even allowing for this impossibility, a tentative guess is possible. This understanding is perhaps mediated by a common—that is, mutually translatable—sentiment regarding "land." The symbol of the "good man" that Tolstoy ultimately arrived at was none other than the "good peasant" who understood the workings of the motherland. Despite differences in manners and customs, broad commonalities existed in agricultural techniques throughout many countries, and naturally there were strong similarities in peasant consciousness. The notion of Russian particularity was not truly separate from the particularity of other nations or peoples but was rather a mere variation that contained universally peasant characteristics. Insofar as faith in the land continued to flourish in one form or another, it was quite natural that pursuit of such particularity led directly to universality. All modern states have embraced a memory of the land as holy as part of the historical background of their formation.

However, the situation is slightly different in the case of Kafka—or rather, beyond Kafka, with regard to Jewish particularity in general. The word "Jew" calls to mind for us only a very abstract concept, one that is perceived strictly through writing, virtually unaccompanied by any concrete image. For Japanese people especially, who do not share the history of anti-Semitism and cannot easily distinguish Jews from other Caucasians based on physical appearance, it is impossible to escape the indirect and false scope of this concept, since it is derived strictly from the words and actions of non-Jewish Europeans.

Judah from the Old Testament; Shylock from Shakespeare's *Merchant of Venice*; Dr. Einstein, who always appears in one section or another in the Lives of Great Men; and, the most familiar example, Jews as the unfortunate victims of racial prejudice and genocide, as symbolized by Auschwitz.

Indeed, the Jews' status as *sacrificial lamb* is certainly one aspect of their particularity. No matter how much this particularity is driven home, however, it does not seem to be easily universalized, unlike the manner in which peasantry in general is extracted from the Russian peasants. Since this is in any case mere *secondary* knowledge, however, let us again hear the views on Jewish particularity directly from the victimizers themselves.

"We must everywhere develop the peasant spirit."[1]

"The urban masses are empty. Where all is extinguished, nothing can be aroused."[2]

"Since the Civil War, in which the southern states were conquered, against all historical logic and sound sense, the Americans have been in a condition of political and popular decay. In that way, it was not the southern states but the American people themselves who were conquered."[3]

This apparent moralist, who seems to speak in the voice of a Narodnik preacher, is none other than Adolf Hitler, the architect of the Holocaust. These are Hitler's own words, as randomly excerpted from Hermann

Rauschning's book *Hitler Speaks: A Series of Political Conversations with Adolf Hitler on his Real Aims.*

Even for Hitler, in other words, the image of the new German aristocracy that would occupy the highest ranks of Nazi power was at most that of peasant landowners. Now let me state here that I have absolutely no intention of engaging in such sophistry as to claim, for example, that Tolstoy and Hitler are thus similar. Just as the power of the peasantry has not always operated negatively upon history, so too has it not always operated positively. Japanese farming villages represent the base of conservative political parties, but in China they were the center of revolution. Che Guevara was aided by the peasants in Cuba, whereas in Bolivia he was ruthlessly betrayed by them. Just as it is false to view the peasants as Hitler's allies merely because of his sense of affinity with them, so too must one avoid regarding them as the kindred spirits of Tolstoy and Whitman.

In any case, it stands to reason that Hitler, who perceived in the good German peasantry the existence of the German *Volk* with its own pure lineage, would recognize something of the city in the hated Jews. In fact, Hitler's image of Jews was that they were diverse, as cities are diverse, and extraordinarily complex, as cities are complex. To put it in the extreme, it was almost as if Hitler regarded everything outside the peasantry as Jewish.

Let me cite once again from Rauschning's book: "The two are as widely separated as man and beast. Not that I would call the Jew a beast. He is much further from the beasts than we Aryans. He is a creature outside nature and alien to nature."[4]

This is clear evidence of a pathological hatred for the unnatural or *artificial.* While attacking Christianity for corrupting the farming villages, Hitler also criticized the atheists in the cities as symptomatic of deracinated Jewish thought. He argued that those members of the working class who were poisoned by cities should not be given the opportunity to receive primary education and be kept illiterate. Hitler also seemed to harbor an immense hatred for those who engaged in various forms of abstract intellectual work, such as the intelligentsia, technicians, and specialists.

Ultimately, for Hitler, Jews were the drab petty officials lurking in government offices, priggish didacticians, liberals, usurers, physicians, speculators, inventors, Romantic composers, financial cliques, lawyers, leaders of the labor movement, natural scientists, university professors, garret writers, and Marxists. In other words, Jews were like an urban demon that could freely transform itself into anything other than German peasants.

Yet the projection of urban characteristics onto Jews is in no way an exclusive idea that originated with Hitler. According to Sartre's *Portrait of the Anti-Semite*, the situation is virtually identical for French anti-Semites: "Intelligence, for the anti-semite, is a Jewish attribute. . . . The *true French-man*, with his roots deep down in his own country, in his own small locality, sustained by a tradition of twenty centuries, benefiting from an ancestral wisdom and guided by tried and tested customs, does not *need* to be intelligent."[5] And again: "Why should *I* . . . be able to understand [Racine]? It is because Racine belongs to me. Racine and my own language and my own *soil*."[6]

Are Jews urban or are cities Jewish? It seems that Jews and cities are so deeply intertwined that I cannot help but ask this question. My theme of the "frontier within" is related to precisely this point.

If it were merely a question of Jews as victims, then perhaps blacks in the United States would be the far more suitable object of this kind of particularity. Actually, there are a number of works from black writers that are worthy of international attention, works in which one clearly sees the principle of movement from particularity to universality. Moreover, prejudice against blacks is far more virulent and nihilistic than anti-Semitism. The Nazis believed that Jews had to be killed, whereas American farmers never even saw the need to kill blacks.

In this sense, the novel *Mandingo* that I read recently is terrifying and quite ominous. If I hadn't known that certain descriptions were of living beings, I might have suspected the characters to be discussing a brand-new sports car. Even when I understood from the mention of limbs and teeth that the characters were referring to living beings, everything convinced me that the topic was something like a well-bred, expensive hunting dog. They were raised cleanly, rationally, and lovingly. In return, they loved and feared their masters to a degree no less than that of loyal dogs. Of course they were not dogs. Rather, the context of such discussions was farms that specialized in the raising of black slaves. If a pureblooded female slave of high quality was obtained, she would be taken to another farm to mate with a man of the same tribe. Women who were especially fertile would be forced by certain measures to repeatedly give birth. Although seldom whipped, slaves received this punishment in such a way that no marks would remain. Veterinarians were immediately called if slaves were even slightly ill. Thus slaves were well cared for and protected until they reached an age where they could be sold at a high price.

Such a cold, inhuman form of interdependence is far more ruthless and cruel than any hatred or genocide. I finished the book with a sense of horror only to find upon glancing through the afterward that the author, Kyle Onstott, was not a professional writer but rather a dog handler who had also written *The Art of Breeding Better Dogs*. I burst out laughing in spite of myself and then immediately felt all the worse. The realization that extreme prejudice and discrimination do not always produce hostility but can indeed take such a form of trust forced me to reexamine the meaning of human relations. I felt stung by a dangerous cynicism. Even if the novel were a purely fictional account that Onstott had written based on his experience raising dogs and which he then applied to blacks, the setting was quite realistic and convincing. In any case, ours is an era in which human relations have grown so complacent that no one feels strange when the peace movement, which is based on humanism, issues statements that sound like slogans from the Humane Society. It might be that a new form of racial prejudice, in which one loves while discriminating just as one loves while being discriminated against, has actually achieved an international universality. This prejudice appears in the form of *lovable dogs*, and haunts everything within us.

In fact, Joseph K., the protagonist of Kafka's *The Trial*, also died like a dog. Yet there is an enormous difference between dying *like* a dog and dying *as* a dog. This might explain why even Hitler could not treat his sworn enemy the Jews in the same manner that blacks in the American South were treated. Far from suggesting any standard for judging the relative superiority or inferiority of Jews and blacks, this point merely reveals the difference in their sociohistorical positions. In reality, blacks recently have overcome all traces of their former status as lovable elite dogs in both the United States and the world in general. They are like an immense stock of black dynamite with a smoldering fuse that runs headlong from discrimination based on contact with whites to a form of equality based on severing such contact.

Classical discrimination survives with a forced smile between friendly nations within each military bloc.

Let us now return to the question of explaining Jewish particularity. Beyond the dimension of mere prejudice or discrimination, there seems to be an essence of particularity itself that is hidden in the way in which Jews have been labeled as distinct from peasants, as incapable of understanding Racine, and as alienated from the land—labeled, in other words, as strictly of the city.

The urban character of the Jews is both a malicious wanted poster fabricated by nativist demagogues and a fact supported by historical proof. No matter how tolerant the king or feudal lord, Jews in their role as the eternal foreigner were strictly forbidden to set foot in the sacred farming areas. They were granted the right to live only in cities (ghettos) and were allowed to maintain symbiotic relations with Christians because of their practice of moneylending—an act considered impure by Christians but which had already become an indispensable part of the state economy. As economies eventually developed, the proportion of the monetary economy gradually increased vis-à-vis that of the object economy, and the role of the Jews within the state economy necessarily expanded as well. Instead of owning land, the Jews gained power in such areas of the credit economy as commerce, trade, medicine, and law, thereby resulting in the consolidation of their urban character, whether they wanted this or not.

For the Jews, however, cities were not a safe refuge. They were squalid areas that were originally seen by feudal lords as mere marketplaces located in the remote frontiers of their domain. Upon realizing that these cities had become the goose that lays the golden egg, however, the feudal lords could no longer silently stand by. Pressure on the Jews was gradually increased: restrictions led to discrimination, which in turn led to rejection. This was perhaps the basis for the emergence of anti-Semitism as well as of the Jews' countermeasure against it, for therein began the consolidation of Jewish religious and spiritual unity.

The proud Zionists would of course strongly protest this point. For them, the self-awakening of the Jewish people did not take place so passively; rather, it must be grounded on the two-thousand-year tradition that began with the Jews' expulsion from Jerusalem. If the Jews had wandered for two thousand years, the Zionists argue, then they had also been persecuted for that long, and yet they had survived catastrophe to finally arrive at the founding of the state of Israel. For the Zionists, it is precisely the weight of this fact that furnishes the best proof that Jews are the "chosen people." Now I have no desire to refute this claim. My focus here is less on the Israelis as object than on the false image of the Jews that haunts the interiority of non-Jews.

What I cannot understand, however, is the strange fact that agrarianist ideas are still constantly reproduced even within the advanced capitalist nations, which are now heavily industrialized and where all the major areas of politics, economics, and culture are concentrated in the cities. Even within cities, one still encounters undiminished suspicion and prejudice toward urban elements.

According to statistics, in 1961 one-third of all Jews in the world lived concentrated in fifteen cities across Europe and the United States with populations of over one million people. This trend likely remains unchanged today. Although control over finance and trade has already been appropriated by the *authentic* native bourgeoisie, the Jews' historically urban character—whose formation and development parallels that of the city itself—remains unchanged.

Must "authentic citizens" appeal to antiurban or native elements in order to preserve their "authentic culture"? Must we for the sake of *our* culture stand barefoot on mother earth and purify the filth from cities?

I don't know if this applies to the time of the Crusades, but the state has long achieved full occupation of the city. There is now absolutely no opposition between state and city. On the contrary, cities are the heart and soul of the state, they have been assigned an indispensable and pivotal role within it. Intolerance toward cities on the part of those who adhere to an ideology of the *authentic* is now completely groundless. Even if one recognizes certain urban tendencies in Jews, to regard everything urban as Jewish is a sign of a persecution complex. But even if everything urban were Jewish, the fact that cities no longer stand in opposition to the state means that prejudice against the city (including its Jewish elements) itself has now become a ghost of the past.

"In fact, civilizations are the descendants of cities. . . . Rulers from the Hellenic period clearly appealed to the foundation of cities in order to promote the fusion between Greeks and Orientals. The height of the Roman Empire corresponds to the founding of many cities in the Empire. In contrast, Latin culture disappeared upon the withdrawal of the aristocracy to their 'farming estates' during the final years of the Empire."[7]

Yet the events at Auschwitz happened only yesterday. No matter how industrialized or how firmly reconciled city and state appear to be, the reality of the modern state may be such that the volcano that is hatred for the city is only temporarily inactive and secretly waiting for an opportunity to explode. Of course we must not discount certain conditions particular to the rise of Nazism, as for example the serious damage sustained by Germany during World War I and the country's relative backwardness at the time. Because of Germany's particular circumstances then, an abstract form of prejudice against the city overwhelmed the city's actual functioning. If the gas chambers were nothing more than the convulsions of a premature infant visited by a past nightmare about faith in the land, and if it were possible to believe that such a nightmare was the last one of this century—then I too might regard Auschwitz as an unfortunate exception and hold out some hope for the future of cities located within national borders.

In the wake of the liberalization of Czechoslovakia, the Kafka scholar and Jew Eduard Goldstücker was elected chairman of the Czech Writers' Union. When I first heard this news, I felt cheerful and optimistic. Several years prior, in fact, I had the opportunity to meet Goldstücker and speak with him privately at the Writers' Union in Prague. This was not a chance meeting; rather, I had specifically requested an appointment, and he kindly obliged. His manner of speaking was unusually sullen, however. Just as Kafka was lonely, so too did Goldstücker appear to be filled with misery, as if complaining of his own loneliness. Something about him seemed to suggest the fate of Kafka and indeed of all Jews in Eastern Europe. For that reason alone, I felt my heart soar at the thought that Goldstücker's election as chairman represented both proof of Kafka rehabilitation and a true reconciliation with the Jews, that socialism had perhaps entered a new era marked by liberation from an ideology of the *authentic*. . . . But that too has ended. I have no way of knowing whether this is true or not, but I heard somewhere that Goldstücker had been removed from his post and subsequently went underground.

Sartre has written that socialist revolution is a necessary and sufficient condition for the eradication of anti-Semitism. In principle, he is no doubt correct. The Soviet Constitution clearly states that all racial discrimination is forbidden, and that both favoritism toward and discrimination against people of a specific race are punishable by law. Bernard J. Choseed of the University of Michigan has also written a paper, entitled "Jews in Soviet Literature," in which he points to the appearance of many leading Jewish writers and analyzes the changes over time in the depiction of Jewish characters in various literary works. Here Choseed clearly shows that a gradual shift has taken place from the ethnic particularity of " 'little' Jews" to universality as an awakened member of the Communist Party.[8]

Yet the gradual emergence of the "socialist hero" is in no way limited to Jewish citizens. It is part of the powerful demand in socialist realism with regard to all literary characters. Choseed's point here is acceptable, however, for this trend is very different from depicting Jews as spies. What is problematic about the paper is that it treats only works written before 1945. In truth, my concern is with the fate of Jewish characters after World War II, in the wake of the purges begun the following year known as the Zhdanov Doctrine. As can be seen in the notion of mighty Russia, there exists in the Soviet Union a raging tide of patriotism and xenophobia, which is far removed from socialism. It seems that many Jews have come under suspicion and at times been sent off to the camps simply for having relatives abroad. I wonder what sort of treatment Jewish characters have received during the long night before the publication of Ehrenburg's *The Thaw*.

However, it seems necessary to first consider the situation of Jewish writers. Precisely because writers are made of flesh and blood, they seem to feel the impact of the storm earlier. Beginning with the attack against Shostakovich in 1936 for his western tendencies, there emerged critiques of "formalism" that were soon accompanied by bloody purges and even assumed aspects of a punitive heresy trial.

One finds random shots against "cosmopolitanism," "rootless wanderers," "modernism," "petit bourgeois interests," "western corruption," "bourgeois objectivism," "liberalism," "decadence," and "nihilism." It occurs to me that such invectives against "formalism" are identical to those used by Hitler, and this makes me uneasy. But one mustn't be rash here. To regard Stalin and Hitler as equivalent based solely on this evidence would be no different from those neofascists in the United States who casually refer to "Nazism as a Jewish conspiracy." Rather, we must factually examine what Stalin and Hitler each tried to attack and protect.

In the case of Hitler, it is clear that from the beginning he targeted the Jews and protected the *"authentic* German peasants."

As for Stalin, let us compress these invectives into one standard image through the process of elimination. What appears, for example, is the concept of the "ethnic-nation." This refers to the definition of socialist realism as "socialist in content and national in form." This formulation strikes me as a bit odd, but it is the phrase used by Stalin himself. We can only assume that this is what he truly believed.

However, what would "national in form" mean in the context of prose fiction? I don't know about folk dances or the local arts, but surely the spirit of prose first emerged from the desire to go beyond the dimension of national form and seek something freer. Fixity in form only restricts possibilities for prose. But perhaps we needn't be so sensitive on this point. First of all, Stalin did not use this term "national" in the same, much more limited way as Hitler did. Indeed, socialist revolution also implied liberation from national form. In Russia, moreover, such set form can only be traced back to Pushkin, who has received official government recognition.

Unfortunately, however, it was precisely this notion that came to be singled out for criticism. This was completely unexpected. Who could have imagined that Pushkin would be the one to set off this explosion?

"When at last the big guns opened fire, the target in the foreground proved to be Professor Nusinov. . . . It was to Nusinov that the term 'passportless wanderer in humanity' was first applied in the postwar period. His study was declared to have derogated from Russian national individuality by constantly comparing Pushkin's creations with abstract, cosmopolitan stereotypes. . . . Pushkin's works on Western themes, moreover, held interest not for what they had in common with Shakespeare, Goethe, and Byron, but because of what was distinctive in them."[9]

There would be no place for Jewish writers if the claims of Slavic superiority and uniqueness were traced back to the time before the Soviet revolution. Jews played no part in the historical formation of the Slavic people and so could not possibly understand the notion of national form. Jews were formalists simply because they were Jews. In this way, many Jewish writers would come to be criticized, silenced, and purged—Boris Pilnyak, Ilya Ehrenburg, Isaak Babel, Yuri Olesha, Osip Mandelstam, Bruno Jasieński—as well as those who were not writers—Vsevolod Meyerhold, Sergei Eisenstein, etc.

The bleakness of a long, frozen season continued until finally Stalin died, anti-Stalin critiques began, and Ehrenburg spoke of signs of a "thaw." This bleakness was testimony to the fatal cultural effects caused by suppression of the Jews. Everyone was hurt: both victim and victimizer suffered deep wounds.

In the Soviet Union, where ethnic or national discrimination is expressly forbidden by the constitution, how was such Nazi-like insanity possible?

The average American would proudly reply, "It's because of totalitarianism. There is something wrong with anyone who would take seriously a totalitarian constitution."

But it seems that the situation is not so different even in the United States. American history is brief, there is a sample box of races, and the black problem is like an active volcano: under these conditions, anti-Semitism might not appear, but similar symptoms seem to exist latently that chronically develop. In their book *Prophets of Deceit: A Study of the Techniques of the American Agitator*, Leo Löwenthal and Norbert Guterman skillfully sketch out a profile of the Americanized fascist: "Nazi propaganda tried to conceal the essentially negative and reactive nature of the 'Aryan' by developing the notions of the biological race and the hemmed-in nation. But these notions, obviously irrelevant to American life, are of little help to the American agitator when he attempts to portray his adherent."[10]

Agitation can thus begin in the following way: "When will the *plain*, ordinary, sincere, sheeplike people of America awaken to the fact that their common affairs are being arranged and run for them by aliens, Communists, crackpots, refugees, renegades, Socialists, termites, and traitors?"[11]

If the interlocutor here is a plain American, then the agitator who is addressing him must himself be an equally plain American. This plain American might appear to be quite bland, but actually "the invention of the Aryan race and the agitator's glorification of the Simple American are symptomatic of similar efforts to strengthen social coercion."[12] This represents the standardized, abridged version of the original Nazi appeal, which contains a universal applicability that "could be used in other countries as Simple Germans, or Simple French, or Simple Britishers etc."[13]

Agitators explain themselves as follows: "I do not understand political science, as an authority from an academic viewpoint. I am not familiar with the artistic masterpieces of Europe, but I do say this tonight: I know the hearts of the American people. [For I am] one of [those] plain old time, stump grubbing, liberty loving, apple cider men and women. [I am thus] an American-born citizen whose parents were American born and whose parents' parents were American born."[14]

As to the aim of this agitation: "Sooner or later the American people are going to be looking for a few flocks of scapegoats. And it's not going to be the Irish, the Spaniards, the Egyptians, or the Hottentots who'll be called to the accounting."[15]

"Indeed, the very idea that any other group could be a scapegoat is almost comical. The agitator knows very well that he need not be more explicit."[16]

Agitators have composed the following list of targets to be attacked: "the Judeo-Marxists, Anglophiles, International bankers, radio commentators, Hollywood, Anti-Defamation League, Anti-Nazi League, Friends of Democracy, Rhodes scholars, *PM*, *Daily Worker*, *Chicago Sun*, *The New Masses*, *The Nation* and *The New Republic*."[17]

So different people have different customs, it seems, and "plain Americans" are extremely friendly and a bit humorous. However, it is clear that they also toss out Jews from their own self-definition as "*authentic* citizens" as well as from the melting pot of mixed races. This type of prejudice is no different from Hitler's gang. Let us thus pose the question once more: what is a Jew from the standpoint of these anti-Semites?

Zhdanov would certainly raise his voice from beyond the grave to protest this term. He would say, "I was not an anti-Semite, nor did I ever engage in so-called 'discrimination.' In the name of my country, rather, I simply eliminated those oppositional elements that stood in the way of party unity. For those who make no distinction between communists and fascists, however, it is perhaps futile for me to now offer a defense of my actions."

But I am fully aware that communists and fascists are different. Perhaps everything was as Zhdanov described. Having recognized this distinction between communists and fascists, however, I would like to repeat that, regardless of their difference in motives, there is one undeniable point of convergence: in both cases, it was the Jews who were driven away and chosen as sacrificial lamb. What then did it mean to be a Jew?

There can be only one answer to this question. Jews are those who could not attach themselves to the land. And those who were not bound to the land were Jews. In other words, Jews were those for whom it was inherently impossible to become "*authentic* citizens." Of course it was possible for Jews to become "citizens," but it was absolutely impossible for them to be "*authentic* citizens." Only this thin film of *authenticity* separated the Jew from the non-Jew, but at certain moments this relationship became one of decisive opposition. It seems, moreover, that this relation is formed irrespective of any particular social system. Thus the real nature of *authenticity* appears to be a condition of the state as represented by the space of territory.

Authentic citizens thus appear in the form of peasants, while pseudocitizens are driven off to the cities. In reality, it is the city that is the backbone of the state; on the scale of *authenticity*, however, the city is merely a frontier within. The figure of the Jew, therefore, is unrelated to the Jew in any racial sense but is rather something that comes to be endlessly reproduced as the destiny of the state that contains the city enclosed within its national boundaries. Even in Japan, where there are no Jews, this Jewish question is quite real. In this regard, the Meiji Restoration can be interpreted as the seizing of the cities by provincial feudal lords. When we think of the Jewish question in this manner, we perhaps come close to identifying the space in which Kafka's particularity comes to be universalized. It seems that this issue needs to be reconsidered in the context of Japan, where there are no Jews, from the perspective of the conflict between the city and anticity.

To repeat: the Jewish question cannot be settled simply on the basis of racial prejudice, for the roots of this disease extend deeply within contemporary society. For example, there is the fact that, without exception, anti-Semites in all nations throughout virtually all periods maintained an image of the *peasants* as "true citizens" while viewing *city dwellers* as the source of all evil. This fact alone should serve as sufficient proof that Jews cannot be a mere other (i.e., racial alien).

The socialist countries, in particular, have supposedly completely rejected and expunged racial prejudice and ethnic discrimination. While these countries of course don't make explicit use of anti-Semitic rhetoric, one does find the hothouse idea that *peasants* represent true citizenship while *city dwellers* are marked as corrupted by the West. Given this fact, it cannot be a coincidence that so many of the so-called antirevolutionaries who suffer persecution have been Jewish citizens.

For example, Jewish representatives from Czechoslovakia who attended meetings in Moscow to discuss the Soviet invasion were stigmatized as Zionists and boycotted. And in Poland, there were signs of a campaign identifying the leaders of the student movement as Jewish, and this was used to suppress liberalization and rationalize the dispatch of troops to Czechoslovakia. Perhaps the student leaders were Jewish. If they were French or Swedish, however, it is doubtful whether they would have been denounced for their ideas and singled out by their ethnicity.

In any case, the basis for anti-Semitism is not to be found in Jewish existence itself; rather, it is symptomatic of a kind of autointoxication, for it lies hidden within the demand for legitimacy that is the notion of "authentic citizenry." Jewish existence did not produce anti-Semitism. On the contrary, the heretical notion of the Jew appears to have been introduced as an artificial illumination of consciousness in order to highlight more clearly the contours of the notion of legitimacy. It is not that Jews existed, but rather that they were made to exist. Now there can be no question that responsibility for this inversion of cause and effect lies not in the heretical essence of heresy but rather solely in the legitimizing essence of legitimacy.

Yet why was the Jew—and only the Jew—specifically chosen as the object of heresy? If this were due merely to religious reasons, then nothing requires that discrimination against Jews be greater than that against Muslims or Buddhists. Indeed, it would have made more sense for atheists, who outnumber Jews, to be beaten. But perhaps the problem is due to Jewish statelessness. If this were the case, however, then Gypsies would be the more orthodox choice. And if there were not enough Gypsies to play the role of enemy, then citizens of other ethnic or national origins could be lumped together and victimized. A shortage of enemies is highly unlikely, particularly when one considers, for example, the case of Beckett (who is Irish) or Ionesco (Romanian), both of whom write in French and have French citizenship. For that matter, there could even be state laws banning all translated fiction. Throughout Europe, and even within royal families, members of other ethnic or national groups have often played important roles and mixed in.

Yet the heretic must always be the Jew; it can be no one but the Jew. Jews are not merely members of a different religion or ethnic group; rather, they are the *chosen* (or cursed) figure of heresy itself. How are we to understand this Jewish quality of incompatibility?

Certain proud Jews, and particularly Israeli Jews (this phrase might sound odd, but the notion of "authentic" Israeli already exists in this country despite the fact that it was founded merely twenty years ago. It seems that these "authentic" Jews tend to treat as somewhat "inauthentic" not only overseas (?) Jews but also those Jews who were only recently naturalized as Israeli citizens), explain this situation as follows: "Subsequently, the Jews, already dispersed before the final exile, left the centers of civilization—Alexandria, Babylon, and Rome—for the 'backward' countries of Europe. They were learned and clever; they felt themselves superior and set their defiance against all eventual rejection. . . . From the Renaissance in western Europe, and much later in eastern Europe, the Jews refused to disappear and sink into semibarbarous societies to which they felt themselves superior."[18]

There are those who explain Jewish ethnic superiority on the basis of the lofty ethics, metaphysical depth, and powerful speculative tendency of Judaism. If they continue with this claim, however, they would be forced to admit that at least half the responsibility for anti-Semitism lies with the Jews themselves. Ultimately, it would not be surprising if this argument were seen as indicative of an inferiority complex borne by an inferior ethnic group vis-à-vis their superiors. In this way, the argument for Jewish superiority reveals itself to be the simple reverse of anti-Semitic thought. It is by and large a form of escapism to pull oneself down to the same level as those who practice discrimination. First of all, the very notion that a two-thousand-year tradition has any validity today is pure fantasy and comes closer to the world of myth than it does to history. I for one find it difficult to accept such logic.

I side with Sartre's view that "the Jew is formed through the mirror of the concept of the Jew as other. This self-evident truth serves as the departure point." For such people as Barnir, however, Sartre's "antinational" definition appears deeply unsatisfying: "Yet how does one explain that Jews from one hundred and twenty countries in the world, spurred on by anti-Semitism, have promised themselves that they would meet in Israel and have done so for two thousand years?"[19] Yet if the Jews were truly an ethnic group beholden to a two-thousand-year-old promise, then that is proof far less of their superiority than of their deplorable stagnation and conservative nature. In the course of two thousand years, many ethnic groups built nations, died out, and disappeared. Even ancient Greece, whose cultural force remains vibrant today, has been reduced to stone ruins. Why was it that only the Jews passively stood by for two thousand years while maintaining their dream of founding a nation? Or rather: how were they able to do this?

It would simply be an excuse to reply that no opportunities existed to found a nation. National borders were far more elastic and vague in the distant past than they are at present. For a long time, Europe itself was merely a region surrounded by a vast "frontier." It is hardly the case that states were built strictly on legendary soil. Indeed, the United States created a new state without legends or traditions less than two hundred years ago, when there were neither memories nor attachments to the New World. For Jews now to go back two thousand years—during which time everything has changed, from the shapes of mountains to the position of coastlines—and speak of a mythical Palestine is, in fact, tantamount to confessing that they lack subjectivity or possess *parasitical* features.

Let us consider a much more familiar example. As based on the various, mixed views regarding the century that has now passed since the Meiji era, we know today that the collapse of feudalism was not entirely a spontaneous event. In other words, the present is not framed by tradition; rather, tradition is shaped by the present. If we consider what, from the diverse and complex vector of the present, will be recognized as tradition one hundred years from now, we know that the present itself has no say in this matter and that it is the exclusive concern of that future world. The past with any real binding force can at most be found three generations prior. The length of this force is perhaps proportionate to the stagnancy of the present environment.

No matter how stagnant the environment, however, it is a slight exaggeration to speak of memory going back two thousand years. If a generation equals thirty years, then that is nearly seventy generations into the past. Assuming that with each generation people lose half of what they inherit from a parent, then Jews today possess only one of the roughly three hundred ninety trillion parts of the blood of their ancestors from seventy generations back. If the equivalent of a mere drop in the ocean is sufficient to bind Jews so tightly to the spell of history, then we can only conclude that their psychic structure reveals symptoms of an excessive rigidity similar to that of coelacanths and salamanders.

But that is impossible. While the excavated remains of the past certainly appear in the form of facts, cultural tradition consists in a community's structural patterns; it is another name for the everyday present. Tradition is precisely the patterns selected by the present, and thus the notion of a land promised two thousand years ago should rightly be seen as the crystallization of a fantasy created by the internal structure of Jews today. Such fantasy reveals, in other words, how much the Jews have suffered from their hunger for history.

In many cases, legitimacy as a citizen is measured by one's participation in the history of state formation. The Jews, however, have been rejected from subjectively participating in anything historical that takes the form of the present progressive. *They might somehow endure present misfortune if they could at least learn the identity of those rejecting them.* It is undoubtedly the case that the Jews chose a notion of *"ultralegitimacy"* in the form of a distant promised land as a countermeasure against the notion of "legitimacy" that so threatened them. This makes sense. It is not that the Jews existed because of this promised land; rather, their self-awareness as heretics opened the path to it.

Sartre also fully opposes the idea articulated by proud "authentic Jews" that they are the chosen people: "But we have shown that the Jews have between them neither a community of interests nor a community of belief. They have no common homeland, and no history. The only tie which binds them together is the hostile contempt in which they are held by the communities surrounding them."[20]

Nonetheless, my greatest concern is that this appeal to a notion of "ultralegitimacy" to counter a notion of "legitimacy" means that the Jews have in fact abandoned their contemporary significance—not in the passive sense of challenging the inequality of state evil though restoring rights to the Jewish people, as depicted by the Zionists, but rather more fundamentally in terms of their role as catalyst in hastening the reform of the very structure of contemporary society.

Insofar as the notion of "ultralegitimacy" represents a belief in legitimacy, it is essentially no different from that of "legitimacy." At most, it is the mirror image of this latter: the same yet reversed. Even if one notion centers its belief on the concrete state while the other merely focuses on the state as an abstract idea, the shared belief in legitimacy naturally means that they will reject each other, just as the like poles of magnets are mutually repellent. There might be some hope if these proponents of legitimacy were separated by a buffer zone in the form of a national border, but unfortunately those who believe in this abstract idea of legitimacy are indifferent to the presence of such a border.

Such confrontation in the same arena not only offers an increasingly favorable excuse for anti-Semites but it also makes their incitement more effective and provides opportunities for it to filter among the people. As goes without saying, it is impossible for the general public to arrive at anti-Semitic ideas spontaneously. It is absolutely impossible for fascism to appear without the presence of agitators and their ambitious appeals to the crowd. As I have repeated several times now, Jews themselves are of course not the direct cause of anti-Semitism. Yet anti-Semitism receives its best weapon when Jews come to be infected by the feverish "myth of legitimacy" and, supported by a sense of themselves as the chosen people, begin boasting that the Jewish community remains indomitable even in the face of diaspora. "Authentic citizens" versus "pseudocitizens," "citizens" versus "unpatriotic individuals," "patriots" versus "traitors," "decent, law-abiding citizens" versus "lawbreakers": this language will gradually escalate and cover anti-Semitism in a kind of wrapping paper of sensuous images. In and of itself, anti-Semitism contains too many leaps of logic and is difficult to grasp, but the claims of Jewish legitimacy provide a rare chance for anti-Semites to convert their ideology into popular language and make it more comprehensible. This explains why the agitators' slogans are in general nothing more than clichéd popular versions of anti-Semitism.

(My sense is that, if we give the devil his due, perhaps even Hitler might be somewhat excused. Strictly in terms of the belief in legitimacy, the relation between Nazis and Zionists is not wholly unlike that of twin brothers. Of course many Zionists abhor violence. Yet is it the case that Hitler must be judged solely for his role in ordering the events at Auschwitz? Were it not for Auschwitz, would the anti-Semitism that still smolders throughout the world today be permitted, even if only tacitly, under the name of freedom of activities to political parties? Just as war [the extremity of violence] is described as one form of politics, it seems to me that there is no great difference whether it involves group slaughter. When one considers the sadistic violence in Algeria on the part of the same French soldiers who had earlier taken part in the Nazi resistance movement, for example, or the enormous consumption of gunpowder in Asia (again) under the pretext of protecting national interests on the part of the sons of those same American soldiers who had once exchanged oaths on Elbe Day, one must conclude that only a slight difference separates politics and violence. Insofar as the state prizes its citizens' "legitimacy" and considers its heresy trials justified from the standpoint of national sovereignty, one cannot help but suspect that it will always regard Jews as an internal enemy and seek to provide refuge for a potential

Hitler, secretly waiting for a chance for him to emerge and take wing. Ultimately, the relation between Zionists and anti-Semites cannot be considered in the same terms as that between *brothers* in the saying "Brothers may reveal themselves to be strangers.")

Having said this, however, I have no intention to criticize these proud Jews, the *authentic* Jewish people. I fully realize that I am unqualified to make such criticism, as my knowledge of the history of Jewish suffering is limited to books. I have taken up this question merely as the subject of my essay, but for Jews this topic represents real anguish, from which they can never escape. Joining the ranks of these "adherents of legitimacy" through belief in a promised land was no doubt an attempt to deal with this pain.

Yet my focus here is not on actual Jews themselves. As I mentioned previously, my sense is that the strange heresy trial that is anti-Semitism is deeply related to contradictions that lie concealed at the base of contemporary society (or in the structure of the era). In other words, I wish to examine not the Jews themselves but rather the nature of "the Jew" as well as the anxiety and resistance brought about by this figure in the heart of non-Jews.

Hence I don't reject Israel, which was finally able to revive the "myth of legitimacy," or those Jews outside of Israel who nevertheless consider the country as their spiritual homeland. Instead I simply would like to avoid these issues while focusing on the discussion at hand. This is not simply because the question of Israel, and particularly the Arab-Israeli conflict, is beyond my grasp; rather, the founding of the state of Israel finally transformed Jews into "authentic citizens," and thus they are completely unrelated to what I am trying to think here under the heading of *the Jew*. From the standpoint of non-Jews, Israelis are simply foreigners. Even the vulgar pamphlets distributed by anti-Semites have no effect whatsoever on Israelis. In fact, American right-wing politicians are far more likely to support rather than oppose Israel. Even the Soviet Union, despite its pro-Arab stance, recognizes the state of Israel and maintains an embassy there. For Israeli Jews, the notion of Jewish poison no longer exists.

In other words, if one believes that the notion of a Jewish threat was simply propagated by neofascist agitators, then the founding of the state of Israel should have marked an end to anti-Semitism and foreclosed any and all excuses to agitate. Even if the Jews engineered some plot, the whereabouts of their base would already be known. In which case, it would be possible under international law to file an official protest against them, just as the Canadian government did against De Gaulle. Even if overseas Jews, like other foreign citizens, suffered discrimination or hardship as members of an ethnic minority, the matter could be easily settled.

In theory that would be possible, but in reality the allergy to Jews has not been eliminated. Even with the antidote of Israel, the poison that is *the Jew* still remains exceedingly potent.

This is not surprising. For this poison is not introduced externally by Jewish intruders; rather, it is something intrinsic that oozes from within the "myth of legitimacy" that is the notion of authentic citizenry itself. Ultimately, the allergy to Jews is nothing other than a kind of autointoxication. The poison of heresy will forever be reproduced insofar as the state seeks its authority in the "myth of legitimacy." Jews just happen to be this poison.

Hence even in Israel today, the formation of anti-Semitism is entirely possible. Of course the term "anti-Semitism" would not be used, but there is no need to attach undue importance to names. What is necessary is the effective image of "heresy" to reinforce and confirm the citizens' sense of "legitimacy." Countless variations exist that correspond to the term "anti-Semitism," from the elaborate, theoretical-sounding "cosmopolitanism" (used in opposition to the "internationalism" so cherished by Stalinists) to such simple terms as *hikokumin,* or "unpatriotic individuals," that were indiscriminately used in wartime Japan. Even the very blunt expression "pseudo-Jew" would be fine if one could guarantee its effectiveness.

Regardless of whether the poison of "heresy" is found among Jews themselves or in areas where there are no Jews at all, it seems to be an unavoidable chronic disease insofar as the state functions as the state.

The Jews themselves are certainly not the poison of "heresy." From the perspective of the products of autointoxication that is the "myth of legitimacy," even the term *Jew* is essentially no different from such other stigmatic expressions for heretics as "unpatriotic individual," "traitor," "proforeign," "cosmopolitan," and "rootless wanderer."

Yet this is not to say that these terms are all identical. The expression *Jew* seems to contain a unique nuance that cannot be replaced by these other words. Perhaps the difference is that the latter sound somewhat bland and less forceful, whereas *Jew* is much more sharply delineated and historically resonant.

This point can be understood when one considers, for example, the term "Jewish culture." "Proforeign culture" or "culture of unpatriotic individuals" may work as critical expressions, but they don't necessarily have any concrete meaning. Yet the term "Jewish culture" actually exists. Not only does it exist but it also occupies a distinguished position throughout contemporary culture as that culture that most sharply reflects the historical era.

If I were to list in no particular order only the most famous of Jewish intellectuals (focusing on writers), I would include the following: Irwin Shaw, Norman Mailer, Saul Bellow, Phillip Roth, Bernard Malamud, J. D. Salinger, Arthur Miller, Arnold Wesker, Harold Pinter, Witold Gombrowicz, Hugo von Hofmannsthal, Franz Kafka, Bertolt Brecht, Franz Werfel, Sigmund Freud, Georg Simmel, Karl Löwith, Ilya Ehrenburg, Bruno Jasieński, and Boris Pasternak. And as for those who were not writers: Vsevolod Meyerhold, Sergei Eisenstein, Charlie Chaplin, Karl Marx, David Riesman, and Albert Einstein, etc. What springs to mind here is the enormous range and magnitude of contemporary culture as incredibly represented by only one ethnic group (presumably).

When I think about it, most of these men are important artists who have strongly compelled my attention. But they have not simply impressed me personally; objectively speaking, it is remarkable that these men are pioneering artists who have powerfully influenced the present era.

If for example Franz Kafka never existed, contemporary literature (and particularly the standards of literary value) would be quite different. And no one can deny that Brecht and Meyerhold have shaped the course of contemporary theater. It would be virtually impossible to speak of the history of cinema without reference to Chaplin. Freud is already one of the major channels flowing beneath contemporary art. Even closer to home, contemporary English theater would be quite bleak without Pinter and Wesker.

Yet some people might question whether these artists can all be lumped together and treated as Jewish. In particular, we Japanese are ignorant of specific Jewish characteristics—this is only natural given the lack of opportunities for contact with Jews—and most of us understand, for example, Arthur Miller's very popular play *Death of a Salesman* less for its strong Jewish undertones than as an instance of American tragedy in its depiction of the general split between dreams and reality.

But actually I don't have any problem with that. The point is that Japanese people have no trouble sympathizing with Miller's work in terms of their own concerns, and there is absolutely no need for them to determine whether he is Jewish or not. However, Americans view the reality of that miserable salesman as something that is typically Jewish. But I wonder if these Americans would not hesitate when asked whether Miller should be referred to as an American writer or Jewish writer. This is a poor example, but in comparing Miller and Brecht the question arises of whether to focus on their difference (American writer vs. German writer) or commonality (both as Jewish). Of course the standard of their works' value is determined by the context in which it is placed, and this question cannot be resolved simply by choosing either their difference or commonality. I think it is best to strike a balance between these two views.

My point here is that even for westerners, who have a highly developed understanding of Jews, the works are singular but nevertheless carry an ability to appeal as based on universal themes and are widely accepted, as they are with Japanese as well. This does not seem to be a reluctant kind of reception, as if to say that even Jewish writers won't necessarily be rejected if they have talent. I know certain influential American editors who are quite insistent on this point. They claim that Jewish writers are the most vigorous and promising (in terms of both literary merit and book sales) in America today, and that they, together with South American and black writers, dominate contemporary American literature. This comment was slightly worrying to me, and I later sought confirmation with other foreign writers and editors only to discover that few disagreed with it. Some stated that the static quality of German literature was due precisely to the decrease in Jews, while others suspected that this problem went beyond Jews and signified more generally the contemporaneity of émigré writers. In any case, the advance of *the Jew* seems to be decisive, at least in terms of the field of art.

Yet it is hardly surprising that oppositional views have emerged, claiming that the lack of any firm ground on which to stand for these wandering Jews has resulted in their talent for producing merely clever, superficial art, one that finds easy acceptance by the average masses. In other words, they believe that the advance of Jewish writers can be attributed to the deceit rather than truth of their work.

In fact, however, Jews have written increasingly like Jews. They have increasingly set forth their own Jewish sensibility in no less a manner than blacks have written like blacks. Thus we might say that Jews have attained universality not despite but rather precisely because of their own Jewish particularity.

Yet it would be a problem if Jewish particularity were too quickly swallowed up within such universality. What is at issue here is utterly different from the notion of particularist superiority (i.e., the myth of legitimacy) found, for example, in the claim that what is most Japanese can also be understood by foreigners. As I have already mentioned, what enabled Tolstoy to appeal to the soul of all mankind while writing from the heart of a Russian was the presence of the shared motif of the *peasant*, as found in all "orthodoxies." This might appear to be similar to the universality attained by Kafka through writing from the heart of a Jew, but in fact it is completely different.

The *Jew* is not the Israeli. While it is possible for the Israeli to write of the history and glory of two thousand years of suffering, joining the ranks of those who believe in legitimacy, what remains for the Jewish writer who is refused all participation in history is to write of today, the eternal present. Yet how was Jewish literature able to attain such universality?

Perhaps the poison of "heresy" is cherished precisely because it is poison. Indeed, an interest in toxicants seems to be a general trend of the present. As industrial society becomes more complex, it creates an impression of chaos while also developing organizational technologies, thereby inciting anxiety in people who feel as if trapped in a maze from which there is no escape. This anxiety causes people to work hard in the hope of good fortune, but it also fosters a cynical contempt for hard work. It is hardly surprising that this sense of disjuncture creates a desire for toxicants, from morphine, heroin, cocaine, marijuana, LSD, and Hyminal to such bleak and prosaic poisons as paint thinner.

As a phenomenon, there clearly seems to be an interest in toxicants. Certain Jewish writers (e.g., Norman Mailer) intentionally provoke readers by advertising their effects. However, a substantial difference exists between such toxicants and the poison of "heresy." The heaven glimpsed through LSD and paint thinner is a world of madness that exists in relation to sanity, but the world glimpsed through the poison of "heresy" represents the hell of awakening. Regardless of whether or not it is flagrantly labeled as toxic, *Jew* means "heresy" and "heresy" means poison. Besides, who would indulge in such a substance that offers only a bleak awakening with no promise of intoxication?

What then is the universality found in the work of Jewish writers? Perhaps this secret lies hidden within the very notion of "legitimacy" itself. The notion of "heresy" was originally created for the self-validation of "legitimacy"; it is a sacrificial lamb devoted to an oath of allegiance to "legitimacy." Thus we can more or less guess the identity of this universality by uncovering the "heresy" that lies concealed within "legitimacy" itself. Since it is the state that tests whether something is "legitimate" or "heretical," one must first inquire into the meaning of "legitimacy" as seen from the state's perspective.

It is actually quite strange that "legitimacy" for the state — regardless of political system — is depicted in terms of middle-scale farmers. Why is it that, even in the advanced industrial countries whose sole economic basis is heavy industry, the *image of authentic citizen* still remains that of the good farmer? In this era where the earth's surface is divided everywhere by national borders, competition between states creates compromise in the form of international agreements, and the temporary cease-fire known as peace barely passes as justice, it is understandable why states demand unity and loyalty from their citizens. But it is utterly unnatural that such unity and loyalty be identified with the peasantry. Putting aside the question of those semicolonial, underdeveloped nations that are forced by other countries to provide raw materials, industrialization has become necessary for all states. In the advanced industrial nations, in particular, industrialization is accelerating at a geometric pace, and an actual program exists that involves a population influx into cities, the explosive growth of cities, and indeed the urbanization of the nation as a whole. Knowing that ultimately this situation results in the branding of cities as "heretical," what does the state have to gain by granting peasants the license of "legitimacy"?

I won't touch on this point in detail since it is not my intent here to provide a theory of the city. However, cities can be characterized by their compressed spatial density. This urban concentration leads to a relative increase in migration efficiency and a diversification in human relations at the same time that it results in growing anonymity. Compared to the fixity of rural life, the lives of those who live in cities assume, to a surprising degree, many of the features of migrant ethnic groups.

It is clear that the state does not approve of this mobility of urban life. For the descendant of the fixed state, which after its long struggle with the frontier has finally succeeded in stabilizing agriculture, it must be horrible to realize that it must now use the cities defined by migration efficiency as its own standard.

Apart from true city folk, who have no particular attachment to fixity, the vast numbers of newcomers to the city who have not yet fully broken with fixed habits also enjoy the city's convenience while at the same time experiencing the anxiety of the temporary resident. In its hatred for the city, the state takes advantage of this anxiety and assiduously fertilizes the unrealistic notion of legitimacy that is "faith in the land." Of course the state does not actually encourage a return to agrarian society. Rather, it continues to maintain the functions of the city while nevertheless encouraging people to construct an illusory community of "legitimacy."

Just as the state once fought against the "heresy" of the frontier and vigorously protected its national boundaries, so too must it now begin the struggle to safeguard the notion of legitimacy against the "heresy" of the frontier within (i.e., migrant society). Heretics might be identified as "unpatriotic individuals," "proforeign," "destroyers of order," "foreign agents," "reds," "the Zengakuren student association," etc. If the state is lucky enough to have Jewish citizens—"those congenital city folk"—play this role, then they will of course quickly become known as "dangerous kikes who ignore national interests."

Illusions are only illusions, however. In the context of this increasing urbanization, any futile repetition of the notion of "faith in the land" can only broaden the sense of emptiness and lack even among those avowed citizens of legitimacy. The fact that Jewish and émigré writers have now begun to exhibit an irrefutably global influence also signals the beginning of the end to the state's pretext of "belief in legitimacy." Just as the foreign invasion of migrant ethnic groups once destroyed the spatial identity of the agrarian state, introducing a *sense of contemporaneity* beyond national borders and providing a new opportunity to leap beyond the stagnation that accompanies fixity, so too might troops intent on destroying national borders now appear from the internal frontier of cities. The state ideology that recognized "legitimacy" in the particularity of farming villages might then be replaced by frontier troops who recognize "legitimacy" in the contemporaneity of cities.

I believe that the first sign of this battle in the field of literature appeared quite early, at the beginning of this century. With Tolstoy's death in 1910, literature based on faith in the land began to decline and was replaced by Kafka, Proust, and Joyce waving the flag of "heresy." But even I am not so naïve as to think that this shift signaled the death of the state. At most, literature can only hasten the onset of the state's autointoxication, but this is better than standing by and doing nothing. Is it not the duty of writers who are conscious of contemporaneity to, at the very least, reject all "beliefs in legitimacy" and attempt an internal defection to the frontier within?

The "festival" celebrating the land is over, but the new plaza is still dark. Che Guevara, who went beyond national borders, is dead, and the Vietnamese who lost their national borders are being burned by the war. But it is too early to despair. The plazas of the city might be dark, but the national borders are darker still. Those who cross borders are in need of something more than light.

THE FRONTIER WITHIN, PART II

I

I casually agreed to this talk today, not realizing how unpleasant it would be to deliver remarks before my play. These talks normally go well, but I fear this one will go badly and that my tempo will be a bit off. I really had no idea that so many people would attend.

In truth, I have been busy directing the play up until the last minute and so really haven't prepared anything by way of remarks. Well, I generally don't prepare much beforehand. If I have a general idea in mind, then I am confident of being able to fill things in well enough, but the problem is that today I don't even have that. I brought something with me, but this is not anything I spent a great deal of time working on. Rather, I happened to find something in a magazine that I thought might be helpful and so simply folded up the magazine and brought it here. My talk will probably be a bit

Lecture given August 17 and 18, 1969, at Kinokuniya Hall, Tokyo.

rambling, but please be patient. The play following this talk will make a lot more sense.

I happened to randomly open this magazine. A book had been wedged into one of the pages, which featured an ad for a Unimat small machine tool. I dog-eared this page because the tool seemed wonderful. It was cheap, and I actually considered buying it. I really wanted to buy this tool.

Now that I have just advertised this tool, it would be very nice for any of you who might be affiliated with the company to give it to me as a gift.

That is a joke, but when I considered buying this tool, I also suddenly came upon an idea for a play. If one wanted, one could write a play about someone who bought a small machine tool.

Perhaps I'll write this play next year, but this tool is great. It can do anything, functioning like a lathe, drill press, slicer, grinding wheel, fret saw, circular saw, screw-thread cutter, and electric drill. Its functions range from metal tools to plastic and wooden ones, tools of extreme precision with an error range of 0.01 millimeters. This is a tool with an astonishingly high performance, priced at only 30,090 yen. You really want it now, don't you? Perhaps some of you don't, but I bet that there are some of you who do.

But I imagine that if you actually bought this tool, you probably wouldn't make anything with it. You'll surely need help when you consider the time and effort involved, no matter how versatile this machine tool might be. If I bought this tool, it would be a real problem. Once I began making something, I would have no time leftover to write fiction, not to mention plays. In the end, it would be faster to buy something ready-made than to purchase this tool. Ultimately, then, I'm interested in the circumstances involved in buying such things as well as what happens after one buys them. Well, capitalist society is defined by the privatization of the means of production. Since machine tools are the very basis of the means of production, I could if I wanted buy this high-precision instrument and use it to make things—not everything, of course—so as to become perfectly self-sufficient. But these things would be so inefficient that the plan wouldn't work. Actually, I'm fully aware of this. It's just that when I see this tool, I want to buy it. Perhaps I will buy it, but I still won't make anything worth mentioning.

Well, despite the fact that I have already spoken so much, I'm sure you don't have a clue as to what this play is about. Don't get me wrong, though. I certainly don't say this to make fun of you.

But I'm not here to speak about machine tools. While reading a page in a magazine that was necessary for my talk, I simply happened to come across this ad. It's a bit of a stretch, I know, but this topic is somewhat connected to my talk. My remarks today are related to my essay "Uchi naru henkyō" [The

Frontier Within], which appeared serially in the journal *Chūō kōron*. As to why I have entitled this talk "The Frontier Within, Part II," it is because urban society has now become a major issue. One constantly hears such phrases as "urban society" or "fall into everydayness." In my own fashion, I wrote about these things under the heading of "The Frontier Within," but I didn't receive the response that I expected. I wrote the essay hoping for a slightly larger reaction, but it was not to be. It thus seemed that I needed to be more persistent in dealing with this matter, which is why I have entitled today's lecture "The Frontier Within, Part II."

I'm sure there are some of you in the audience who have not read this essay, so let me simply mention that the theme focused on the question "What are we human beings?" When we inquire into the nature of our society, status quo and present, we begin to see that a sense of security of everydayness (in which today appears like yesterday and tomorrow appears like today), as for example the sense of security one feels in a community, pervades us. We then gradually extend the continuum of everydayness until we finally enter the framework of the state. Everyone has now grown used to the fact that such frameworks as the native hometown or household come naturally to be destroyed and reorganized. Upon encountering the state, however, the particular sense or perception one has is that it possesses a different level or character than such frameworks as family, native hometown, society, or school. Ultimately, the question here concerns what exactly this means.

Recently, however, the expression "I am a stateless person" appeared in both the slogans from the Zengakuren student association and the dialogue between Mishima Yukio and the Zenkyōtō movement at Tokyo University. I myself of course more than sympathize with such a notion of transcending and negating national borders; indeed, this is a basic premise of my work. This was precisely the theme of my essay "The Frontier Within."

But in such talk of transcending national borders, I wonder if the pain, difficulty, and hardship involved in this act are not casually watered down by empty oratory. Although I did my best to claim that possibilities existed to transcend these borders, that fissures in the state could be seen right in front of us—indeed, even within our very everydayness—those who insisted from the beginning that they were rejecting the state found my appeals to be all too obvious, and they seemed to have no effect whatsoever. But I wonder if such a view of the state is not somewhat naïve.

For example, we find ourselves in a money economy. The value of things is measured not by themselves but by money. Thus we live in an age where everything is measured by money rather than by bartering or commodity exchange. Well, this point is quite obvious.

There are various theories that reject the money economy, however, beginning of course with Marxism. Such rejection is easy. "But I have no luck with money!" some might say. So you have no luck with money. I know that, and I'm sure that you have considered cutting yourself off from money, believing that you have no relation to it. And then you'd go someplace like the book stall below Kinokuniya Bookstore and say only that you now have nothing to do with money. I imagine there might be some problems.

In other words, money has created a certain universality of value. Compared with the era of commodity exchange, money has led to a far greater universalization of value. To this extent, the penalty for destroying money has become commensurably severe. No matter how much one confirms for oneself one's detachment from the money economy, actualizing this idea makes one a thief.

Just as money is merely a piece of paper or concept while also containing a theoretical and objective principle, the state clearly holds some kind of value for us. Even if one personally abides by a theory of rejecting the state, it is nonetheless an established fact that the state, like money, exists in reality as a universal value or force. Just as one would be immediately penalized if one actively trampled on money, the state possesses the same power. As some say, the formation of the state and the formation of the money economy are really two sides of the same coin.

The state has now arrived at the status of universal idea. Yet it seems to me that the actual existence of the state's universal value and power must be conceived as separate from its accompanying attributes (such as patriotism or people being forced to act in certain ways for the state).

It is not that I am agitating here for the means to overthrow the state, nor was I attempting to do so in my *Chūō kōron* essay. Rather, I wish to consider the state's attributes or relativity as based on these undeniable facts. In truth, all our actions and measures are very much bound by these attributes. For example, people are bound by money, as can be seen in the fact that all of you here had to pay 250 yen to get in. Regardless of whether one is conscious of this or not, the fact is that the presence of the state already announces itself here. Your actions themselves have already been stamped by the state. We live without being especially conscious of this fact. Instead, the state's attributes very powerfully appear in our consciousness. Of course rejection of these attributes does not amount to rejection of the state. That is completely unrelated, but my aim in writing "The Frontier Within" emerged from the need to thoroughly expose the real strangeness of these attributes.

In that essay, I sought to demonstrate that the state is ultimately a form of fixity or settled condition, something that was constructed especially against the background of agrarian society. I then went on to discuss those multiple concepts that were constructed upon agrarian society: the connection to the land, the mystification of the land, and the sense of loyalty toward landowners who ruled over the land. These concepts also produced the notions of hatred and negation of the city.

Jews, for example, were confined to the city, and one of the reasons behind the emergence of anti-Semitic discrimination was the fact that they were then unable to live elsewhere. Today people freely drift toward the city. This isn't simply free movement, however, for the population influx there is also a demand of capital. Yet in feudal society, a phenomenon that was strictly unique to Japan and Europe could be seen in the fact that cities were places of confinement. People did not flee to the city; rather, they were trapped there. For example, Jews were strictly denied the right to buy land. They were denied the right to engage in any labor involving land. Instead, they could enter the moneylending business, for instance, which was then very small in scale due to the fact that the money economy was not yet highly developed. Christians, in particular, had a code of morals in which involvement in moneylending was regarded as impure. This is precisely why they permitted Jews to engage in such work. In the general scope of the economy at this time, the field of moneylending occupied a very small place.

As a rule, society develops. With the increasing power of the money economy, those Jews who had been confined to the city became increasingly powerful. Cities had previously been mere dwellings for the luxury of regional feudal lords and landowners, but now they acquired special meaning. Despite the fact that moneylending violated Christian law, these businesses were also confiscated from Jews. This era clearly marked the beginning of the Holocaust.

Hence the desire to expel the Jews had less to do with racial discrimination than this dense economic background. There was no such opposition in the case of Japan, where the gradual process of urban expansion went smoothly.

In Japan, the relation between merchants and warriors was such that, by the end of the Edo period, merchants were no doubt effectively judging these overlords by the amount of their crop yields. In principle, a commodity exchange economy ruled, but what actually took precedence was the money economy. Samurai were as a result forced to go to the moneylenders in town to exchange their salary (which was measured in rice) for money. Ultimately, samurai were controlled by the merchants. This led to the emergence of a kind of samurai stock, which was purchased by many merchants as a symbol of their success and given to their sons and grandsons. In this way, merchants became samurai. If one looks at such figures as Katsu Kaishū, one finds that there were in fact many samurai whose families had been merchants several generations earlier.

Most of the outstanding figures who emerged from the backward samurai class at the end of the Edo period originally came from merchant families. These men provided new blood. The so-called samurai became a mere guarantee of social position, one that could be bought and sold with money. By infusing this class with new merchant blood, the samurai class was also able to harness the energy that in part shaped the period.

In the case of Japan, the conflict between merchants (i.e., those who controlled money) and those who ruled over land did not emerge as flagrantly as it did in Europe, with the result that no figure comparable to the European Jew ever appeared. Of course theories of racial difference exist as well, and I do not necessarily deny them, although I have no evidence. When one asks Europeans about this, however, they reply that it is generally difficult to determine whether someone is Jewish simply by looking at their face, although there are exceptions to this. They add that they can tell after speaking with someone for five minutes. More or less recognizing whether someone is Jewish after five minutes means that they cannot determine this at a single glance.

As proof, there is for example the Yiddish language, which is spoken by many Jews. Yiddish is actually a special regional dialect from southern Germany. In terms of word form, it is simply German. While there are many Jews who speak Yiddish, the difference with the German language is so slight that these Jews would be able to communicate with someone from southern Germany. Of course there are also Jews who speak Hebrew, but many more speak Yiddish.

In fact, there are many Jews who live in the region stretching from central Europe to southern Germany. It is unclear why this is. Or rather, the question of whether these people were originally Jews or a group that was widely considered to be Jews is virtually impossible to answer. Perhaps this was simply a case of religious discrimination. It is difficult to verify anything here.

One hears that the Jews, confined within the city, *acquired* the ancient traditions of urban society, but that is untrue. The point is that the Jews were confined within those traditions. During periods in which rule over land predominates, residents of cities are in a sense alienated. Although this trend is reversed with the advance of urban society, the conditions for building a uniquely urban Jewish culture—which was absent in both Europe and Japan—were in any event long imposed from outside. This actually led to the extreme universalization of Jewish culture.

For that period marked by rule over land has now imperceptibly disappeared. Our age is nearly everywhere characterized by urban society. Even farming villages, for example, are dominated by structures that are quite urban in nature. Having now arrived at a period in which urban structures dominate the state, the ideas and cultural forms of the Jews, which were previously considered peripheral, have now become quite universalized.

In the case of America, for example, eighty or possibly even ninety percent of the country's famous fiction writers are Jewish. This includes a very broad swath of writers, from urbane and sophisticated writers like J. D. Salinger to such wild and unruly writers as Norman Mailer. The range is considerable, but Jewish writers have become a significant presence in America.

What this means is that Jewishness has gone beyond Jewish society and has come to be accepted among non-Jews as a certain universality.

In the case of Europe, there have been a large number of Jews working at the core of revolutionary movements. It was for this reason that many Jews poured into Russia, but with the rise of Stalinism, they were eventually driven out and exiled, with many fleeing to America and England. With the exception of such figures as Ilya Ehrenburg, then, the early Soviet Union also saw a great number of Jews engaged in cultural activities. Many were later vindicated.

In Hitler's anti-Semitic diatribes against this Jewish culture, however, it is clear that his image of the good German was really an image of the good farmer. This point appears in his own writings.

I have already written about this, but in the Soviet Union during the Stalinist period Tolstoy was more readily accepted than Dostoevsky. Neither writer was seen as part of revolutionary literature, but Tolstoy was regarded more favorably. This was due to the fact that Tolstoy saw the future in terms of the peasants. In contrast, while it might be too much to say that Dostoevsky saw the future in terms of the urban lumpen proletariat, he did perceive a certain kind of history. The Soviet Union thus began supporting the policy of one-nation socialism through the mediation of the state as Jews and other urban elements gradually came to be hated and boycotted.

A similar phenomenon can be seen in Japan. People's experience very much differs according to age, and I am sure that all of you react with quite different nuances of feeling, but there are two types of people: the first associates the good and beautiful with the earth or land, that is, the rural. This type senses or feels that good things can be found in the countryside, whereas the second type finds only brutal and vicious things there. Even among us, it is actually more common to regard the city as the root of all evil. I suspect that all of you would feel this way if confronted with the same choice.

When one looks at such paintings as Millet's *The Angelus*, everything appears blissfully peaceful, with a peaceful bell ringing and people praying for the bounty of the earth. Yet we must sharpen our sensitivity to our surroundings so as to perceive all manner of brutal and vicious evil here. If we don't sharpen our sensitivity, in fact, I fear that we will become unable to investigate such horrible attributes of the state as its dangers and deceits. Hence I wrote about this at length in my essay "The Frontier Within."

In other words, what role has land played throughout history? Also, what historical role has been played by landless peoples or ethnic groups, as for example the equestrian tribes of central Asia? What is the difference between the laws and morals established by these equestrian tribes and those morals set forth by agrarian tribes, whose existence was more settled? The point here concerns which type of laws or morals is more suitable to the city—which type does the city require?

To come right to the point, it seems to me that cities actually require morals that are closer to nomads and equestrian tribes than to the more settled agrarian tribes. I also believe that any discussion of going beyond the state is only so much empty talk if people lack the ability to not only understand but viscerally internalize such morals as their own.

Although this is not directly related to my topic, the other day I read a book called *Dōketsugaku koto hajime* [*Introduction to Speleology*]. This book of course focuses on various explorations of caves. The image of caves calls up many artistic associations as well. I'm sure that this word alone evokes various images among all of you. Such images differ among individuals, from the innocent association of treasure and completely other worlds to the more shady and sexual. These kinds of things are not to be found in the book, which is completely scientific in nature. But what really fascinated me were the various things one learns while classifying those insects that live strictly in caves. No one has ever researched this topic, so one is forced when classifying these insects to distinguish between different and similar species. As a matter of habit, we first think about differences when comparing things. For example, we perceive differences in the shape of fangs or the distance between the eyes. Of course it is true that differences are important.

In the case of people, what little I have seen of all of you is enough to reveal that you are each individually different. While there may be some of you with the same width or distance between your eyes, the width of your nose might be different. All people are slightly different in some sense. It would be frightening if people were identical to one another.

Yet if one didn't actually discover some commonalities within these differences, it would be impossible to classify the latter within a single species or genus. Such things as small insects that live strictly in caves are of no great value, and so they have not been accurately classified. As to why there is a need to study these insects, however, the fact that they never appear on the earth's surface is useful information not only in terms of the history of caves—as, for example, when they were first formed—but also in geological considerations. Thus the classification of insects is revealed to be meaningful. In the case of criminal investigations, however, there are as many different types of fingerprints as there are people. All fingerprints are different, which distinguishes this from insect classification. Yet in order to differentiate according to species and genus, commonalities must be discovered. No matter where one looks, however, there is hardly any mention of commonalities. This book contains various research results and quite fascinating observations. Different features are used as criteria, as for example jaws and eye width. In truth, however, the key to solving this mystery can be found in the number of hairs found on the insect's posterior section. No one had ever realized this before. Actually, it is not that one grasps that commonalities are to be found in the number of hairs on the insect's posterior section; but rather that, upon making this discovery, one can now systematize and brilliantly analyze these previously disparate classifications. This point is quite fascinating.

In the real world, we too distinguish and discriminate between things. To discriminate—this word might be too strong given the link with such phrases as racial discrimination, but that is ultimately where I'm leading—means to distinguish or discover differences. We do this all the time and it is not always wrong. Indeed, it is necessary. In particular, when we are in a community, it is in fact necessary to discover the difference between who belongs to the community and who does not so as to discover who is the enemy—that is, who exists outside the community.

Agrarian society would be an example of a community with a clearly defined frame or border. The borders of land must be quite distinct. For agrarian peoples, therefore, trespassing has long been a serious offense. In urban society, however, the attachment to land has gradually faded. Of course one can say that everyone wants to buy land, but such desire to buy land and build a home is completely different in character from the farmer's attachment to land.

When one enters urban society, the clearly defined frame or border of community as found in rural society quickly disappears. For example, when one imagines daily life within these very insular and closed rural areas, how many people can one discuss things with? When one compares this with the number of people whom each of you speak with as urban residents, the difference is considerable. But perhaps this gap is not so great. When one considers how many people one happens to see every day, however, the difference becomes unimaginable. If one includes such people whom one happens to see in the city as part of one's everyday contacts, then the number is extraordinarily high. These contacts are virtually infinite, in contrast to the finite number of community contacts one has in rural society. For better or worse, this difference in human relations brings about a change in the concept of community.

It might seem easy to acknowledge this point, but one cannot be so blithe. In fact, various contradictions and points of resistance arise here. Internal conflicts emerge within communities, the same land-based communities in which we have long been confined. These land-based communities have affected our culture in various ways; they permeate so deeply that we barely notice them. This creates a great deal of anxiety.

At the same time, however, we also sense the cramped and suffocating nature of community. For example, gangster films typically depict men who become drifters and leave their village. Although this is fine in and of itself, these men then invariably begin to feel anxious and find it impossible to remain as drifters. Rather, they feel the need to belong somewhere. There is currently a labor shortage in Japan, so it is easy to find a place to belong, but in the past the absence of labor shortages made such belonging difficult. Those men who had fled a certain community would then find other communities to enter. And the easiest community to enter was the gangster organization. Gangster films thus have a strong sense of realism to them; they possess a certain reality. Here we see an extremely sad self-contradiction: one flees someplace in order to gain entry elsewhere. At the same time, it is also fairly easy in the gangster world to enter somewhere in order to flee. Yet it is not my intent here to extol gangster films; rather, it is simply undeniable that these films reflect a certain reality.

To make an extremely needling remark, I would say that there is essentially no difference between working in a company somewhere and leaving the countryside to become a gangster and look cool. It might be a bit of an exaggeration to claim that no difference exists between these two things, but the difference is not great. In contrast, the notion that we need to cultivate concerns the state of sustained flight. What does this mean? Whereas settling down somewhere is a basic condition, remaining in a state of sustained flight is a process. We carry within ourselves a prejudice that this process invariably involves settling down somewhere. My point here consists in shedding doubt on this prejudice. Such doubt arises only with great difficulty.

If we wish to create such morality, then we must formulate ways to rediscover human relations as based on commonalities rather than on discriminations or distinctions between people. Otherwise urban life will be virtually buried by contact with strangers. In other words, urban life will feel as if one has been thrown among mere others. One often hears the expression "loneliness in the big city," in which loneliness is used in a negative sense. But I wonder if this usage is correct. We must rethink this prejudice.

The city is certainly a hodgepodge, something that is all mixed up. It also doesn't provide the same sense of safety or security that one feels in rural communities. This is precisely why cities are good. I wonder if one cannot see that cities thus contain the potential to act as a bridge to the future. I would like to ask these questions. We casually speak now less about morality than about our inner sense of alienation. "People who live in cities suffer from a sense of alienation": these words are of course used negatively. However, it is unclear whether such alienation is negative in a logical sense. Is it not simply the case that we feel lonely at an emotional level? The fact that we are so easily given to such expressions as "urban alienation" suggests that we somehow feel ourselves to be already part of an ancient communal morality. Also, what would be the nature of a state outside loneliness? This is a state in which one forms companions, but that is not easy to do. In order to clarify things, one first forms enemies.

In other words, one establishes who it is that exists outside the community. If you yourselves in any way subscribe to such an approach, it can quickly be taken advantage of. For example, in Japan there is no concept or actual presence of "the Jew," so fortunately this has not become an issue here, but anti-Semitism immediately makes use of this approach. Surprisingly enough, anti-Semitism often appears among those who live in cities. Although city dwellers realize that they cannot return to the village, they nevertheless continue to view urban life from this village perspective. The sense of alienation and loneliness is here transformed into a weakness.

For example, I propose that we posit the various notions as expressed by such words as "lonely" and "alienated" as mere objective facts and to refer to them without feeling or emotion. Of course, other people are quite unpleasant. In truth, I myself am not a particularly sociable person. I don't always act cheerful when I'm with others, but I don't believe there is any need to. My point, in other words, is that we must try to break out of a naïve idea of the other in which those who do not act cheerful or display the stamp of ally are simply regarded as the enemy.

This might sound as if I were propagating Christianity, but in fact the reverse is true. To clarify things, Christianity actually speaks of increasing the number of neighbors. That is fine, but everybody cannot be a neighbor. In other words, it is strictly because there exist people who are not neighbors that one can steadily increase the number of neighbors as far as possible. The desire to increase the number of neighbors is predicated on the border between neighbors and others. It is perhaps best to reject the neighbor from the start. Such rejection of the neighbor causes us to experience a kind of internal, visceral pain. I believe that we must fight against this visceral quality. That is, we must fight it as a cultural rather than political concept. If we disregard this point and simply reject the state conceptually, then we will fail to do it much damage. Hence I want to question whether the wall that is the state represents the final wall while at the same time point out the danger of idle talk if we simply negate the state without confronting this problem at an internal level.

In truth, this talk is nothing more than an introduction. The play will be staged later, so this setup is a bit embarrassing. I'm afraid that it might appear rather impudent on my part to direct my own play in addition to giving a talk beforehand. I am quite conscious of how incredibly brazen this must seem, but the play is very short. This is my first time to do something like this, since I've actually never delivered a paid lecture before. It is not the case that I added the play because I feel so bad about this. Rather, I need to do both the lecture and play in order to fill the allotted time. That's why I added the play. The mood or atmosphere of the play and lecture are completely different. There is no intermission, so please forget all that I have said during my talk and simply watch the play with an open mind. Thank you.

II

There should of course be no one here today who also came yesterday. Yesterday, in fact, I felt some stage fright. It was the first time in my life that I got nervous giving a speech. Something was a bit off. That was the first time in my life that I felt this way, although it is not as if I began giving speeches while still a baby. Fortunately, I don't feel any stage fright today. Well, I at least feel comfortable enough to look at my notes. What I have before me now, however, are not notes but actually the budget sheet for the play.

Nerves can cause a great deal of damage. First of all, I simply spoke as I pleased yesterday without explaining the reasons why we were holding this event. And then I got nervous, and these nerves spread to the actors, with the result that things were quite a bit off. One really must avoid getting nervous.

The reason why I felt such stage fright was that it was my first time directing and the play, which I wrote and directed, is being put on after the talk. I hadn't realized how unpleasant it would be to give a talk beforehand. I suppose it was a case of a lack of imagination. I was all set to take on this challenge only to discover that I felt nervous and had trouble breathing. I soon began trembling and it was all quite awful. I feel calm today, however, since I have already told myself that things will be awful.

The flier for the play you will see afterward lists my opening lecture in large print while the words "Trial Performance of the Play *Kaban* [*The Bag*]" are barely legible. My real intent was for the lecture to supplement the play, since it's the play that I want you to see. I'm very sorry that it has turned out this way. For me, of course, the lecture that now appears first is clearly the supplement. Nonetheless, I would like to briefly introduce the Drama Department of Tōhō Gakuen College. Tōhō Gakuen is the first professional acting school in Japan and was created as a university. Four years have passed since it took over the training school of the Haiyūza Theatre Company. In truth, such professional acting schools exist in all countries, where they are generally state run. The training of actors costs a lot of money. This is not something that can be run privately, but the school has managed to overcome various adverse conditions. The actors today have received four years of training and may rightly be considered semiprofessional. I don't want to engage in any more self-advertising, but I will simply mention now that, as part of my own seminar, I will be directing there in the fall my *Bō ni natta otoko* [*The Man Who Turned into a Stick*]. Since I'm a bit worried about the opening performance, as I've never directed before, I decided to do a practice run here. I firmly believe that people can do anything if they have one talent, and that's why I took this on.

I'll explain this point later, but I'm finally going to direct. I'm trying this because I was a bit worried. I think that things have gone surprisingly well. Generally, trial performances are performed only at the school, but I wanted this to be seen by an outside audience. Fortunately, many students or people around the same age often come to this playhouse—well, it is a play house, since the space is too small to be a real house. I decided that the play should be seen in a theater.

The directing here is completely different. Today's play is only the first scene of *Bō ni natta otoko*, which will be performed in November, but the direction is utterly different. I'm sure you will see for yourselves how varied it is.

I sent Mishima Yukio an invitation to come today, but of course I knew that he wouldn't. He called to tell me that he wouldn't be able to attend. It's fine that he's not here. He mentioned that he's been directing a Kabuki play, which will debut on November 5. "So it's a contest, then. It seems that I'm always competing with you," I replied. "But it's Kabuki," he said, "so I only have to direct for five days." I told Mishima that I am now going to start preparing for the play in November, which means rehearsing for the next three months. He answered, "I don't get involved with all that tiresome stuff." "If you have enough time to spend with the Self-Defense Forces," I replied, "then why don't you work on making more effective plays?" "Stop messing around," he said. "This is not just a hobby. I participate in the Self-Defense Forces for my country." To which I responded, "Then it can't be helped. I'll focus on the art of a ruined nation while you go ahead and fight for the country." This explains why one corner of the reserved seats is empty.

Of course I'm only joking, but compared with the Self-Defense Forces, plays may well represent the art of a ruined nation. Yet I've come to believe, in fact, that the art of a ruined nation is something positive. This is all the more reason for me to speak today about a ruined nation. But I know that such exaggerated talk will only bring about negative effects later. It will affect the play. I had some stage fright yesterday and so became a bit too excited and ended up speaking about very difficult things. Of course the play has its flaws, but it is actually a comedy. Yesterday, however, the audience didn't react as if they were watching a comedy, and that was a bit disheartening, to be honest. I suspect that this was partly because my lecture raised the pitch of things, so today I'm trying to lower the pitch.

Very broadly, then, Mishima focuses on the Self-Defense Forces while I work on plays. The Self-Defense Forces is certainly much more effective. They carry weapons and would respond powerfully if you ran into them. But if one wishes to destroy the nation, then art is the more powerful. I call this art of a ruined nation because it matches up well against the Self-Defense Forces.

Although this expression "ruined nation" is a mere figure of speech, I hadn't heard it in a long time and so actually felt rather nostalgic when Mishima used it. But I suspect that the nuance of this expression will in the future come to affect us in various ways. That is to say, this notion corresponds to its opposite, which has gradually achieved a certain effectiveness. When discussing the question of the usefulness of art, for example, there is nobody in Japan, for better or worse, who claims that making art more useful will help rally a spirit of patriotism. Nevertheless, art was often used for this purpose in the past, and there are still countries that use art in this way. In general, however, art is intrinsically not something that serves the state; rather, it must ruin the nation. I don't believe that art that ruins the nation exists alongside art that makes the nation flourish. In speaking with Mishima, I again realized that what we call "art" must ruin the nation, but let me conclude this point.

In a word, art is quite plainly expression. Art is also knowledge, but knowledge can be transmitted simply through essays and reviews. I of course have no intention today to comment on the play, for such commentary is extremely unpleasant. It seems that everyone assumes that writers understand their works best. I always find it off-putting when people ask me about the aim or theme of my work.

I recently spoke with Donald Keene, who remarked that Shakespeare was very fortunate in Japan. When I asked why, he replied that it was because Shakespeare doesn't appear in Japanese textbooks. As I'm sure all of you know, one immediately forms a negative impression of writers whom one hears a lot about through textbooks. Students encounter many pages and are forced to write summaries at the end. From this perspective, literary works appear quite silly. In England, one typically learns about Shakespeare in textbooks from childhood, with the result that one grows fed up. In Japan, this would be similar to—actually I don't know what materials appear in textbooks these days. Apparently some of my work is included, but I find this quite regrettable. Only a small portion of my work appears, however. As for those writers who appear frequently, I too received a permanently negative impression of them as a child. Many English people grow up in such a way as to come to appreciate Shakespeare's value only after graduating and reaching adulthood.

Appearing in textbooks is of course something negative and unfortunate; one is characterized as an authority and part of the orthodoxy. This is bad because students are immediately forced to interpret and summarize these works.

Yet it seems that some of Donald Keene's writings also appear in text-books, with the note that these are passages written by a foreigner, and students are asked to correct the mistakes. That sounds about right.

These textbooks include my "Akai Mayu" [Red Cocoon], which is a short piece. Students are nevertheless asked to summarize it, which is quite depressing. There is just no way to summarize a story like that.

I thus won't offer any commentary on the play but simply say that it is an expression. As an expression, I cannot project the play onto a surface of knowledge. I have no desire to summarize, interpret, or outline it.

As to why I have decided to direct plays, there are of course many directors in the world. There is really no need for me now to so arrogantly begin directing. As a matter of principle, I believe that writers should not direct, for this results in a limitation of images.

In other words, it is the conflict between writer and director that makes it possible to create new images. If one directs one's own work, then, there is a danger that one will become absorbed by set images. This is why I oppose as a matter of principle writers' directing their own work. Despite this premise, however, I felt something else in my desire to direct. I began to suspect that, in the case of writing—or literature in the broad sense, which includes plays—there might be two ways of emphasizing expression: writing and style.

The difference between writing and style can be found not in the encyclopedia but rather in the *Kōjirin* and other such dictionaries. My original plan was to research this and then very grandly inform you of the results, but I'm afraid I ran out of time. In fact, I don't have a very rigorous grasp of this difference myself, but I thought I might speak intuitively and define these terms in my own fashion.

In terms of the meaning of writing, there are people known as fine writers. Here it would be sufficient for you to call up your own image of fine writers. This is an expression with a certain meaning. It refers to whether or not writing skillfully expresses a given content. A good writer is thus someone who writes skillfully.

However, one doesn't typically say that someone has a skillful style. As for what I specifically mean here by this notion of style, I would like you to think about translated novels, although this is perhaps not the best example.

Translation never transmits the author's writing as such. Yet the style is conveyed. When we read the novels of Dostoevsky, for example, the Japanese and Russian are completely different. Despite this difference, Japanese people are fond of Dostoevsky's novels and have been greatly influenced by them. How is this possible? It is due to the fact that one goes beyond writing to the style that lies behind it. Style is structure: it conveys structure through language. Writing conveys a sentiment—this might sound odd, but it conveys something mysterious about expression. Style conveys that structure.

Seen in this way, translated novels of course become something very different for us. Such languages as Japanese, Russian, French, and English each have their own unique expressions and traditions, which cannot be conveyed as such. Yet Japanese culture would become quite impoverished and shallow if translated novels were completely removed. With no difficulty whatsoever, the reception of these novels has gradually increased. I suspect that this is because style is more important than writing for the expressing subject. If you agree with this point, I'm sure you will understand what I mean by this notion of style.

This is a bit of a leap in logic, but writing individualizes the details of something by means of various individual, detailed expressions. In contrast, style might be described as an operation of universalization. This may suggest that writing contains an appeal to more nuanced emotions or feelings, unlike style, but it is not the case that our emotions themselves are so individualized and expressed. Rather, it is communication as or through various structures that actually strikes our emotions and touches our soul. Translated novels thus possess something appealing to the soul in a way that differs from merely following a story or reading a philosophical text. This is not just an expression, for structures themselves have the potential to trigger something within our souls.

When I thus refer to style as structure, as complicated as this sounds, I am in no way suggesting that it is anything unique or unrelated to our everyday sensibility.

I would like to consider this shift from writing to style as one of the defining features of contemporary art. This might appear to be a leap in logic, but it seems to me that directing plays can also be divided into the writerly and stylistic. I feel that directing in Japan today is too writerly, and that there is a real need to establish a stylistic type of direction. It might be a bit of an exaggeration to use the word "establish" here, but I thought that I should at least try, without knowing if this is possible. I feel that I've gone a bit too deep into this.

I suspect that part of the reason behind this shift from writing to style is that it is characteristic of the present age. The novel is now gradually tending to surpass national borders. That is to say, if one compares Japanese novels with French or American novels, one can now more often find commonalities in works between these countries. If, for example, French novels contain elements A and B while Japanese novels contain elements A′ and B′, there might be more commonalities between A and A′ than between A and B. Japanese literature is still separated out from world literature in the Japanese edition of the *Complete Works of World Literature*, but I believe that this division is gradually disappearing.

Rather than bracketing American writers together and dividing literature between French novels and American novels, for example, one must recognize that it is not at all unusual to find greater commonalities between certain American and French writers.

I spoke about this yesterday, actually, and so won't touch upon this subject again today, but there are various opinions both for and against the transition from the cultural forms of agrarian society to those of urban society. Yesterday I spoke very much in favor of this transition, but I'm going to avoid such talk today. Although I approve of this transition, I would like to leave aside the question of pro and con. One thing that can clearly be said about this period change is that regional links and commonalities are extremely powerful in agrarian societies whereas urban societies center much more on temporality, that is, contemporaneousness, a shared sense of the age. In other words, a shared sense of the age is much more powerful in urban societies than a shared sense of land. Although regional distinctions, divisions, and differences do in fact exist, it is a much more important task for us to discover common traits through the filter of the age, which transcends such differences. Our own sensibility is already moving in this direction.

It thus seems to me that the most suitable expressions for our age are those shaped by style, the sense of linguistic structure, rather than the analytically individualized form of writing. In short, it is not so much that stylistic expressions have come to be demanded more than writerly expressions as fit for this age. Rather, it is the age itself that demands this change.

While it is true that various artists and authors each write in their own way, artistic expression is something in which the age itself is forced to express itself. At such times, the age speaks through people's hearts and mouths. Artists just happen to be the receiver and transmitter. If the age remains silent, artists can do nothing regardless of how much they struggle. The age itself now demands stylistic expressions. The age speaks through style. The artist receives this message and is forced to choose these expressions.

More generally, it is extremely important in agrarian society, where one shares a certain sense of community, to create a shared sensibility with one's neighbors—that is, those people who recognize one another regionally or locally. Hence festivals create a shared sensibility among people who know one another by means of detailed regional conventions. Today, however, what we need is a shared sensibility of the age and of the other.

This can be seen in our daily lives, in fact. For example, those of you here probably recognize at most five people in this venue. The rest are complete strangers. Even in such a small place as this, it would not be at all strange if you developed a common sensibility with these strangers. I don't particularly wish to use the term "urbanization" here, since people use it both positively and negatively, but in our present age urbanization is such that a shared sensibility with others is required.

This shared sensibility of the age that we have with others will of course go beyond regional communities and national borders to spread throughout the world. Detailed analysis of this point is difficult and various theories exist, but the student movement, for example, has spread largely throughout the world at the same time. Revolution in underdeveloped countries has in the past typically taken the single form of a national liberated front, but one now finds an image that goes beyond national borders, as can be seen in the liberation movements taking place in Latin America. This surpassing of national borders has been accomplished fairly smoothly.

Also, the problem of Vietnam War deserters has now appeared. You are perhaps not very shocked when you read about this in the newspaper. Yet in the past, during wartime, for example, people would have been shocked by such news as if suffering from an allergic reaction, no matter where the deserters were from.

In other words, escaping or betraying the state would have been seen as horribly shocking, the greatest of evils. Deserters would have been regarded as loathsome and unfit as human beings. If deserters had appeared on the American side during the war with Japan, Japanese people would have viewed them with tremendous scorn. Today, however, news of deserters is reported rather casually, comparable to news of earthquakes and typhoons. A difference in our sense of the age—a certain kind of shared sensibility—has unconsciously emerged in such a way that the act of desertion or renouncing the state is now reported as a cold, objective fact.

Various explanations are offered about this different sensibility: it is a result of urban alienation, we have become disassociated from others, etc. It is true that urbanization has led to greater disassociation among us, but is this fact so sad and disturbing? On the contrary, it is only because of this disassociation that the demand for and imagining of a shared sensibility with the other first emerges.

Although the expression "shared sensibility with the other" sounds very abstract, it means that we have come to possess a shared sensibility of the age by shifting away from an age of space to one that is shaped around time—what I have called "style" or the structure of the age. The change from a shared sensibility of space to a shared sensibility of contemporaneousness seems to have prompted, whether one likes it or not, an artistic shift from writing to style. If I were to use the phrase "avant-garde art," such art must be stylistic if it is to be truly avant-garde. This expression "stylistic art" is abstract and imprecijse, but I would insist that defining such art as avant-garde means that contemporary art—that is, art that truly fits our present age—must be avant-garde art.

It's strange that the time should have passed already, but it has not. I can end this talk at any time, but I feel as if I've just finished.

I can't really do anything about that, so let me return to the topic that I discussed yesterday.

Speaking of shared sensibility, I read a fascinating study the other day. This has nothing at all to do with literature. The book I read was a study of caves, entitled *Dōketsugaku koto hajime*. In sum, a person who likes to climb mountains decided to explore caves. The more he studied caves, however, the more he came to realize that what first appeared as very particular actually led to the formation of a universal type of research.

That is to say, there were insects that lived strictly in caves. Having evolved in a very particular manner, these insects would die upon emerging on the earth's surface. Given that these insects evolved exclusively in caves over a very long period of time, their existence helps us understand how long ago it was when these caves first appeared. If those insects did not exist, then that would prove various things, as for example the fact that the caves sank into the ocean at a certain point in time. In sum, it is by examining the distribution of insects that live strictly in caves that we can understand changes in Japan's long geological age as well as the extremely complex structural changes in the earth's crust under Japan. In this way, universal facts can come to be discovered on the basis of apparently trivial research. It seems that there have not been many instances of such research.

This point is interesting in and of itself, but what I also find fascinating here is that the undeveloped field of entomology is such that it is quite difficult to determine the criteria for species distinctions, as for example whether insects truly belong to the same species or if, despite certain similarities, they actually belong to different species. One variously examines cave-dwelling insects from around the world—for example, small rice insects of some kind. By examining documents from other countries, one determines which insects are the same. One could see the shape of their jaws or whether they have three eyes or two. In fact, there are insects with three eyes. One would then look at such features as the distance between their eyes, and on this basis one could variously classify them. But this manner of classification is inconsistent and logically disjointed. In studying this problem more deeply so as to identify the most crucial point in determining species, one comes to focus on the number of hairs on the insect's posterior section. It has been discovered that classifying the genus of insects as based on the number of hairs on their posterior section is actually the most systematic. No one had ever realized the importance of these hairs since this feature seemed so trivial. Researchers had instead focused on the eyes.

The fascinating point here concerns how easy it is for us to discriminate or differentiate, whereas it is very difficult to discover the commonality of belonging to the same genus. You might not be able to tell with this lighting, but I just returned from the sea and am now darker than most people of the yellow race. But I don't think anyone really suspects me of being otherwise. I'm sure people look at me and think, "Well, he's probably Japanese."

Among all of you here, no individual looks like any other. It is surprisingly easy to discern differences, for this is what we tend to focus on. However, it is very difficult to discover commonalities. This is the gist of the book that I have been reading with such excitement.

For example, racial discrimination arises all too easily. There are obvious, very clear differences between us and black people. But it is actually quite difficult to discover commonalities between us. Today we must shift from a regionally shared sensibility to a shared sensibility based on contemporaneity. If we try to accomplish this and learn about our shared sensibility with others, we must discover not distinctions and discriminations so much as essential commonalities. This point about discovering essential commonalities struck me while I was reading the book about caves. If I may sing my own praises, I believe that this is how the book must be read.

I don't need to boast, but it is in fact crucial in our daily lives to discover essential commonalities. We Japanese people are opposed to racial discrimination in the abstract and don't really have an actual, everyday sense of it, but everyone is highly sensitive to this issue. However, it is surprisingly difficult to discover these commonalities. It's very hard. We must be extremely perceptive and observant. We must work hard at this.

For we are part of a very old agrarian society with a long commitment to the land. We thus share commonalities as a community bloc, and yet differences can be seen, for example, in language. The Japanese language contains various dialects and regional differences. Some people tend to stress these distinctions. While I won't mention any names, those who praise the beauty of the Japanese language typically emphasize such differences.

More important, however, if for example older people from Kagoshima and Aomori met and suddenly began speaking to one another, they would not be able to communicate. (Young people would understand one another, given the spread of television.) They would have no idea what the other was saying. Yet people from Aomori and Kagoshima possess the same linguistic structure. This is indisputably the Japanese language. It is this commonality that is crucial.

There are those who claim that standard Japanese is frail, while regional dialects possess vitality, but I disagree. Such dialects do not possess much vitality but rather have a writerly quality. However, what is crucial is style or structure. This structure remains the same whether one writes in an Aomori or Kagoshima dialect, which is minor.

We are sensitive to distinctions and don't make efforts to see commonalities, perceiving them as suspicious. We thus feel uncomfortable to speak about urbanization. There seems to be something dubious about it. But this is absolutely false. It is not simply that urbanization is inevitable. Rather, it marks our inner anticipation of an ideal future, in which a narrowly spatial shared sensibility gives way to a shared sensibility based on contemporaneity.

As a process, urbanization is clearly part of our reality. As I mentioned yesterday, for example, few people are sensitive enough to regard Millet's painting *The Angelus* as anything other than peaceful and beautiful. I would feel a great deal of respect for anyone so sensitive as to perceive in this work an awful brutality, something suggestive of the Nazis. But this is how the painting must be seen.

This gesture of praying to the land is virtually always appropriated by right-wing forces. Both Hitler and Stalin appropriated this image. Throughout every age, such images as the sweet-smelling and beloved land have been appropriated by such people, while the city has been used as a symbol of evil, something suspicious and negative. Yet this is impossible.

For example, although one hears about the frequent crime in Tokyo, the percentage is negligible when one considers how many people live here. I believe that human beings are basically peaceful. Now consider the amount of crime in rural areas as based on this same percentage. Surely there should be many more murder cases. The rate is surprisingly small. People have been very rapidly forced to live in close contact with the other. All of you are probably only three or four generations removed from village life, where people lived strictly among neighbors. Or five generations if your family married early, but there is perhaps no one like that here. Nevertheless, you have already grown accustomed to this contact with the other—or rather, you have overcome this difficulty. The question remains, however, whether this represents an unhappy development for us.

People are unhappy at all times and in all places. Isn't this why people from rural areas long to leave and come to Tokyo? Aren't there many popular songs about longing for Tokyo? That is why people come. All people from rural areas long for the city. Once here, they take part in surveys and complain that the city is too noisy and the people too cold. But it is hardly the case that people in rural areas are so warm. Rather people are cold wherever one goes. But that doesn't mean one would just kill everyone.

I once wrote a short piece called "Hakuchō goroshi no uta" [A Song of Swan Killing] based on someone who had killed a swan in Kichijōji or some such place. I can empathize with this person's feelings. That is, I would not kill a swan if I couldn't understand his feelings. The only reason why people don't kill swans is because they have no such opportunity or are afraid of botching the job and getting arrested. Would you let something like that live? Swans are not so important. A person's life is much more valuable than a swan's. Yet the story focuses on someone who killed swans being regarded as more evil than someone who killed people.

Regarding the desire to kill swans, one must feel a certain disgust in one's love for them. There must be a certain sense of revulsion in the idea that it's natural for one to consider the beauty of swans and wonder why anyone would want to kill something so beautiful. That is one way to develop a method or sensitivity required to go beyond the neighbor and connect directly to the other. I wrote somewhat sarcastically that the role of art consists largely in killing the swan, but the piece was mostly ignored.

In a manner of speaking, this seems to more or less illustrate the difference between writerly art and stylistic art.

However, the play will suffer if I take such a high-handed attitude now. Fortunately, my time is now at an end so I'll finish up.

I already explained the circumstances of this lecture at the beginning of my talk but hope to have similar opportunities in the future. All of you here seem quite young, and this is perhaps the first time for many of the actors in our play to perform under these conditions. This represents a chance to interact with the other. The actors typically perform at school in front of people they know, such as their parents. There are many of you here today who know the actors, but also many who do not. This is an excellent chance for these actors to broaden themselves, professionally and otherwise, through interacting with others.

These actors are in acting school, of course, and are not amateurs. So please don't be afraid to scrutinize them and view their acting critically. At the same time, they are not yet full professionals, so please cheer them on critically yet generously, to use a strange phrase. I don't mind if you critique my directing. We will now take a five-minute break and then begin. Thank you.

NOTES

INTRODUCTION

1. "Miritarī rukku," in *Abe Kōbō zenshū* (*Collected Works of Abe Kōbō*) (Tokyo: Shinchōsha, 1997–2000), 22:130–31.
2. Gilles Deleuze and Félix Guattari, *Anti-Oedipus: Capitalism and Schizophrenia*, trans. Robert Hurley et. al. (Minneapolis: University of Minnesota Press, 1983), xiii.
3. *Suichū toshi, dendorokakariya* (*The Underwater City, Dendrocacalia*) (Tokyo: Shinchō bunko, 1973), 129–75.
4. For a recent example of such cultural particularism in the study of fascism, see Alan Tansman, *The Aesthetics of Japanese Fascism* (Berkeley: University of California Press, 2009).
5. "Uchi naru henkyō," in *Abe Kōbō zenshū*, 22:209.
6. Jean-Paul Sartre, *Les temps modernes* (August–September, 1946): 196–97. Abe, a close reader of Sartre, whom he cites regularly and with admiration, doubtless knew this passage himself.
7. I try to untangle some of the strands of this logic in the context of war memory in "Abe Kōbō no 'Tanin no kao' ni okeru sensō no kioku to jinshu mondai" (War

Memory and Race in Abe Kōbō's *The Face of Another*), *Quadrante*, no. 14 (March 2012): 175–83.

8. "Zoku, uchi naru henkyō," in *Abe Kōbō zenshū*, 22:334.

9. "Hōhō toshite no Ajia" (Asia as Method), in *Takeuchi Yoshimi zenshū* (Tokyo: Chikuma shobō, 1980), 5:115, trans. Richard F. Calichman, *What Is Modernity? Writings of Takeuchi Yoshimi* (New York: Columbia University Press, 2005), 165. Let me simply state in passing that the thought of Abe and Takeuchi reveals a great many important similarities, particularly in terms of Takeuchi's notion of resistance (*teikō*).

THEORY AND PRACTICE IN LITERATURE

1. Karl Marx, *A Contribution to the Critique of Political Economy* (General Books, 2010), 12.

2. V. I. Lenin, *Materialism and Empirio-Criticism: Critical Comments on a Reactionary Philosophy* (New York: International Publishers, 1927), 139.

3. Karl Marx, *Grundrisse: Foundations of the Critique of Political Economy*, trans. Martin Nicolaus (New York: Vintage, 1973), 163. Originally published in 1953.

4. J. V. Stalin, *Marxism and Problems of Linguistics* (Moscow: Foreign Languages Publishing House). Originally published July–August 1950. See marxists.org /reference/archive/stalin/works/1950/jun/20.htm.

5. Mao Zedong, "On Practice: On the Relation Between Knowledge and Practice, Between Knowing and Doing," in *Selected Works of Mao Tse-tung* (Beijing: Foreign Languages Press), 1. Originally published July 1937. See http://www .marxists.org/reference/archive/mao/selected-works/volume-1/mswv1_16.htm.

6. Ibid.

7. Ibid.

8. Ibid.

9. Lenin, *Materialism and Empirio-Criticism*, 142.

THE HAND OF A CALCULATOR WITH THE
HEART OF A BEAST: WHAT IS LITERATURE?

1. In *Modern Russian Poets on Poetry*, ed. Carl R. Proffer (Ann Arbor: Ardis, 1976), 104.

2. Maksim Gorky, "The Reader," *Poet Lore* 15, no. 2 (summer 1904): 44–47.

3. Lu Xun, "Literature and Revolution," in *Selected Works of Lu Hsun*, trans. Yang Hsien-yi and Gladys Yang (Beijing: Foreign Languages Press, 1956–1960), 3:22.

4. *Modern Russian Poets on Poetry*, 115.

5. Lu Xun, "Zenme xie" (How to Write), in *Lu Xun zuopin quanji* (Taipei: Fengyun shidai, 1992), 11:17–19.

DISCOVERING AMERICA

1. Graham Greene, *The Quiet American* (New York: Penguin, 1996), 163. First published in 1955.
2. Jean-Paul Sartre, "New York, the Colonial City," in *Literary and Philosophical Essays* (London: Hutchinson, 1955), 123.
3. Tsurumi Shunsuke, "Nihon chishikijin no Amerika zō," *Chūō kōron*, July 1956, 176.
4. Jean-Paul Sartre, "Présentation," in *Situations, III* (Paris: Gallimard, 1949), 131–32.
5. Jean-Paul Sartre, "American Cities," in *Literary and Philosophical Essays*, 108–12.
6. Nakaya Ken'ichi, "Chibeishugi no teishō," *Chūō kōron*, July 1956, 120–21.
7. This appears to be one of the verses of a "counting song" from the Freedom and Popular Rights Movement, attributed to Ueki Emori (1857–1892).
8. Greene, *The Quiet American*, 184.
9. Nakaya, "Chibeishugi no teishō," 124.
10. Saitō Makoto, "Minshushugi no fūdoka" (The Localization of Democracy), in *Iwanami kōza: Gendai shisō* (Tokyo: Iwanami shoten, 1957), 6:35.
11. Tsurumi Shunsuke, "Puragumatizumu no hattatsu gaisetsu" (A Survey of Developments in Pragmatism), *Chūō kōron*, July 1956, 236.
12. *A Face in the Crowd* (1957), directed by Elia Kazan.
13. Nagai Yōnosuke, "Masu demokurashii to seijiteki taishū undō" (Mass Democracy and Political Mass Movements), in *Iwanami kōza: Gendai shisō*, 6:202.
14. Tsurumi, "Puragumatizumu no hattatsu gaisetsu," 242.
15. J. Hector St. John de Crèvecoeur, *Letters from an American Farmer and Sketches of Eighteenth-Century America* (New York: Penguin, 1981), 70. First published in 1782.
16. Donald Richie, *Gendai Amerika bungaku shuchō*, trans. Kajima Shōzō (Tokyo: Eihōsha, 1956), 40.
17. Johann Wolfgang von Goethe, *Faust: A Tragedy* (New York: Norton, 2000), 36. First published in 1808.

THE MILITARY LOOK

1. The correct lyrics, of course, are "It was twenty years ago today / Sergeant Pepper taught the band to play / So let me introduce to you / the one and only Billy Shears."

PASSPORT OF HERESY

1. Julius E. Lips, *The Origin of Things: A Cultural History of Man* (London: Harrap, 1949), 291–92.

THE FRONTIER WITHIN

1. Hermann Rauschning, *Hitler Speaks: A Series of Political Conversations with Adolf Hitler on His Real Aims* (Whitefish, Mont.: Kessinger, 2010). The translation is directly from the Japanese, since it is unclear to which passage in Rauschning's book Abe is referring.
2. Ibid., 63.
3. Ibid., 76.
4. Ibid., 238.
5. Jean-Paul Sartre, *Portrait of the Anti-Semite*, trans. Erik de Mauny (London: Secker & Warburg, 1948), 18.
6. Ibid., 19–20.
7. Jean-Bernard Charrier, *Citadins et ruraux* (Paris: Presses Universitaires de France, 1964), 10.
8. In *Through the Glass of Soviet Literature*, ed. Ernest J. Simmons (New York: Columbia University Press, 1953), 110–58.
9. Ibid., 110, 265–66.
10. Leo Löwenthal and Norbert Guterman, *Prophets of Deceit: A Study of the Techniques of the American Agitator* (New York: Harper, 1949), 106.
11. Ibid., 1.
12. Ibid., 106.
13. Ibid., 136.
14. Ibid., 109, 120.
15. Ibid., 62.
16. Ibid.
17. Ibid., 61.
18. Dov Barnir, "Les juifs, le sionisme et le progrès," in *Les temps modernes: Le conflit israélo-arabe*, ed. Jean-Paul Sartre, no. 253 (1967): 420–22.
19. Ibid., 418.
20. Sartre, *Portrait of the Anti-Semite*, 76–77.

GLOSSARY

ARAGON, LOUIS (1897–1982), French writer affiliated with surrealism and communism whose works focus largely on political and social critique.

BABEL, ISAAK (1894–1940), Russian short-story writer known for such works as *Red Cavalry* (1926) and *Odessa Tales* (1927).

BALZAC, HONORÉ DE (1799–1850), French novelist regarded as the founder of realist fiction; author of the masterpiece *La comédie humaine*.

BARNIR, DOV (1911–2000), Belgian-born Israeli politician who authored several books on art and politics upon retiring from the Knesset.

BECKETT, SAMUEL (1906–1989), Irish-born French writer best known for his absurdist plays; awarded the Nobel Prize in Literature in 1969.

BELLOW, SAUL (1915–2005), Canadian-born Jewish American novelist whose works include the 1953 *The Adventures of Augie March*; won the Nobel Prize in Literature in 1976.

BRECHT, BERTOLT (1898–1956), German dramatist whose notions of theater have been enormously influential in both literature and film; works include the 1928 *The Threepenny Opera*.

BROOM, ROBERT (1866–1951), Scottish South African paleontologist most noted for his discovery of *Paranthropus robustus*.

CHAPLIN, CHARLIE (1889–1977), Hollywood icon born in England most famous for his creation of the Tramp character. Pressured by McCarthyism to live outside the United States in 1952.

CRÈVECOEUR, J. HECTOR ST. JOHN DE (1735–1813), French author who lived in America and whose experiences as a farmer and traveler are reflected in his works.

DARWIN, CHARLES (1809–1882), English naturalist whose 1859 *Origin of Species* set forth the theory of evolution on the basis of natural selection.

DASSIN, JULES (1911–2008), American filmmaker who relocated to France after being blacklisted under McCarthyism; works include the 1955 *Rififi*, for which he won Best Director at Cannes.

DOS PASSOS, JOHN (1896–1970), American writer whose novels include *Manhattan Transfer* (1925) and the trilogy *U.S.A.* (1937).

DOSTOEVSKY, FYODOR (1821–1881), Russian novelist, author of such works as *Crime and Punishment* (1866) and *The Brothers Karamazov* (1879–1880).

DUNHAM, KATHERINE (1909–2006), American dancer and choreographer who is recognized today as one of the pioneers of African-American dance theater.

EHRENBURG, ILYA (1891–1967), Soviet novelist and poet whose 1955 work *The Thaw* was openly critical of life in the USSR.

EINSTEIN, ALBERT (1879–1955), German-born American physicist who introduced his theory of relativity in 1918; awarded the Nobel Prize in Physics in 1921.

EISENSTEIN, SERGEI (1898–1948), Russian filmmaker known for his influential montage techniques; works include the 1926 *Potemkin*.

ENOMOTO BUYŌ (1836–1908), samurai who fought on the side of the Tokugawa shogunate against the newly formed Meiji government; subject of Abe's 1965 novel of the same name.

FAULKNER, WILLIAM (1897–1962), American novelist and short-story writer whose works employ stream of consciousness techniques and deal with problems of the American South; received the Nobel Prize in Literature in 1949.

FLAUBERT, GUSTAVE (1821–1880), French novelist whose naturalist works include *Madame Bovary* (1856) and *L'éducation sentimentale* (1869).

FREUD, SIGMUND (1856–1939), Austrian founder of psychoanalysis whose theories of the unconscious included insights into repression, hysteria, and dreams.

FUKUZAWA YUKICHI (1835–1901), social reformer, author, and educator; one of the leading advocates of Japan's "civilization and enlightenment." Founded Keio University in 1868.

GAZZO, MICHAEL V. (1923–1995), American playwright who later acted in film and television; wrote the 1955 Broadway play *A Hatful of Rain*.

GOLDSTÜCKER, EDUARD (1913–2000), noted Kafka scholar and first Czech ambassador to Israel who participated in the Prague Spring of 1968.

GOMBROWICZ, WITOLD (1904–1969), Polish novelist known for his realist fiction, in particular his 1937 work *Ferdydurke*.

GORKY, MAKSIM (1868–1936), Russian writer who emerged from the ranks of the proletariat; author of *The Lower Depths* (1902). Helped found socialist realism.

GREENE, GRAHAM (1904–1991), English writer whose works range from novels and short stories to plays and travel books; *The Quiet American* appeared in 1955.

GUEVARA, CHE (1928–1967), Argentine physician, intellectual, and Marxist revolutionary who helped lead the Cuban Revolution.

HEIDEGGER, MARTIN (1899–1976), German philosopher whose influential notions of ontology were introduced in his 1927 *Sein und Zeit*.

HEMINGWAY, ERNEST (1899–1961), American novelist and short-story writer most remembered for such works as *The Sun Also Rises* (1926) and *A Farewell to Arms* (1929).

HIJIKATA TOSHIZŌ (1835–1869), coleader of the Shinsengumi who died in battle fighting against the imperial forces of the Meiji government.

HOFFMEISTER, ADOLF (1902–1973), Czech poet and novelist who briefly served as ambassador to France before running afoul of the communist regime.

HOFMANNSTHAL, HUGO VON (1874–1929), Austrian playwright and poet whose works explore the difficulties inherent in linguistic expression.

INFORMEL PAINTING, postwar art movement centered in France that valued spontaneity as part of its critique of formal structure.

IONESCO, EUGÈNE (1909–1994), Romanian-French playwright and one of the central figures of the theater of the absurd; elected to the Académie Française in 1971.

ITARD, JEAN-MARC GASPARD (1774–1838), French physician famous for treating the so-called Wild Boy of Aveyron.

ITŌ SEI (1905–1969), novelist and literary critic who translated *Lady Chatterley's Lover* into Japanese; awarded the Kikuchi Kan Prize in 1963.

JASIEŃSKI, BRUNO (1901–1938), Polish poet and one of the leaders of the Polish futurist movement who was executed in a Moscow prison.

JOYCE, JAMES (1882–1941), Irish novelist and short-story writer whose use of interior monologue and invented words can be seen most prominently in *Ulysses* (1921) and *Finnegans Wake* (1939).

KAFKA, FRANZ (1883–1924), Austrian novelist whose works explore issues of alienation, absurdity, and family tension; author of *The Metamorphosis* (1915) and *Amerika* (1927).

KAMEI KATSUICHIRŌ (1907–1966), nationalist critic who committed *tenkō* in 1935, the same year he cofounded the journal *The Japanese Romantic School*.

KATSU KAISHŪ (1823–1899), Japanese statesman knowledgeable in western military technology who served as commissioner of the Tokugawa navy.

KAUFMAN, GEORGE S. (1889–1961), American playwright and drama critic who won a Pulitzer Prize for the 1932 musical *Of Thee I Sing*.

KEENE, DONALD (b. 1922), noted scholar and translator of Japanese literature whose works include the 1984 *Dawn to the West*.

KELLER, HELEN (1880–1968), American writer whose memoirs and essays recount her own experience as both blind and deaf.

KHRUSHCHEV, NIKITA (1894–1971), Soviet head of state from 1958 to 1964 whose leadership was marked by a growing period of de-Stalinization.

KONDŌ ISAMI (1834–1868), Japanese Tokugawa government official and commander of the Shinsengumi.

LENIN, VLADIMIR ILYICH (1870–1924), Russian communist leader who successfully led the revolution of 1917, leading to the creation of the Soviet Union.

LIPS, JULIUS E. (1895–1950), German ethnologist who fled Nazi Germany to teach in the United States; works include the 1947 *The Origin of Things.*

LONDON, JACK (1876–1916), American writer known for such adventure novels as the 1903 *The Call of the Wild.*

LÖWITH, KARL (1897–1973), German philosopher and student of Heidegger who was forced to flee Nazi Germany for Japan and the United States; author of the 1949 *Meaning in History.*

LUCIAN OF SAMOSATA (ca.120–200), Greek satirist and author of such works as *A True Story* and *Dialogues of the Gods.*

LU XUN (1881–1936), the pioneer of modern Chinese literature whose many short stories and essays offer a critique of traditional Chinese culture; educated as a medical doctor in Japan.

MAILER, NORMAN (1923–2007), American writer and multiple Pulitzer Prize winner who first emerged on the literary scene with his World War II novel *The Naked and the Dead* (1948).

MALAMUD, BERNARD (1914–1986), American novelist and short-story writer whose works often deal with Jewish life; author of the 1966 *The Fixer.*

MANDELSTAM, OSIP (1891–1938), Russian essayist and poet of the Acmeist school persecuted under Stalinism.

MAO ZEDONG (1893–1976), chairman of the People's Republic of China from 1949 to 1959.

MARX, KARL (1818–1883), German socialist whose critique of capitalism and theories of dialectical materialism were expounded in such works as *Das Kapital* (1867).

MATHIEU, GEORGES (b. 1921), French painter associated with lyrical abstraction and the Informel school.

MATSUKAWA INCIDENT, series of events in which a fatal train accident that took place in August 1949 was blamed by the government on the Japan Communist Party.

MAYAKOVSKY, VLADIMIR (1893–1930), Russian futurist poet whose work, such as the 1914–1915 "A Cloud in Trousers," was noted for its break with the symbolists.

MCLAREN, NORMAN (1914–1987), Scottish-born Canadian film director and animator known for his innovative techniques combining animation and sound.

MELVILLE, HERMAN (1819–1891), American novelist and short-story writer best known for his 1851 masterpiece *Moby Dick, or The Whale.*

MEYERHOLD, VSEVOLOD (1874–1940), Russian theater director who experimented with the use of symbolist techniques; author of the 1913 *On Theatre.*

MILLER, ARTHUR (1915–2005), American playwright whose best known work, the 1949 *Death of a Salesman*, depicts the sense of failure and eventual suicide of its protagonist, Willy Loman.

MILLET, JEAN-FRANÇOIS (1814–1875), French painter and one of the founders of the Barbizon school; known for his paintings of rural life and peasants.

MISHIMA YUKIO (1925–1970), Japanese writer and right-wing nationalist who committed ritual suicide; author of such novels as *Confessions of a Mask* (1949) and *The Temple of the Golden Pavilion* (1956).

NADER SHAH (1698–1747), military leader who united Persia and ruled as king of Persia from 1736 until his assassination.

NAKAYA KEN'ICHI (1910–1987), Japanese scholar of American history at Tokyo University whose wartime research focused on the Philippines.

NIETZSCHE, FRIEDRICH (1844–1900), German philosopher who criticized systematic philosophy and Christianity for its rejection of life; author of *Beyond Good and Evil* (1886) and *Thus Spake Zarathustra* (1883–1885).

NUSINOV, YITZHAK (1889–1950), Russian literary critic whose disagreements with the Stalinist regime led to his death in prison.

ŌE KENZABURŌ (b. 1935), Japanese novelist and short-story writer whose works, such as the 1967 *The Silent Cry*, helped earn him the Nobel Prize in Literature in 1994.

OLESHA, YURI (1899–1960), Russian novelist and short-story writer best known for his 1927 work *Envy*.

O'NEILL, EUGENE (1888–1953), American playwright known for his psychological insight and innovative use of symbolism; works include *The Emperor Jones* (1920) and *Mourning Becomes Electra* (1931).

ONSTOTT, KYLE (1887–1966), American novelist whose experiences as a dog breeder informed the writing of his most famous work, the 1957 *Mandingo*.

PASTERNAK, BORIS (1890–1960), Russian poet and novelist, best remembered for his 1957 work *Doctor Zhivago*; awarded the Nobel Prize in Literature the following year.

PAVLOV, IVAN (1849–1936), Russian physiologist whose widely influential notion of conditioned response led to his winning the Nobel Prize in 1904.

PICASSO, PABLO (1881–1973), Spanish artist and one of the cofounders of cubism; painted *Guernica* in 1937.

PILNYAK, BORIS (1894–1941), Russian novelist whose elaborate prose can be found in such works as his 1928 *The Naked Year*.

PINTER, HAROLD (1930–2008), English dramatist influenced by Kafka and Beckett whose major works include *The Birthday Party* (1958) and *Betrayal* (1980).

POE, EDGAR ALLAN (1809–1849), American short-story writer and poet whose best works include the 1845 "The Purloined Letter."

PROUST, MARCEL (1871–1922), French novelist whose notions of time and memory appear powerfully in his masterpiece, the 1913–1927 *Remembrance of Things Past*.

PUSHKIN, ALEKSANDR (1799–1837), Russian writer who created lasting works in poetry, fiction, and theater; author of *Eugene Onegin* (1831) and *Boris Godunov* (1825).

RACINE, JEAN (1639–1699), French playwright and one of the cornerstones of French literary tradition whose works include the 1677 *Phèdre*.

RAUSCHNING, HERMANN (1887–1982), German conservative who broke with Nazism and defected to the United States, where he became one of Nazi Germany's most influential critics.

RICHIE, DONALD (b. 1924), scholar of Japanese culture and film best known for his work on Kurosawa Akira.

RIESMAN, DAVID (1909–2002), American sociologist and educator who attacked social conformity in the United States in his 1950 *The Lonely Crowd*.

RILKE, RAINER MARIA (1875–1926), German poet whose works powerfully influenced the young Abe; wrote *The Duino Elegies,* published in 1923.

ROTH, PHILIP (b. 1933), American novelist whose works often deal with such themes as male sexuality and Jewish identity; his *Portnoy's Complaint* was published in 1969.

RYSKIND, MORRIE (1895–1985), American dramatist and screenplay writer who won a Pulitzer Prize for the 1932 musical *Of Thee I Sing.*

SAIGŌ TAKAMORI (1827–1877), one of the leaders of the Meiji Restoration whose unsuccessful rebellion against the central government in 1877, known as the Seinan War, forced him to commit suicide.

SALACROU, ARMAND (1899–1989), French playwright who experimented with temporal sequence in his works; his *La terre est ronde* was published in 1938.

SALINGER, J. D. (1919–2010), American novelist and short-story writer who won enormous critical and popular acclaim for his 1951 *The Catcher in the Rye.*

SARTRE, JEAN-PAUL (1905–1980), French philosopher, novelist, and playwright and one of the founders of existentialism; declined the Nobel Prize in Literature in 1964.

SASAKI KIICHI (1914–1993), Japanese literary critic who translated György Lukács and helped launch the journal *Kindai bungaku.*

SHAW, GEORGE BERNARD (1856–1950), Irish playwright, essayist, and social reformer known for his socialist views and attacks on conventional morality. Awarded the Nobel Prize in Literature in 1925.

SHAW, IRWIN (1913–1984), American writer who produced novels as well as works for radio and television; author of the 1948 *The Young Lions.*

SHINSENGUMI, group loyal to the Tokugawa shogunate who were charged with the task of preserving peace in Kyoto during the 1860s.

SIMA QIAN (ca. 145 B.C.–86 B.C.), Han-dynasty official remembered for founding the field of Chinese historiography; author of *Records of the Grand Historian.*

SIMMEL, GEORG (1858–1918), German sociologist and philosopher who wrote theoretical works on culture and society, such as the 1903 *The Metropolis and Mental Life.*

SPILLANE, MICKEY (1918–2006), American writer of detective fiction who created the character of Mike Hammer; known for the graphic violence in his works.

STALIN, JOSEPH (1879–1953), Russian political leader who succeeded Lenin, ruling as premier from 1941 to 1953.

SUGAWARA TAKASHI (1903–1970), Japanese dramatist and director who studied theater at Columbia University; translated and staged *The Death of a Salesman* in 1954.

TOLSTOY, LEO (1828–1910), Russian novelist and social reformer known for such works as *War and Peace* (1865–1869) and *Anna Karenina* (1875–1877).

TSURUMI SHUNSUKE (b. 1922), philosopher and social critic who wrote on such diverse topics as American pragmatism, *tenkō,* and popular culture; cofounder of the Institute of the Science of Thought (1946).

Twiggy (b. 1949), English model and actress who gained fame in the 1960s for her thin frame and short hair.

Werfel, Franz (1890–1945), Austrian novelist, playwright, and poet who fled the Nazis in 1938; author of the 1941 *The Song of Bernadette*.

Wesker, Arnold (b. 1932), English dramatist whose strong socialist beliefs inform much of his work; author of the 1962 *Chips with Everything*.

Whitman, Walt (1819–1892), American poet known for his democratic convictions; wrote his masterpiece *Leaves of Grass* originally in 1855.

Zengakuren, leftist student league in Japan that was first officially organized in 1948.

Zenkyōtō (All-Campus Joint Struggle Council), student movement during the 1960s and early 1970s that protested against such issues as the Vietnam War and the Japanese university education system.

Zhdanov Doctrine, cultural policy set forth in the Soviet Union in 1946 that resulted in tighter government control over the arts.

Wang Anyi, *The Song of Everlasting Sorrow: A Novel of Shanghai*,
translated by Michael Berry with Susan Chan Egan (2008)

Ch'oe Yun, *There a Petal Silently Falls: Three Stories by Ch'oe Yun*,
translated by Bruce and Ju-Chan Fulton (2008)

Inoue Yasushi, *The Blue Wolf: A Novel of the Life of Chinggis Khan*,
translated by Joshua A. Fogel (2009)

Anonymous, *Courtesans and Opium: Romantic Illusions of the Fool of Yangzhou*,
translated by Patrick Hanan (2009)

Cao Naiqian, *There's Nothing I Can Do When I Think of You Late at Night*,
translated by John Balcom (2009)

Park Wan-suh, *Who Ate Up All the Shinga? An Autobiographical Novel*,
translated by Yu Young-nan and Stephen J. Epstein (2009)

Yi T'aejun, *Eastern Sentiments*, translated by Janet Poole (2009)

Hwang Sunwŏn, *Lost Souls: Stories*,
translated by Bruce and Ju-Chan Fulton (2009)

Kim Sŏk-pŏm, *The Curious Tale of Mandogi's Ghost*,
translated by Cindy Textor (2010)

Xiaomei Chen, editor,
The Columbia Anthology of Modern Chinese Drama (2011)

Qian Zhongshu, *Humans, Beasts, and Ghosts: Stories and Essays*, edited by
Christopher G. Rea, translated by Dennis T. Hu, Nathan K. Mao, Yiran Mao,
Christopher G. Rea, and Philip F. Williams (2011)

Dung Kai-cheung, *Atlas: The Archaeology of an Imaginary City*,
translated by Dung Kai-cheung, Anders Hansson, and Bonnie S. McDougall (2012)

O Chŏnghŭi, *River of Fire and Other Stories*,
translated by Bruce Fulton and Ju-Chan Fulton (2012)

Endō Shūsaku, *Kiku's Prayer: A Novel*, translated by Van Gessel (2013)

Li Rui, *Trees Without Wind: A Novel*, translated by John Balcom (2013)

GPSR Authorized Representative: Easy Access System Europe, Mustamäe tee
50, 10621 Tallinn, Estonia, gpsr.requests@easproject.com